Penguin Handbooks

Helping Your Handica

Janet Carr read psychology at Reading University and, after gaining a diploma in clinical psychology at the Maudsley Hospital, worked in mental hospitals and child guidance clinics. She carried out a longitudinal study of children with Down's Syndrome, which led to a Ph.D. at the London University Institute of Education.

From 1970 to 1978 she was a lecturer in the Psychology Department of the London University Institute of Psychiatry and Senior Psychologist at Hilda Lewis House, a hospital-based unit for the assessment and treatment of severely mentally handicapped children. She became involved in the teaching of behaviour modification and as a result has run numerous courses, for professionals and parents, both in this country and in Sweden.

Janet Carr is currently Senior Research Officer in the GLC Spina Bifida Survey. Her publications include *Young Children with Down's Syndrome* and (co-editor with W. Yule) *Behaviour Modification for the Mentally Handicapped*. She is married to a psychiatrist and they have two sons and a daughter.

Janet Carr

Helping Your Handicapped Child

A Step-by-Step Guide to Everyday Problems

Illustrated by Posy Simmonds

Penguin Books

Penguin Books Ltd, Harmondsworth,
Middlesex, England
Penguin Books, 625 Madison Avenue,
New York, New York 10022, U.S.A.
Penguin Books Australia Ltd, Ringwood,
Victoria, Australia
Penguin Books Canada Ltd, 2801 John Street,
Markham, Ontario, Canada L3R 1B4
Penguin Books (N.Z.) Ltd, 182–190 Wairau Road,
Auckland 10, New Zealand

First published 1980

Text copyright © Janet Carr, 1980
Illustrations copyright © Posy Simmonds, 1980
All rights reserved

Typeset, printed and bound in Great Britain by
Hazell Watson & Viney Ltd,
Aylesbury, Bucks
Set in Monotype Plantin

To Karl, Katy, Paul, Ruth, Chris, Carla, Jane, Lisa, Howard and Graeme: and to all the other children who go to Dysart School, Kingston-upon-Thames, for whose parents this book was originally written.

Contents

Acknowledgements

I owe a great deal to the late Professor Jack Tizard and to Dr Elizabeth Newson for their helpful and constructive criticism of the manuscript; to Glyn Murphy who wrote the first draft of the chapter on play besides reading and commenting on the rest of the manuscript; to my family who put up with me while I was writing it and who are on two or three occasions pictured within; and finally to the Parents' Group at Dysart School, Kingston-upon-Thames, without whom this book would not have been written.

1. About This Book

To most people, the news that their child is mentally handicapped comes as a tremendous blow. As a parent has said, 'Being told for the first time that one's child is retarded may well be the most severe shock that one may experience in a normal lifetime full of trying experiences'.*

When the first shock is past, most parents want to know what they can do for their child. How can we help him? How should we teach him? What should we teach him? What will he be able to learn? How can we give him the best possible opportunities so that, even if his abilities are limited, he can make the most of them?

Until recently there were not many answers to these questions, and the answers that there were seldom came the way of parents. With little help or guidance available many parents fell back on the only rules they knew: bring the child up as normal. (Indeed this not specially helpful advice has often been handed out by professionals.) For some mentally handicapped children this approach suffices: the children learn reasonably well what they need to learn and their parents have few problems with them. But with others, the ordinary ways of bringing up ordinary children are less successful. Many mentally handicapped children do have special difficulties in learning. In particular, although normal children pick up a great deal from their surroundings and from watching what other people do, the mentally handicapped child often cannot. Because of this he may seem unteachable and may be written off as incapable of learning. In fact the mentally handicapped child *can* learn, but he may need special teaching and special teaching methods to do so. This book is concerned with one such teaching method, behaviour modification.

* 'A parent discusses initial counselling', H. Raech, *Mental Retardation* vol. 2, 1966, pp. 25–6.

What is behaviour modification?

Behaviour modification methods consist of a set of ways aimed at changing – modifying – what someone does – his behaviour. By 'behaviour' I mean anything that the child does; a wave of the hand, a kiss, a kick, jumping into a puddle, saying 'bye-bye'. This isn't quite the way the word is used ordinarily, when it tends to cover a longer period of time, as in 'Tommy behaved well today'. This slightly specialized use of a word is not unusual in discussing technical matters and we shall come across it again with other words in the book, but as it is always pretty clear what is meant it need not bother anyone. However, perhaps I should stress that the behaviour I am talking about is not, primarily, a matter of what the child may be thinking or feeling (though, of course, this too is important), but of observable things – what he does. The methods I will be discussing here are very practical.

Behaviour modification is based on the idea that what we do is influenced by what happens immediately afterwards. If, when we do something, what happens next is something pleasant, we will be likely to want to do that thing again; if it is not, we will be less likely to want to do it again.

So, when we want a child to learn, we look very carefully to see what he particularly enjoys; then we try to make sure that he gets one of these enjoyable things when he does what we want him to do, and that he does not get it when he does something we would rather he did not. Suppose, for example, the child loved praise and attention, and suppose we wanted to teach him to put things in a box and not to throw them round the room; then we would make sure that when he put something in the box he gets lots of praise, while if he throws things around he does not get any attention at all – we might even look away from him, apparently bored.

Behaviour modification also lays stress on teaching methods that are adapted to suit the child. When we have decided on something we want the child to learn – say, using a spoon or putting on a sock – if we find it is too difficult for him, then we break the task up into smaller bits and teach them to him one at a time. As each bit is learned it is joined up to the next, until finally he succeeds in the whole task that seemed so impossible at the beginning. We may need to observe progress, to record and chart it, since over a short period change may not be easily perceived. All this is less difficult than it sounds, and in later chapters there is plenty of practical guidance on how to go about it.

By this time some readers may be getting a bit uneasy. What about the ethics of all this? Isn't behaviour modification a bit like brain-washing? Maybe it would be all right with normal children, but is it right to use it with someone as vulnerable as a mentally handicapped child? I would like to discuss this uncertainty both because of the very real fear it expresses and because in showing the fears are mistaken we shall see more clearly what behaviour modification does aim to achieve.

One of the most important things it sets out to do is to help the child understand what we are trying to convey to him by simplifying the messages we give him. Normal communication is a complicated process, but with normal children this simplification is not usually necessary: they are able to take in and respond to the jumble of signals we give out by gesture, facial expression, emphasis of speech, and to sort out what matters and what doesn't. For the handicapped child this may be just too difficult, and he may fail to respond not because he *can't* but because he doesn't *understand* what we want him to do. Behaviour modification helps us to sort out our messages, to make them simpler and clearer, so that the handicapped child has a better chance of understanding and responding.

Secondly, behaviour modification is a way of opening up to the mentally handicapped child a whole range of interesting and useful experiences. A normal child can be introduced to these in words; we can tell him about new things, or explain why we think it is a good idea for him to learn this or that. He may or may not be convinced by our arguments, but at least he knows about them and can decide for himself. The mentally handicapped child, however, often has a special problem with language. He may be unable to understand what we say, to grasp an idea, to think about it and make up his mind whether or not he will give it a try. By using behaviour modification methods we can introduce the child to things he might otherwise never experience – riding a bike, putting on records, playing with toys. When he has tried out these new experiences then he can decide whether or not they are for him.

I think it's important to emphasize this – the potential enrichment of the child's life and the limitations of the method. By its use we can help the child to understand what we want him to do and to enjoy doing it, but even if we wanted to we cannot force behaviours from him. What we can do is to make them available to him, enable him to choose to do them. The aim is to free him as far as possible from the restrictions of his handicap, to help him become more independent and able to make decisions for himself. Behaviour modification methods can help.

I have stressed that behaviour modification methods are especially important in teaching mentally handicapped children, but they are used a great deal, too, with normal children, to help them learn, pay attention in class, become toilet trained, get over temper tantrums and sleeping difficulties, and hundreds of other ordinary and not-so-ordinary childhood problems. I myself used one of these methods, a token programme (see chapter 4), to help my son work for an exam he wanted to pass. Many parents who have used these methods in order to help a handicapped child have gone on to use them with their other children too. There is nothing strange about behaviour modification; it is just a very careful way of teaching.

Some people may feel that they are being asked to behave in a rather artificial and unspontaneous way, but this may be necessary only for the particular problem they are tackling; otherwise life goes on as normal, as loving and caring, friendly or cross, organized or disorganized as ever it was. Moreover, once the problem is behind them, most parents will be able to slide gently back to more normal ways of behaving, but at the same time they know that if new problems arise they can return to behaviour modification to help them over this new hump; while some parents may find that certain methods become more or less second nature to them and will use them more often than not – paying attention to the good things the child does, perhaps, or affecting indifference to tiresome behaviour. Others will not want to use behaviour modification methods at all, some may use them quite briefly, some for a bit longer. For those who think behaviour modification might help them this book offers some guidelines on how to go about it.

Getting started

The book falls into two main parts. In Part 1, which is about ways of teaching, chapters 2–7 are concerned with behaviour modification methods in general and chapter 8 with making records and graphs. In Part 2, which is about teaching particular things, chapters 9–14 are about some skills which parents often want their children to learn and chapter 15 about helping children get over fears. Finally, chapter 16 has some suggestions about continuing the work.

What to teach?

Behaviour modification, being a teaching method, tells you *how* to teach, not *what* to teach. You can teach your child what you think he needs to learn, whether it is an everyday activity like feeding or dressing (described in chapters 9–14) or whether it is something quite different. Whatever you decide on you can, if you want, use behaviour modification methods in your teaching.

Some people find it helps to make a list of the things they would most immediately like the child to learn to do and not to do, and put them in order of priority. As a rule it is a good idea to work on only one or two to begin with – too many at a time can be muddling – and to work on a positive, learning-to-do, project at the same time as a learning-not-to-do one. There are usually plenty of positive things to teach, and it is enjoyable for everybody to see the child making progress in something new.

How much time each day?

How much time you will need to spend on teaching depends, of course, on the kind of problem you are tackling and on the other demands on your life. As a rough guide other parents have usually spent between five minutes and half an hour a day. With a very distractible child five minutes may well be enough. Little-and-often is a good general rule: two sessions of five minutes are probably better than one of ten.

Some behaviour, such as throwing things about, can't be dealt with in a single session each day at a particular time. You just have to deal with it when it happens. If it doesn't happen too often – only once or twice a day – you may be able to deal with it any time it occurs. Similarly, if the best treatment is a fairly easy one to use, like time-out from your attention (turning your head away, or in some way refusing to pay attention to what the child is doing), you may be able to use it every time the behaviour occurs. If, on the other hand, the child's bad behaviour happens very often, and you have decided that you should use a treatment method like restraint (holding the child quite still for a short time) which demands your full attention, so that it is impossible to do if the behaviour happens just when you are pouring tea for a nervous aunt or dealing with a pan of boiling fat, then you may at first decide to deal with it only in certain situations.

Supposing, for instance, the bad behaviour was throwing things and you had decided to use over-correction (in which you make the child clear up not only the mess he has made but a good deal else as well). You might decide that first thing in the morning is too hectic a time for you to do this, but you could manage it between 4 and 6 p.m., after your child gets home from school and before you start on the evening meal. If you kept careful records over the weeks of how often the child threw things during the 4–6 treatment time, you would be able to see whether the method you were using was a useful one – that is, whether the child was throwing things around less often. If this were the case you might find it possible to extend the treatment into a little more of the day – success works wonders.

The important point is that the methods described in this book are meant to help your child and you, not to make life difficult. What you decide to do must be possible, given your life and situation. You too have a life, so has your wife/husband, and so have your other children. I am not asking you to spend every available minute with your handicapped child, to dedicate yourself body and soul to him. He might indeed learn a great deal by such intensive teaching, but you might end up so exhausted that you had to give up teaching him altogether, so the benefit would be short-lived. Many teachers (and of course I include parents in this term) have found that a mentally handicapped child can gain a great deal from a short amount of teaching each day geared to his special needs. I hope also that in reading this book you will discover ways of casual, informal teaching and of responding to him (for instance by noticing and appreciating tiny bits of 'good' behaviour) that can go on for most of his waking hours without making undue demands on your time and energy.

Brothers and sisters

Parents with other children may wonder about the effect on them of all this work with the handicapped child. Of course, I hope the work will not take up so much time that the other children feel badly neglected. All the same this is a question to think about. In general there are three main things you can do:

1. Give time to the other children on their own. This is fairly obvious. Most parents are aware of the need to give some time to the other children and do their best to fulfil it.

2. Give the other children a programme of their own. This is on the whole most suitable for young brothers and sisters. They may be included because their parents see that these children, too, can benefit from behaviour modification methods – one sister had a programme to help her keep her bedroom tidy and another little brother a similar (very successful) one to help him not to wet his bed. Or the other children can be included just so as not to feel left out. When Hugh was going to be given sweets for washing and dressing himself in the morning his mother was asked whether she thought this would cause any upset with his very small sister. 'Oh, no,' she replied, 'that won't be any trouble. She can get sweets for putting her toys away, or helping me around the house. We'll think of something. We'll make sure she doesn't lose out.'

3. Include the other children in the teaching. This is where older brothers and sisters come in. Many parents feel, rightly, that they do not want to over-burden their other children with responsibility for the handicapped child. But brothers and sisters are often glad to do something positive and can enjoy helping to keep records or run teaching sessions (even if, like one mother, their parents boggle at their being involved in dealing with the 'bad' behaviour; 'I'm not having her bossing Tess about'). If a brother or sister wants to do some of the teaching it is a good idea for him or her to do one or two sessions alongside the parent, to make sure that things are being done in the same way, records kept, and rewards given.

Brothers and sisters can be very good teachers and can get a great deal of satisfaction from teaching and helping the mentally handicapped child in the family.

How long will it take the child to learn?

This can vary a lot from problem to problem and child to child. Sometimes a child can take months to learn something that looks quite simple, like matching colours; sometimes a really daunting problem, like putting uneatable things in the mouth, can be overcome quite quickly. One child took nearly a year to learn not to wet his bed, another became dry over a period of a few weeks. There is no real way of telling in advance how long it will take to overcome a problem completely, but progress along the way is very encouraging.

What, though, if things don't go well, or go very slowly?

When things don't go right

It is helpful to realize that irregular progress in this kind of teaching is quite common. Several good sessions can be followed by a terrible session, even two or three together. The progress chart, instead of being a smooth steady upward slope like a telegraph wire going up a mountainside, resembles instead the Atlantic in a force eight gale, climbing up and plunging down.

There may be some reason for the child's dropping back – he may be unwell, or some change in his surroundings, like a new teacher at school, may be disturbing him. If you are fairly sure you are working along the right lines it may be best simply to persist with the programme. Evan, who was learning not to wet his bed, had kept it dry up till 9.30 in the evening six nights out of seven for about nine weeks. All of a sudden, for no apparent reason, the dry beds dropped to five and then wavered about between five and two for five more weeks. His mother persisted and Evan went up to six dry beds and then, again for no special reason that she could see, suddenly, for the first time in the nine years of his life, began to be dry not only through the evening, but also frequently still at 7 in the morning.

Here persistence paid off, and we should not give up too easily. But what if things continue to go badly? First of all, don't get discouraged. Don't think:

'It's my fault' (I'm not able to do this sort of thing well enough).

'It's his fault' (he's too retarded/stubborn/wicked ever to learn).

'Behaviour modification doesn't work' (just like all the other methods).

Find someone to discuss it with.

What you need here is a change of tactics. And to do this you need someone to discuss your problems with. Perhaps another member of the family would help – a son or daughter, perhaps, if both parents are already involved, or a grandparent, aunt or uncle; or perhaps a friendly neighbour or interested friend. One of them might discuss the problems with you, read over the relevant parts of this book and help you plan new strategies. What one person does not understand the other may find reasonably clear and be able to explain. When one is flagging the other may be able to inspire fresh enthusiasm.

The two-heads-are-better-than-one approach paid off for this family: 'We wanted to teach Tess not to put everything in her mouth. We wondered whether we should use time-out for her, but I couldn't see how you were supposed to do it. Then my husband and I read through that part of the chapter together and talked it over, and then I found I could understand it and we used it with Tess. It worked too – she hardly ever puts things in her mouth now.'

So, first stop, family and friends. If things are complicated or if you feel it might help anyway you could try professional help.

Professionals

You might find it useful to discuss tricky points with a psychologist who is interested in behaviour modification and is using these methods with handicapped children. If you have any difficulty the British Psychological Society will try to put you in touch with someone in your area. Write to: British Psychological Society, St Andrews House, 48 Princess Road East, Leicester LEI 7DR.

If your child is at school his teacher may be able to help and may anyway be interested to hear what you are trying to do. Other interested people – your doctor or social worker, speech- or physiotherapist, people at the Toy Library, nursery school, clinic, hospital, Day or Training Centre – might be glad to know what you are doing and, where possible, may tailor their efforts to fit in with yours. Love makes the world go round but communication gives it a good push in the right direction.

If you feel like not only getting help for yourself but also helping others and sharing problems and victories in a big way you could think about contacting other people to form a group.

Getting a group together

If you don't know other parents with handicapped children, your Regional Officer for the National Society for Mentally Handicapped Children may be able to put you in touch with other parents in your area. To find the address of your Regional Officer write to: National Society for Mentally Handicapped Children, 117 Golden Lane, London ECIY 0RT.

Finally, behaviour modification has helped some parents to see their children in a new light.

'Since I have been using these methods I feel more able to control Evan and find it easier to be one jump ahead of him. Mentally handicapped he may be but he's aware of what he's doing and knows right from wrong. I think, too, that he wasn't stretched enough. I was doing too much for him; now I expect, and get, more from him and I'm pleased, and he's pleased I'm pleased!'

'Behaviour modification shows you how to sort your problems out and stops you getting too cross with the child so you can build up a better relationship between you.'

'We are such good friends now, Ann and I, we do so much more together. I find her so much more rewarding now. It just changes your whole attitude.'

Children with special handicaps

Behaviour modification methods can be used to help all sorts of children whether handicapped or non-handicapped. However, children with special handicaps, whether blindness, deafness, cerebral palsy, autism, spina bifida or any other form of special handicap, do have special problems which may affect their learning. It is not possible in this book to go in detail into ways of tackling all these different kinds of problems, but you can get a great deal of help from the various societies listed in the Appendix at the back of this book. A number of books dealing with particular handicaps are also listed in Appendix 3.

The practice problems

At the end of each chapter you will find a short section called 'Practice problems'. These were at first intended as light relief, and if you like you can treat them as such. Later it became clear that they might have a more useful purpose: they can be used as a way of working out methods and solutions for problems other than those you are immediately concerned with, giving you the opportunity to think about new situations and to try to be flexible and imaginative about them. So, if you like, work out your own answers to the 'Practice problems', perhaps as revision.

In some of the 'Practice problems' I have suggested you look at your own situation in your family, and only you will know the answers to these. In others, the ones which are starred, the questions are more general and have some general answers. These are given in Appendix 1. But remember, the 'Practice problems' were originally included for a bit of fun and relaxation, so don't take them too seriously.

Part 1: Ways of Teaching

2. Observation: Watching and Counting

Observation is the cornerstone of behaviour modification. Everything we do starts with observation, and depends on observation. From observation we decide on the problem, what we should do about it, and whether what we are doing is making any difference.

How to observe

The main reasons for wanting to make observations are: first, to get things clear – to define the 'good' or the 'bad' behaviours; secondly, to get them expressed in precise rather than vague words; thirdly, to pin them down to events or patterns of behaviour which can be counted.

Suppose a mother says, 'What *can* I do about Jill, she's really awful these days'. We would ask in what way Jill is awful. 'Well, she never leaves me alone, she's always following me around – and she won't do a thing I tell her to do.' Supposing we know that Jill is about 8 years old – that is, she is not a tiny child in whom this kind of behaviour would be fairly normal – we would want to know more. Is there any particular time that Jill follows her mother around – does she do it more in the morning before school, or in the evening, or at weekends? Is she said to be disobedient at school? Does she follow her father or other adults too? Is she disobedient to her father? Are there any special requests that she won't obey? or that she will – if her mother says 'Help yourself to a biscuit', does she disobey that? Does she follow her mother (or other people) only at home or in other places as well? Does it make any difference if other people are present? What does her mother do when Jill follows her around? or won't obey her? How does Jill react to this?

By now we should have a fairly clear idea, from the mother's description, of Jill's difficult behaviour. Ideally we would now watch Jill and her mother together for some time to see what actually happens, though you can be sure that if we were sitting around waiting to see Jill being tiresome she would behave like an angel all afternoon. (Outside observers often turn out to alter the behaviour they are there to observe, though if they stay long enough and don't chat to the person they are observing things usually go back to normal.) One way or another we should be able to collect enough information to make a clear definition, with her mother, of the tiresome things Jill does. This will be helpful to anyone taking records, as it makes it easier to decide whether any particular occurrence 'counts', and if two people are trying to record the behaviour at the same time a clear definition is essential.

'Following round' might be defined as Jill being close to her mother – say within about three feet of her – and not occupied with something on her own (not counting times when Jill and her mother are going somewhere or doing something together, like going shopping or for walks). 'Disobedience' might be defined as any time that Jill is asked or told to do something and she does not begin to do it within about five seconds of the request. These definitions sound quite reasonable, though we may find that as we begin to use them we have to redefine them again and again, to get them clear.

Having decided on and defined the kinds of behaviour we want to work on we are now ready to begin to count and to record how often they occur.

Recording observations

There are several reasons why you should put your observations down on paper, rather than keep them in your head. Keeping written records will help you to make the observations more carefully – it seems to matter more what we observe if the observations are going down in black and white; it makes the observations permanent, so that you can look back on what happened days or weeks ago without having to rely on memory; and, following on from this, it cuts out the arguments between different people as to when or how much of the behaviour really occurred.

Different ways of recording

1. Continuous recording

This is the 'diary' method. *The observer tries to write down everything that happens.* Since it is physically impossible to write everything down, he records some things and misses out others so of course two people observing the same child at the same time would not necessarily record the same things. It is also an exhausting procedure, and is not much used in behaviour modification. Nevertheless it can be a good way to make preliminary observations of a child's behaviour, especially for someone who does not know the child well, like a new nurse or teacher.

2. *Event recording*

The observer selects one or more particular kinds of behaviour, and records every time they occur. For instance, we could record how many times a child came when he was called, or used his potty, or threw something, or took off his socks. The record may be taken over any period of time: if the behaviour happens only occasionally the record may be taken over the whole day, if frequently it may be more convenient to record it over a particular half hour or hour. Jill's disobedience could be recorded like this: her mother could record how often Jill did not comply with a request from the time she got up in the morning until she left for school, and again when she came back from school until, say, 6 in the evening or until she was in bed. Times can be chosen which are convenient for the person doing the recording.

Event recording is a simple straightforward procedure and used a good deal in practical situations.

3. *Duration recording*

The observer records how long a certain piece of behaviour lasts. This is used for the kinds of behaviour that are not exactly events as they are not on–off affairs, like a throw or a kick, but once started normally last for some time, like running; in this case it may seem better to record not how often the bit of behaviour happens but how long it lasts. For instance, we would use duration recording to record how long a child spends smiling, or playing with a toy, or riding a bicycle. Jill's mother might use this method for the 'following round' problem: she might record how much time Jill spends within three feet of her, or she might record the time Jill spends further than three feet away from her, if this were likely to be less. Again, Jill's mother could choose to suit herself the times in which she would keep her records.

A stop-watch is a help in duration recording, but not essential. Paula's mother, who was trying to teach her to keep her mouth closed to stop her constant dribbling, used to sit opposite the kitchen clock for her five-minute sessions, and record the number of seconds in the five minutes that Paula's mouth was actually closed. (Once the record showed that it had been closed for eight minutes: 'it was going so well, and all that time she was *swallowing*, I just didn't stop'.)

4. *Interval recording*

The observer divides up the time in which he will make his observations into certain periods, or intervals – say, five minutes, ten minutes, thirty seconds, one day, or whatever he chooses. Then *he records whether or not the behaviour happened at all during that interval.* It would make no difference to his record whether the behaviour happened once or fifty times in any one interval: the record simply states that the behaviour had or had not happened.

This is a simplified form of recording which can be used instead of either event or duration recording. It also makes it easier to record more than one piece of behaviour at a time. Jill's mother could divide up the time after Jill gets back from school into quarter-hour intervals: she could then record, for each quarter hour, whether Jill had, at any time in the quarter hour, been further than three feet away from her, and whether she had obeyed any request. (Jill's mother chose to make her records this way: that is, instead of counting the bad behaviour, 'disobedience' and 'following round', she counted how often Jill behaved well, 'obedience' and 'not following round'. She thought this would be easier – 'there'll be nothing on the charts'. She was surprised to find that she was not quite right about this, and that Jill *was* sometimes obedient and did not *always* cling to her like a limpet.) A tick would show that Jill *had* been more than three feet away, or had obeyed a request, and a cross would show the opposite. In the 'obedience' row a nought (o) would show that Jill's mother had not asked her to do anything in that interval. The record might look something like this:

| | 3.30–4.30 | | | | 4.30–5.30 | | | 5.30–6.30 | | | |
	3.30–3.45	3.45–4	4.–4.15	4.15–4.45							
Distance	x	x	x	√	√	x	√	x	x	x	x	x
Obedience	o	x	√	x	x	o	o	x	o	x	x	x

So for these three hours it would be clear that Jill had moved away from her mother in three of the twelve intervals, and had obeyed a request in one. We can also see a hint that Jill became more clinging and disobedient towards the end of the evening, though more records would be needed to discover whether this was a regular pattern.

The tricky part of this kind of recording is that the observer has to keep alert to the passing of time, or several intervals may go by without the behaviour being recorded. It can also require a lot of concentration, especially if the behaviour does not occur, as this means that the observer has to keep on watching like a hawk throughout the entire interval (whereas if the behaviour occurred he could record a tick and then relax for the rest of the interval).

It helps to set a kitchen timer to go off at the end of the interval, re-setting it each time it goes off.

5. *Time-sampling*

Here too the period under observation is divided up into intervals, but in this case the observer records whether the behaviour is happening at one moment *only*, usually at the end of the interval. So Jill's mother might record whether Jill was more than three feet away from her at the moment before 3.45, 4 o'clock and so on.

The advantage of this method is that if two people – say, a mother and a father, or a brother and sister – are recording the child's behaviour at the same time, then if each of them records independently that they observed a particular piece of behaviour at the one moment, it is extremely likely that they have recorded the same piece of behaviour. So by using a time-sampling method of recording it is possible to get a good measure of the reliability of the observations. By contrast, if two people used any of the other four recording methods I have discussed they could not be nearly so certain that they had recorded the same pieces of behaviour. Using interval recording, for instance, both of them might record that a certain piece of behaviour had taken place during the interval, but one observer might have seen and recorded it happening at the beginning and the other at the end of the interval.

So time-sampling is the best method to use to check on the reliability of the observations. It is still possible to measure reliability of the other recording methods (event, interval, etc.) and see how far the records of two people recording at the same time agree; but with these methods we are not so certain that they have recorded identical things.

The importance of reliable records

When we know that certain observations are reliable we know that different observers saw and recorded much of the same behaviour: they agreed on what happened. So if there are changes in the records over time we know that this is due to changes in the child's behaviour, and not to changes in the observer or to mistakes made by him. All sorts of things can make somebody an unreliable observer. He may be tired, or upset, or not particularly interested in the task, and so be careless: he may have some particular bias, such as being very fond of the child, and so want to present him in as good a light as possible: if he knows that no checks will be made on his record it will seem to him less important if he makes a few slips. When a second observer is present mistakes like this would show up in disagreements between the two records.

Another thing that makes it more difficult to get reliable records is poor definition of what is being observed. It is quite common for two observers, finding that their records differ, to discover they have been recording slightly different things. In one case two people set out to count the number of tantrums a little girl had. Later they found that one counted it as a tantrum if the little girl burst into tears while the other only counted it if she also stamped her foot, screamed or lay down on the floor and kicked. Discussion and clarification usually result in closer agreement, though it is not unusual for the behaviour to have to be redefined several times before sufficiently close agreement is reached.

Reliability is worked out by counting up the number of times the two observers agreed, dividing this by the total number of observations (the number of times they agreed plus the number of times they disagreed) and multiplying by 100 to put the figure as a percentage. For example, in 75 observations the observers agree 23 times and disagree 52 times: divide 23 by 75, multiply by 100 which gives you 31 per cent. Reliability is usually accepted as satisfactory at 80 per cent or above, so clearly these observers have some work to do. Probably not many parents do, in fact, concern themselves with the reliability of their observations on their own children. Nevertheless it could be interesting for the parents to do a reliability study between them, or for a brother or sister to do reliability checks every now and again.

Baselines

The most important reason for making and recording observations is to enable us to judge whether what we are doing is having the effect we want on the child's behaviour – whether he is any 'better', following our efforts, than he was before. This means that you need a record of what he was like before you started to teach him something to compare with later records. The record of what the behaviour is like before we start trying to change it is called a *baseline*.

Graphs

In order to get a clear picture which we can see at a glance of how things are going it is often helpful to set out the figures from our records on a chart, or graph. We put down on the graph how much the child did each day, or in each of our teaching sessions, and then join up the points with straight lines. The days, or sessions, go on the horizontal axis: and the kind of behaviour on the vertical axis. So, if we want to teach a child to use his potty, before we start teaching him we might take a baseline of how many times a day he has wet pants. Supposing in the first week he has four wet pants the first day, four the second, six the next, then five, then seven, then four, then five. Our baseline graph would look like this:

Wet pants

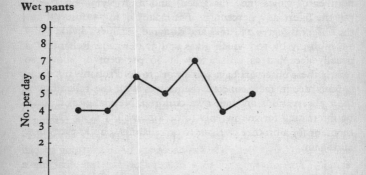

We try to make the graph perfectly clear, giving it a title and labelling the two axes so that anyone who looks at the graph can pick out the information without having to ask what it means. (There is more about records and graphs in chapter 8.)

Our baseline, then, is a record of what the child's behaviour was like before we did anything to change it. Sometimes people are reluctant to spend time taking a baseline, especially when the behaviour is very unpleasant or destructive, such as self-injury. In these cases we may want to start working to discourage the behaviour as quickly as possible, but as a rule a baseline is helpful because with it we can see more clearly the effect of working with the child. Baselines are seldom nice straight lines but, allowing for a bit of wavering, they fall into three broad categories: ascending, descending or stable. Examples are shown below:

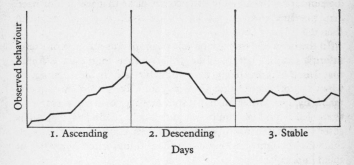

1. Ascending   2. Descending   3. Stable

Days

An ascending baseline is not an ideal one from which to begin a programme if the behaviour is of a kind that we want to increase (for instance, the number of words the child can say); as the behaviour already, for some other reason, is increasing it is hard to tell whether what we are doing has made any difference – or indeed whether it was necessary to do anything special at all. The same applies to a descending baseline charting a kind of behaviour we want to discourage. In one case, some nurses at a hospital wanted to treat a boy who was banging his head. They decided to take a baseline, simply recording how often he banged his head each day. To their amazement as they began to record the baseline he began to bang his head less and less until he finally stopped doing it altogether. They never found out for certain what brought about this change, though they suspected that, in some strange way, the boy was affected by the fact that every time he banged someone in the room reached for a pencil and made a mark on paper, but it did mean they did not need to embark on 'treatment'.

The ideal baseline for most purposes is a stable one. Since the behaviour is happening at a pretty regular rate, any changes that take place following the beginning of the programme are probably the result of what we have done.

So if we find we have an ascending baseline for a behaviour we want to increase, or a descending baseline for a behaviour we want to decrease, we go on taking baseline records until either the graph levels out, in which case we can then begin our programme; or, alternatively, it becomes clear that we do not need a programme at all – and few things could be more delightful than that.

In the ordinary way the baseline can give us all sorts of useful information. In her baseline Jill's mother might have found that Jill was more likely to be difficult late in the evening, or when visitors came: that she was more likely to obey requests made by her father than by her mother, or vice versa. One thing Jill's mother would be quite likely to find is that Jill is actually rather more obedient and less continuously difficult than she thought. Just counting these things often helps to put them in perspective.

If we want to be completely sure that it was our efforts that caused the change, and not something quite unrelated to what we were doing, like a spell of fine weather or a visit from Granny, we can discontinue the teaching for a while. We will then see whether the child's behaviour goes back towards what it was before we started (in which case the changes probably were due to our efforts) or continues in the changed direction (in which case it may have been due to something else). This way of taking a baseline, starting teaching, and then stopping the teaching, is called a *reversal design*, and leads to charts like this:

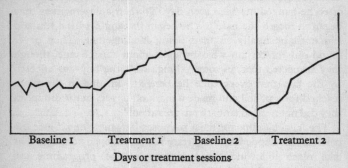

| Baseline 1 | Treatment 1 | Baseline 2 | Treatment 2 |

Days or treatment sessions

In this case the kind of behaviour was a 'good' one that the teacher wanted to encourage: if it were a 'bad' one that we wanted to discourage we would expect to see the last three parts of the chart the other way up – the curve going down with our teaching, up again in the second baseline, and down again in the second teaching phase. Notice, too, that the teacher doesn't give up at the end of Baseline 2 but puts the teaching into effect again so that the child finally benefits from it.

Many people dislike using a reversal design, as it goes against the grain to encourage or deliberately allow a child to slip back. There are other ways of tackling the problem of making sure that it is our teaching that is changing the behaviour (and we need to be sure so that we know whether it will be worth using this method another time). The main one is a *multiple baseline design*. In this we choose three or four kinds of behaviour that could be treated in the same way, do baselines on all of them, but treat them one at a time. Then, if each time we begin work on it the behaviour in question changes, while the others remain much the same, it is highly probable that what we are doing is responsible for the changes. In this case we get a chart something like this:

Speech training: teaching single words

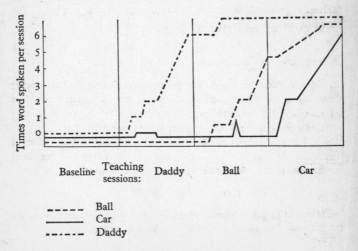

Keeping records can seem a tiresome chore at the time but later on it can be very gratifying to look back and see how much the child has progressed. As one parent has said: 'The keeping of regular records is useful as one sometimes does not realize how quick progress has been; it also helps one to spot difficulties and areas where one should try a new approach'.*

The main points

1. In making observations we want to:
    (a) be quite clear about exactly what the child does
    (b) describe what he does clearly, not vaguely
    (c) describe things that he does that we can observe and count (not feelings or thoughts which we can't).

2. We should write down our observations rather than just try to remember what happened.

3. There are five different recording methods; the most often used are event, duration and interval recording; the other two are continuous recording and time-sampling.

4. To see whether what we are doing makes a difference to what the child does, we take a baseline wherever possible.

5. Figures obtained from the records give us the information more quickly if presented as a graph.

Some practice problems

1. Keep a record of some unimportant happening in your home: how often one child goes upstairs or into the garden; or says 'Please' or 'No' – anything you like.
Use any one of the recording methods suggested.
Do it for any length of time you like – all day or only part of each day. If you decide to use only part of a day use the same part or parts each day you make your observations.

2. Try setting your record out on a graph.

3. If possible get a second observer to do two or three (or more

* *One in Seven is Special*, Ronald Brown, N S M H C, 1974, 30p.

if you like) observations alongside you to check on the reliability.
If you do this, be careful to make your observations quite
independently of each other at the time you are doing them
(but make sure you both start and stop at the same time).
Don't discuss them while you are doing them, though, of
course, you can afterwards, at the end of the observation
period.

3. Reinforcement: 'You've done it – Hurray!'

Reinforcement is a familiar word. We talk of reinforcements for an army, of reinforced concrete, of reinforcing the seat of a small boy's pants. In each case what we are talking about is strengthening something: extra troops to bolster up those already in the field, iron girders set into concrete to toughen it, extra material in that part of the pants where strength is most needed. When the word *reinforcement* is used in behaviour modification it has the same meaning, but since what we are talking about now is behaviour, in this case the meaning is, *reinforcement strengthens behaviour*.

Reinforcement is anything which, when it follows a piece of behaviour, results in an increase in that behaviour in the future:

Adult says: 'Sit down'	Child sits down	Adult says: 'That's lovely', and gives a kiss	Child sits down more readily next time he is asked
	Behaviour	*Reinforcement*	*Result*

Everyone depends to some extent on reinforcement for their actions. If you think carefully about any aspect of your everyday life you will see that most of what you do is in the expectation of some form of reinforcement (though sometimes this may be something that will happen well into the future).

The same is true for mentally handicapped children. They too need reinforcement, especially when the things we would like them to do are not particularly interesting or enjoyable to them. We may need to plan reinforcement deliberately for the mentally handicapped child because there may not be many things in his life that he enjoys so much that he is willing to work for them –

that is, that are reinforcing to him; he may be less able than we are to look to the future or to wait for reinforcement; and he may be less able to get reinforcement from very small things happening around him – for instance, a slight smile on his mother's face. So it often turns out that the mentally handicapped child does not get much reinforcement. When this happens he may give up expecting to get it at all, and feel there is little point in making an effort to do things: he then seems to be lazy, and we say 'he won't try'.

Reinforcement is one of the keys to learning for the mentally handicapped child. When we reinforce him after his good behaviours we help him to learn. Many parents do this anyway when a child is learning something new. For instance a child just learning to use his potty may get a delighted hug and a kiss from his mother the first time he actually performs in it; this makes it more likely that he will use his potty next time he sits on it. Of course it does not make it certain, but, providing of course that he likes hugs and kisses, it makes it more likely than if he had not been reinforced.

You will remember that reinforcement is *anything* that makes a piece of behaviour more likely to occur. We should never assume that any particular thing is a reinforcer for any particular person, though some things *are* found to be reinforcing for most people. Many retarded children are willing to make an effort if they know that this will be followed by a sweet or a biscuit, but some are not. So in every case where we want a child to learn we have to find out what *he* is sufficiently keen on that he will work for it. When we have found it, that is a reinforcer for him.

Positive and negative reinforcement

Up till now we have been talking about *positive reinforcement*. This is the most important and frequently used kind of reinforcement. With positive reinforcement a piece of behaviour is followed by *giving something good*. With *negative reinforcement* a piece of behaviour is followed by *taking away something bad*. Negative reinforcement is seldom deliberately used with children, though adults quite often find it working on them. Supposing Rupert hears the chimes of the ice-cream van and runs to his mother: 'Mum, can I have a lolly?' His mother doesn't think he should have one and says so. 'Oh, go on Mum, let me have a lolly, I *do* want one. *Everybody's* out there, I'm the *only* one in the street who isn't getting a lolly! Go on Mum, I haven't had one for *ages*. It's only 7p. I'll be ever so good if you let me. *Go* on Mum.' And so on and on. At last his mother gives him the 7p. Rupert runs off, the pestering stops and his mother thinks, 'Well it was worth letting him have the money for the lolly, it will keep him quiet for a bit'. Her giving in is negatively reinforced, through the relief it brings her from the pestering. She may be more likely to hand over the lolly money more readily next time. (Unless, of course, she tumbles to the fact that at the same time Rupert is being positively reinforced for pestering and is likely to pester more. Once she realizes that she may decide to take a firm stand.)

The man who banged his head against a brick wall and when asked why said, 'Because it's so nice when I stop', was negatively reinforcing himself.

Negative reinforcement is not much used with children, and I shall not discuss it further. The thing to notice is that it *increases* behaviour, and is *not* the same as punishment; in behaviour modification 'punishment' means anything which *decreases* behaviour (this is discussed in chapter 7).

Kinds of reinforcers

There are four main kinds of reinforcers:

1. *Primary reinforcers*

These are the things that are necessary for life – food, drink, warmth, sleep. The first two are often used with retarded children, the third and fourth hardly ever. Food and drink are powerful reinforcers because they are such basic needs. Primary reinforcers, naturally enough, work better when the child actually needs them – food when he is hungry, drinks when he is thirsty. However, he is unlikely ever to be so hungry or so thirsty that just any food or drink will do; we have to look around for his favourites to use them as reinforcers.

2. *Secondary or generalized reinforcers*

These are things that, although not useful in themselves to the child, become valued because they make it possible for him to get what he wants. Money is a good example of a secondary reinforcer. In itself it does nothing for us but it can be exchanged for goods and so it has great representative value. Similarly, tokens or stars or points that the child earns can be exchanged in the same way. Secondary reinforcers are not always easy to use, especially with very retarded children, but if they can be used they have some special advantages.

Using secondary reinforcers is described more fully in chapter 4, 'Tokens'.

3. *Social reinforcers*

Praise, smiles, hugs, kisses, cuddles; anything that involves giving attention. Just a glance or a raised eyebrow can sometimes work as a reinforcer, and even crossness can be a reinforcer: if

the child desperately wants attention, angry attention may be better than none at all. He may also find it very simple to get angry attention just by behaving badly.

4. Stimulating reinforcers

There are a number of things which a child can find reinforcing which are neither primary, secondary, nor social: toys, games and activities; music; bright lights; other kinds of sights, sounds and sensations. These seem to be reinforcing because the child enjoys the stimulation, the interesting experience, he gets from them.

Finding reinforcers for the individual child

Many children enjoy and will work for food reinforcers. Sweets, of course, spring to mind, and if that is what the child likes best then they may be what we have to use. Sweets and sweet things are, however, bad for the children's teeth and liable to make them fat, so wherever possible we look for other foods that they like – cheese, crisps, fruit, sultanas, carrots. Drinks too are often reinforcing to children: soft drinks, milk, tea, coffee – sometimes just water.

Other children love attention, praise, hugs and kisses – the social reinforcers. In many ways these are the reinforcers that most of us would prefer to use wherever possible. We can show the child how pleased we are with him at any time, whereas it is more complicated to have to carry round the special toys or bits of apple. Moreover, social reinforcers are the ones we get in normal everyday life for most small successes; a child who responds to them is that much nearer his fellow human beings than one who does not. Because of this it is always to be hoped that a child who is not interested in social reinforcers can learn to enjoy them, so they should always be given alongside any other kind of reinforcer that we use. A child who is not specially interested in praise from an adult but is mad on ice-cream should when he has done what is required of him be given a hug and told, 'That's splendid!', and then given a spoonful of ice-cream. Eventually we hope that the two kinds of reinforcement – the social and the edible – will become linked in his mind, he will come to enjoy the praise and the hug, and both will become reinforcing to him.

Some children show little response to praise and attention, and may not be particularly interested in food. In this situation we have to explore other things that may be reinforcing, and may have to be imaginative and ingenious about it. Here are a few things that have been found reinforcing for some children:

Music – records, tapes, singing.
Clapping.
Stroking, tickling, patting.
'Frolicking' – being bounced or jumped.
Bright lights – a torch to switch on.
Hand cream rubbed on to the child's hand.
Sucking an ice cube.
An electric toothbrush.

You will see that most of these come under the heading of 'stimulating reinforcers'.

Where it is very difficult to think of anything that the child is really keen on we may make use of the *Premack Principle* (David Premack is an American psychologist who first defined the principle). According to this, any activity that the child does frequently when left to himself may be used as a reinforcer. For instance, if a child spends much of his time running around, or rocking, then we may allow him to run or rock *only* when he has performed some task that we want him to do. Probably most of us would not ordinarily think of these things, running, or rocking or, in the case of Timmy, twiddling a plastic cup on his thumb (see pages 209–10) as particularly reinforcing, and would not think of using them as reinforcers. But if a particular child demonstrates a 'preferred activity' – that is, the child behaves in a particular way whenever he can – then it is a hint that his own behaviour could be used to reinforce his learning of other things. So if we want the running-about child to learn to sit still he may learn to do so if he is only allowed to run when he has sat still for a short time. It sounds mad, but it can work.

You will see that selecting a good reinforcer for a child is a matter of very careful observation of what he enjoys most and of what he likes best to do. Parents are often very good at this, as they know the child so well, and may notice things about him that other people miss.

It is important to remember that a reinforcer, which increases the behaviour it follows, will have this sort of effect on any kind of behaviour, good or bad. No one sets out deliberately to make a child do bad things more often, but we may, in fact, do so without realizing it. For example, a child who enjoys adult attention may find that a certain way to get attention is to throw ornaments through the window, or attack his baby sister – people rush to his side, they hold him, look earnestly at him, make gestures and talk to him. For some time following his action he can rely on being the centre of attention. Next time he feels in need of attention, wham goes another flower vase.

Of course, nobody would deliberately increase the number of times a child did these things: but if he is reinforced by attention, and if his bad behaviour is followed by attention, this behaviour may continue or become more frequent. Once we have identified the reinforcers for a child we should try to make sure they follow his good behaviours, and not his bad ones. (See also chapter 7, p. 96.)

How to give reinforcement

1. Reinforcement should be given when the child does what we want him to and not, as far as possible, at other times; this helps to keep him interested in the reinforcer. Of course, I don't mean that if attention is the reinforcer we never attend to the child unless he (say) puts the yellow brick in the yellow box. That would be absurd. Of course he receives attention in the ordinary way during the course of the day. But in the ten minutes or so that are set aside to teach him he gets our

warmest praise, our most enthusiastic hugs and kisses, for those times when he does the thing we want him to learn. So, during most of the ten minutes we remain our calm friendly selves, but when the yellow brick goes in the yellow box we go really wild.

Where the reinforcer is something other than attention it may help if we see that the child does not get too much of it at other times. Jay's mother, after discussing a programme that was having only moderate success, said thoughtfully, 'I think perhaps she's getting too many biscuits and sweets at other times. If I cut those down a bit she may be more excited about them when we do our sessions.'

2. Reinforcement should be given *immediately* after the good behaviour. Even quite a short delay (five seconds) between the behaviour taking place and the reinforcer being given can hinder his learning. This means that we need to have the reinforcer ready to hand – actually in our fingers – to give as soon as the child has done what we want.

3. Reinforcement should be given *clearly*. This applies particularly to social reinforcement: praise should be enthusiastic,

smiles delighted, hugs and kisses warm. Besides being exciting and enjoyable to the child (most children anyway) this also lets him know without any doubt that he has done the right thing (see also page 86).

Schedules of reinforcement

When the child is learning something new he should be reinforced *consistently*, every time he does it. Later when he becomes more skilful, and succeeds with the task quite often, it is better to give the reinforcement only every now and again. So for building up a new kind of behaviour use a consistent, or *continuous* schedule of reinforcement: for keeping it going once he has learnt it an *intermittent*, every-now-and-again, schedule is best.

Intermittent schedules can be of various kinds: the reinforcement can be given according to the number of times the good behaviour occurs (ratio schedules); or according to the passage of time (interval schedules). Ben who is reinforced for each brick he puts into a box is being reinforced on a *ratio* schedule, while Molly who is reinforced for every thirty seconds that she sits still is being reinforced on an *interval* schedule.

Either kind of schedule may be fixed or it may be variable. On a *fixed* schedule the reinforcement is given regularly, after a certain number of responses or after a certain length of time; Ben, as he gets better at putting in the bricks, may be reinforced for every second brick, or every third, or sixth, or tenth; while Molly, becoming more able to sit still, may be reinforced after every forty seconds, sixty seconds, two minutes, five minutes and so on.

On a *variable* schedule, the same overall amount of reinforcement is given but the number of responses made or the amount of time that goes by before the reinforcement is given is varied. So, if Ben were on a VR2 (variable ratio schedule, every second response reinforced on average) he might get reinforcement for the first brick he put in the box, then for the third after that, then the second after that, then the next, and the next, then the fourth after that: at the end of this little session he would have put twelve bricks in the box and received reinforcement six times, but dodged about so that Ben was never quite sure when the reinforcement would come. Similarly Molly could be reinforced on a VI 30 seconds schedule – at variable intervals averaging out at thirty seconds. It seems to be the unpredictability of the varied intermittent schedules that makes them best for encouraging the child to keep up what he has learnt thoroughly.

Very precisely worked-out variable schedules are difficult to use in everyday life. In practice you are likely to give intermittent reinforcement in a much more haphazard way, just every now and again. If reinforcement is not to be given continuously (after every right response) the important thing is to remember to give it often enough. This is especially important just after moving off a continuous schedule. A child who has been accustomed to getting reinforcement after every response may get discouraged and give up trying if the reinforcement is delayed too long. In the example above, Ben twice got the reinforcement after only one response: it may be helpful to remember to do that occasionally, especially at first.

The main points

1. Reinforcement is anything which, when it follows immediately on a piece of behaviour, makes it more likely that the piece of behaviour will occur again.

2. Positive reinforcement works by following the behaviour by giving something good: negative reinforcement by taking away something bad.

3. The kind of reinforcement we use in working with children is almost always positive.

4. Reinforcement may be:
   primary – things to eat or drink
   secondary – money, tokens, stars
   social – praise, attention, hugs and kisses
   stimulating – toys, activities, sensations.

5. We look for whatever the child is *really* fond of, fond enough to be willing to work for it, to use as a reinforcer for him.

6. The *Premack Principle* means using as a reinforcer anything that the child does frequently when left to himself – a preferred activity.

7. Reinforcement should be given only for the kinds of behaviour we want the child to show.

8. Reinforcement should be given:
   when the child shows the good behaviour
   immediately he shows the behaviour
   clearly – especially the social reinforcers.

9. The best reinforcement schedule for teaching the child something new is a continuous schedule.

10. The best reinforcement schedule for keeping a behaviour going once it has been learnt is a variable schedule.

Some practice problems

1. List some things that you think may be reinforcing for your child.

2. List some things you think would be reinforcing for you. Which of the four headings (primary, secondary, social, stimulating) would each of these come under?

3. Can you think of any time when, without meaning to, you reinforced one of your child's bad behaviours?

*4. Can you think of some everyday activity of yours that does not bring you much reinforcement from other people? (i.e. the reinforcement normally comes only from your own feeling of having done it well). How much difference would it make if somebody reinforced you for this every time you did it? Or just now and again?

* 'Practice problems' marked with an asterisk throughout the book are more general and have some general answers. These are given in Appendix 1, pp. 243–58, at the back of the book.

*5. *Scene :* A hotel lounge. A guest is lurking in the background (writing this book actually). Enter a mother and father and pretty little girl of about three.

Child : Mummy I've got a pain.

Mother : Where does it hurt?

Child : (indicates an improbable area near her armpit)

Father : Never mind, have a sweetie. (Addressing the guest) We find that soon cures it.

Guest : (thinks)

Who here is being negatively reinforced? and who positively? What do you think will be the outcome? Would you (if asked) suggest that the parents do anything differently?

4. Tokens

Tokens are one kind of reinforcer. Using tokens, however, is rather different from using other kinds of reinforcer.

When I talk about 'tokens' I am referring to all sorts of secondary reinforcers: points, stars, counters – anything which the child can be given when he does something we want him to do and which he can later exchange for something he particularly wants.

In themselves the tokens do nothing for the child. He cannot eat, drink, or, except to a very limited extent, play with them. If they alone were to be given to a child following something he did it is most unlikely that he would then do that thing more often. If, however, the child finds that if he gets tokens now he will be able to exchange them for something he wants later, the tokens will come to represent the things he wants, and may then become reinforcing. In this case when they are given following something he does he is indeed likely to do that thing more often.

Before discussing how to use tokens, let us look at some of the objections that are sometimes raised against using tokens at all.

The way tokens work for the child is similar to the way money works for most of us. Money is in itself a useless commodity, but is valued because it can be exchanged for the things we need or want. In the same way the child may be reinforced by tokens.

It may be partly this parallel with a cash economy that makes some people jib at the idea of using token programmes with children. It may be, too, that the memory of some 'Token Economy' programmes in some large institutions have seemed to epitomize a manipulative and 'inhuman' approach to human beings. But there is no need for a token programme, any more than any other way of giving reinforcement, to be inhuman. Instead, it can bring particular benefits, especially that of being able to reinforce, and so teach, the rather brighter handicapped child. Indeed, tokens can be used to help the normal child (as I did with my son, see page 12). I have even run a very successful token programme on myself to get rid of a tiresome habit (nail biting) which years of self-reproach and self-exhortation had failed to eradicate. What I found, and what my son found, was that the effect of reinforcement available *now this minute*, and not in some vaguely imagined future, made all the difference to our being able to alter our behaviour in the way we wanted it altered. The token programmes were a very real help.

Some people feel that using tokens smacks of bribery: the child is only doing as he is asked because he is paid for it. On the surface, of course, it does look like that, at least at first. If we look a little deeper we can see that the normal person also does as he is asked because he can foresee, consciously or unconsciously, that this will have some pleasant result – that people will be pleased with him (which pleases him); that there may be some practical advantage to him in their goodwill or simply that he will enjoy knowing that others have benefited. The handicapped person on the other hand may be much less able to envisage all these things: he may not be able to foresee what benefits he could get from doing as he is asked, so he cannot make a realistic choice between doing it and not doing it. When tokens are used to help him to do what we ask we enable him to experience the other advantages of doing so, and eventually these may be enough for him to continue the new behaviours – tokens do not have to go on for ever. For example, 18-year-old Colin attended a centre for handicapped people and sat there, rocking, day after day. It had been impossible to get him to participate in the centre's work training scheme. Then a programme was set up whereby Colin got tokens for joining in with the work, and could exchange the tokens for his favourite orange juice. Colin came to enjoy the work so much that within two to three weeks he no longer needed the tokens – in fact the work itself became reinforcing and he would do other useful things in order to be allowed to go to work. The tokens had enabled him to experience working, and to find how much he liked it.

So tokens can help the handicapped child. Besides helping

him to learn they may also help to make life pleasanter for him and for his parents. Parents who have found themselves driven to nagging the child into doing something can let the tokens take over; the nagging stops; the child has a straightforward choice between doing what he is asked and getting a token for it or not doing the task and foregoing the token. Without the nagging, life becomes more peaceful. For the parents, too, giving the tokens is a useful reminder to give social reinforcement ('Here's your token, Gary: well done, you did do that nicely!') so the child benefits in both ways. Of course the parents could have given the praise all along without waiting for the token programme. But parents are human, too; in everyday life opportunities seem to slip by, while having a definite programme to follow may make it more likely that the opportunities will be taken. Many parents who have tried a token programme have been surprised and delighted at the change in the child, at how much more eager and willing he is to cooperate pleasantly when the reinforcement he wants actually comes his way.

Many people will not want to use tokens or token programmes. Many will have no need of them, or of the other suggestions in this book. Others may still feel that they do not want to use this method, and they should not concern themselves with this chapter. But for some children, and their parents, tokens offer another and often highly enjoyable kind of help.

Why we use tokens

Token programmes are especially useful with older or rather brighter children. For these children many of the reinforcers discussed earlier (chapter 3) are of little interest: these children are not thrilled by bites of food, sips of drink or snatches of music. What they are interested in is, perhaps, something more substantial: pop records, a transistor radio, new clothes, extra swimming sessions or meals in a restaurant. If the child is really keen on these things we want to be able to make use of them as reinforcers, but because they are large and expensive things, or because they may be difficult to give quickly we cannot use them in the same way as pieces of cheese or crisps: we cannot give a child a transistor radio each time he tidies his bedroom, or take him swimming each time he is helpful in the house. Instead the child can work towards his chosen reinforcer, earning tokens (or stars or points or whatever) for each piece of good behaviour, until at last he has enough tokens to exchange for the reinforcer.

Another reason for using tokens may be to save the interruption that using ordinary reinforcers entails. For instance, instead of giving Becky a tiny piece of biscuit every time she puts in a piece of puzzle her teacher may give her a token: when Becky has saved up, say, six tokens she can exchange them for a (larger) piece of biscuit. In this way Becky can work for a much longer time before she stops work to eat the biscuit.

Group work is easier with tokens. Instead of having constantly to remember who likes orange and who likes biscuit, and who likes a few moments with the Jack in the box, the teacher gives a token to each child for good work or good behaviour. At the end of the session each child gives up his tokens and chooses his particular reinforcer.

Teaching the child to understand tokens

If the child can understand speech well we can explain to him that he will get tokens for his good behaviour, and that when he has saved up a certain number he will be able to exchange them for his particular reinforcer. If he does not understand speech but we want to use tokens in the way Becky's teacher did we may have to teach him what the tokens mean.

Joe was very fond of crisps and would work well in order to get them, but his teacher thought it would be easier if she could use tokens with him, particularly when she was teaching him in a group of children. He could then exchange his tokens for crisps rather than getting the crisps continuously throughout the lesson. Joe had never had anything to do with tokens so his teacher began by handing a token to him. Immediately she asked and prompted him to give it back and gave him in exchange a piece of crisp. Joe was pleased with the piece of crisp and ate it. After doing this two or three times Joe's teacher handed him a token and told him that he should hold on to it. Joe did not really understand this and was eager to give back the token and to get his piece of crisp. His teacher kept returning his hand with the token in it to his lap. After about ten seconds she asked for the token: Joe handed it over and was given a piece of crisp. Joe soon learnt that he should keep the token and that his piece of crisp would still be given in exchange for it.

Next his teacher taught him to put the token down on the table during the time between the earning and the exchanging of it. Next, when Joe had taken the token and put it down on the table, the teacher, instead of exchanging the token for the crisp, gave him another token and asked him to put that, too, on the table. Joe was puzzled by this but was quite happy to hand over the two tokens this time for two pieces of crisp.

So the programme continued until Joe was able to take and store four tokens before exchanging them for four pieces of crisp. To help him to know when he had the right number to exchange Joe's teacher constructed a little form-board with four token-shaped pieces drawn on it: every time Joe was given a token he put it on to one of the spaces in the board, and when the board was full he emptied it and exchanged the tokens for the pieces of crisp. Other ways to store tokens are a rack or plastic tube, with four spaces marked on it. This can be made like the diagrams that show how the church fund is progressing:

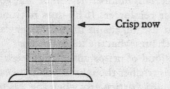
Crisp now

The tokens are put into the tube until they reach the mark which shows there are now enough to be exchanged for the reinforcer.

You will have noticed that up to this point Joe had not done anything to 'earn' his tokens; they had simply been given to him. All his teacher had been doing so far was teaching him what the tokens stood for; that 'tokens now' meant 'crisps later'. Now it was time to begin linking the tokens with his work. Joe's teacher gave him some work to do – colouring shapes in a drawing book. When he had coloured one section she gave him a token, then another for the next section, and so on. When he had completed four sections Joe exchanged the tokens for pieces of crisp. Since he realized that he would get the crisp when he had the four tokens he was encouraged by being given the tokens to do his work, as was shown by his greater attentiveness to his work and the care and interest with which he did it.

Each time she gave him a token Joe's teacher made a point of pairing the token with praise or affection: at the same time, as she gave him a token, she also said how well he was doing, stroked his hair or gave him a quick hug. The idea here is that eventually these social reinforcers might take over so that Joe would happily work for them alone and the tokens become unnecessary (see page 63, 'How to end a token programme').

Token programmes for the brighter child

There are four main steps in setting up this kind of programme. We have to decide on:

1. The kind of behaviour we want to change.
2. How many tokens will be given for the things the child does.
3. The exchange reinforcers – what he can get for his tokens.
4. How many tokens are to be given in exchange for the reinforcer.

1. Deciding what behaviour we want to change

We can use tokens just like other reinforcers, either to encourage or to discourage something the child does: either to increase the number of times he behaves well, for instance by being friendly to his brother or getting dressed in the morning; or to decrease the number of times he behaves badly, perhaps grinding his teeth or swearing. If we want to increase the incidence of a good behaviour we have to make as careful a definition of it as we can and follow the good behaviour with a token. If we want the child to stop doing something we may either take away tokens when the bad behaviour occurs (see 'Fines', page 57); or we may use DRO – *Differential Reinforcement of Other kinds of behaviour* (see page 104). If we use DRO, instead of defining the bad behaviour that we want to get rid of we focus on others that we want to encourage to take the place of the bad behaviour. In many cases these 'Other' kinds of behaviour that we want to increase will be the opposite of the bad behaviours that we want to decrease: we would reinforce the child for *not* grinding his teeth or for *not* swearing. For example, Ann was very disobedient and disobliging, and her mother wanted to help her get over this. She set up a token programme in which Ann was given a star to stick on a chart every time she was obedient – that is, every time she began to do what she was asked within five seconds of her mother asking it. Dino, who made a great deal of trouble in class, was given a token for every half hour in the classroom in which he had not caused trouble. ('Not causing trouble' had to be rather carefully defined: not leaving his seat without permission, not interfering with other children, not disobeying a teacher, grumbling or whining.)

2. *How many tokens to give*

At the beginning of a programme, when a continuous schedule is used, this is quite easy: a token is given for every good piece of behaviour, or at regular intervals of good behaviour. It gets more complicated when we want to ask the child to do more for his tokens. This is discussed under 'Adapting the programme', page 58.

3. *Deciding on the exchange reinforcers*

One of the advantages of a token programme is that we can use all sorts of reinforcers and be as imaginative as we like. I have already suggested using quite large reinforcers (transistor radio, new clothes, etc.). Parents quite often do something of the sort anyway: promise, for example, a bicycle if the child will do this or that over a period of time – pass an exam, be good until Christmas. But unless the child is very strong-willed this sort of promise often does not lead to a consistent change in his behaviour, because the reinforcer is so far away from what he is doing here and now. By giving a token for each of the individual things he does you can bring the whole idea of the reinforcement nearer, making it more real to him.

Privileges of one sort and another can be used as reinforcers: a special visit to the cinema or other treat. Sometimes, however, it's very difficult to find extra things that a child likes enough and that you can afford and you may then have to use ordinary, everyday things that he is fond of which might ordinarily be regarded as his by right.

If the child himself asks for help, you may be able to agree with him on the use of his normal rights as reinforcers – my son readily agreed that the reinforcer for his programme should be his pocket-money. If you have to use these normal 'rights' or privileges in this way, make sure that the child can obtain the privilege quite easily, especially at first, so that he doesn't lose out.

All sorts of things may be used as reinforcers for children for whom 'extras' cannot be found; anything that the child is interested in or enjoys. Sue, who was expected to mix with the other children at her school in the normal way, very much liked to be able to get away from them and to spend time in her bedroom by herself. This was not usually allowed as school rules said that bedrooms were out of bounds during the day but she was able to use her tokens to 'buy' time to spend in her bedroom. Rachel, on the other hand, used hers to get the chance to watch her favourite TV programme. Other children may like to earn outings, visits to the zoo, the chance to go swimming, time to spend with a favourite person, staying up later in the evening. The important thing, as with all reinforcers, is that it should be something that the child is really keen on and willing to work for. In Ann's case, for example, the psychologist working with her mother at first suggested using Ann's pocket-money, with a little extra added, and giving her one penny of her pocket-money in exchange for every four stars. At first this worked well, but one morning her mother found that Ann had ripped all her stars off her chart.

Sometimes a child will spoil his star chart in a fit of temper, wanting to show he doesn't care about it. If we think this may not be the true reason we carry on for a while, substituting a new chart onto which any surviving stars can be re-stuck, and see whether he continues to tear up the charts or whether he really enjoys getting the stars and exchanging them for what he wants. On the other hand, the chart-spoiling may be an indication that the stars are not reinforcing for the child because the exchange items are of little interest to him. This is what happened with Ann. Her mother realized that the pennies Ann was earning in exchange for stars were simply not sufficiently reinforcing. She also knew that Ann very much wanted a particular pop record, so this was substituted as the exchange reinforcer. As it was an expensive record she told Ann that she would have to get sixty stars in order to earn the record, and although it took longer to get the record than the pocket-money, the record was a much more effective exchange reinforcer, and Ann went to work with a will. Not only did she obey with alacrity almost every request made of her but her mother was bombarded with offers of help on every possible occasion. Although at this point Ann was being obliging in order to get what she wanted, it was very pleasant for her mother, who in her turn responded more warmly to Ann, and the whole relationship became a happier one.

4. Exchange rates

There is no set way of doing this; it is a matter of trial and error. Each child, his problem, the rate at which he can earn the tokens, and the exchange reinforcer that works for him, is different. We have to make an intelligent guess at a reasonable exchange rate, and then be prepared to change it if we get it wrong.

One general point is that the exchange reinforcer should be sufficiently within the child's reach: he should expect to get it with lively anticipation. To a large extent this depends on his ability to measure time, especially future time, and children vary in this. Even very severely handicapped children can wait for half an hour or so to exchange their tokens: others can wait for half a day, exchanging their tokens at mid-day and again in the evening: others again can wait for a whole day, or two days, or a week, or, as in Ann's case, for several weeks. A longer wait will tend, naturally enough, to go with better (i.e. more expensive) exchange reinforcers: Lynn exchanges her tokens once a day for an apple or a bar of chocolate while Philip (see page 105) exchanged his every four days for a small toy. However we arrange things, we should make sure that the child continues to be keenly aware that he is, in what for him is the foreseeable future, going to get the reinforcer.

Fines

One of the possible advantages of a token programme is that it allows for tokens to be taken away in the case of bad behaviour as well as given in the case of a good one: that is, we can use punishment alongside a reinforcement system. This makes tokens different from other kinds of reinforcement – we cannot take away a child's sweet when he has already eaten it. The fining system can be used in one of two ways: either tokens which have been earned for good behaviour can be removed if 'bad' behaviour occurs: or, if we are working only on a 'bad' behaviour, we can give the child a certain number of tokens as his supply for the day and these can be taken away if his 'bad' behaviour occurs. In either case it is very important to remember that the motive power behind these programmes is the availability of positive reinforcement, so the programme should be arranged in such a way that the child is unlikely to reach the situation in which he has no reasonable chance of getting reinforcement. Mandy's programme, which was aimed at reducing her temper tantrums, came unstuck because she lost tokens so fast that at the end of every day she had no tokens left with which to obtain her particular reinforcer – special biscuits for tea. So the tokens themselves quickly lost their reinforcing value for her, she stopped caring whether or not she lost them and went back to having as many temper tantrums as before.

Some American psychologists have thought of an ingenious way to help with the problem of children losing tokens and becoming upset when they do so.* By their method a child who has to lose tokens for bad behaviour is given a chance to earn some tokens back *immediately*, by doing something good: 'It's a pity you threw that dishcloth at me because that means you lose 500 points; but you can earn back 50 points right now if you pick up the dishcloth and wipe down the sink with it.' (The Americans tend to work with astronomical numbers of tokens.) Although the child in this case was of normal or near normal intelligence this approach may be worth remembering.

I think I should say that, on the whole, I have not been very successful with using fining systems with mentally handicapped children. Although these systems may appear attractive and to attack problem behaviours directly, they often break down. I have found token programmes more effective when the tokens were given for good kinds of behaviour than when they were taken away for the bad ones.

Adapting the programme

At some time in the programme we may want to make changes, either because we have not got it quite right in the first place, or because the child makes progress and we want to move things along a bit. Whichever it is, we may do one of two things: either change the schedule of token reinforcement (give more, or fewer, tokens for the same piece of behaviour); or alter the exchange rate of tokens for exchange reinforcers (make the 'token price' of the exchange reinforcers higher or lower).

Making it a little easier to get reinforcement

Changes in which the child is given more tokens, or is charged fewer, are usually made because it becomes apparent that we have set our sights too high. Either by giving the child too few for what he does or by expecting him to give too many in exchange (or perhaps by both) we have made it too difficult for the child

---

* 'Teaching important social skills to children and youths', M. M. Wolf. Paper given at the International Behaviour Modification Workshop, University College of North Wales, Bangor, 1973.

to get the reinforcement, with the ensuing danger that he will despair of ever being able to get it and give up trying to earn the tokens. In this case we either increase the number of tokens the child gets or reduce the number he has to give for his reinforcers. If the child has more tokens he will be better able to 'buy' the reinforcers: or if the token price of the reinforcers is lower he will have a better chance of being able to afford them. In either case the reinforcers become within his reach, and the tokens are seen as leading directly to the reinforcers. The tokens themselves then become reinforcing and the child will make an effort for them.

Making it a little harder to get reinforcement

The situation is rather different when the child makes good progress with his programme, begins to get plenty of tokens and is often able to exchange them for the reinforcers. Not that we regret this state of affairs: it is precisely what was hoped for. It shows that the task we have set him is possible for him and that by doing it he is able to get the reinforcement. The question arises, though, of whether, if he is able to get the reinforcement so easily, he may not be doing as much as he could; alternatively he may get too much of the reinforcer too quickly and get tired of it (satiated). So we may feel that it would be better if he had to put out a bit more effort, or if the reinforcers were spaced out a little more.

The way we do this is either to decrease slightly the number of tokens given for a particular piece of behaviour (so that the child has to do more to get the same number of tokens): or to require slightly more tokens for the reinforcer. In theory it makes little difference which of these methods we choose, but in practice it often seems easier, and less likely to cause trouble, to require more tokens in exchange for the reinforcers.

How to change the programme

If we are using the tokens with a child who can count sufficiently well we can simply tell him that he needs more tokens for the reinforcer. If the child is not very good at counting but has his tokens stored in a rack or a tube or on a stick, then we can move the mark, which measures the number of tokens he needs in order to exchange them, up a couple notches. If he is earning stars which are put on a chart it is probably best to complete one chart and then the new one can be made a bit bigger, with extra spaces for stars; the new chart, like the old one, has to be filled up before it can be exchanged, but now it carries more stars before the goal is reached.

Again we have to be careful when adjusting the programmes that the reinforcement is not put too far out of the child's reach. The aim should always be that the child should receive adequate, even plentiful, reinforcement. After all, that is what is going to make him willing to do the things we want him to do. If we can achieve that everyone will be happy: the child getting plenty of fun and enjoyment and behaving pleasantly, cooperatively, helpfully. If the programme is adjusted because the number of tokens that the child is able to get has steadily increased, and consequently the amount of reinforcers that he can obtain, then the number he has to give for the reinforcer should be adjusted to that point where he gets less reinforcement than at present, but can get at least as much as he got at the beginning of the programme. We should not price him out of the market. In the same way, if we increase the number of tokens he has to give for the reinforcer because we think he may be getting reinforcement so easily that he loses interest in it, then we should reduce the amount of reinforcement he is able to get but not by so much as to make it impossibly difficult for him to get it.

Another way of painlessly scaling-up the number of tokens the child has to get in order to get his reinforcer is to use new exchange reinforcers. This may be a good idea in any case in order to keep up the child's interest in his reinforcers. If a new reinforcer is brought into the system then the number of tokens needed to get it can be made rather higher than the comparable number for the reinforcers the child was getting before. For example, Ann's first exchange reinforcer was a record, for which she had to get sixty stars. Later when she had become very friendly and cooperative and was getting stars by the dozen she wanted to work for a pair of pretty knickers. Although these were much cheaper to buy than the record she was told she would need to get eighty stars for them. Compared with the record they took a lot of tokens but because Ann now gained stars quickly through her cooperative behaviour, she was able to 'buy' the knickers in about the same time that it took her to get the record.

Cheating on the programme

I am talking here about cheating by adults.

Charlie's parents had asked for help with getting Charlie to dress himself. He was slow, dreamy, and, as his parents said, 'lazy'. It would take them an hour and a half each morning to nag him into putting on some of his garments and eventually his mother would dress him in the rest of them in order to have him ready to go to school. Charlie had no actual difficulty with managing his clothes – he was quite able to put them on and do them up himself – so a token programme was set up by which Charlie would be given a token for each garment that he put on himself within a twenty-minute dressing time. Each token was exchangeable for a little sweet which Charlie could take with him to school.

When the psychologist went along at the end of the week to see how things were going she found that the programme was no longer in operation. She asked, why not? had it not worked?

'I'll tell you why not,' said Charlie's father. 'He was having us on. He could do it perfectly well all the time. He came downstairs with all his clothes on that first morning and he's done it every morning since. Today I said "That's enough my boy. I'm not having any more of this." All those sweets! He just couldn't be bothered, that was all there was to it. I've told him from now on he can dress himself like anybody else, to help his mother, not because he's bribed to.' When the psychologist visited the following week Charlie was once again being slow and awkward about his dressing. His father thought the whole episode proved his point – that Charlie was simply lazy.

When we set up a token programme with a child it is in the nature of a contract with him: the child will perform certain actions, we undertake in return to provide exchangeable tokens. The contract is drawn up on the basis that the child will be able to get a certain minimum number of tokens in order to get his exchange reinforcers. We recognize that the reason for the child's future willingness to work for his tokens – that is, to to produce the behaviour that we want of him – is that he will, by means of the tokens, be able to obtain the exchange reinforcers. So it is essential that we should not duck out of the contract when we find that the child is successfully earning his tokens and getting his reinforcers. If we do so, not only will we have been guilty of not honouring the contract, but the child may feel, more strongly than before, the hopelessness of his ever getting reinforcement.

When adults 'cheat' like this it is not as a rule because they are miserly, or that they consciously grudge the child reinforcement. The reasons are more subtle. What Charlie's father felt was typical of many in his position: that he had been conned into setting up the programme and providing the reinforcement, that Charlie was fully capable of doing what was required of him and that therefore he ought to be doing this for no reward at all but just because it was his duty as a member of the family.

Of course it is true that most children dress themselves each morning as a matter of routine and for no other reason but to allow themselves to get on with the business of the day. Let us look a little more closely at this. The child who dresses himself in order to get on with the day's business looks forward, when he is dressed, to all manner of things – an enjoyable breakfast, his comic coming with the newspapers, friends to see at school. Charlie, on the other hand, besides not being very good at looking forward, had rather little in his day to look forward to. His one real pleasure, which he could be sure he would always get, was the prolonged attention that his mother gave him over getting dressed.

What we see here is, first, that even children who apparently perform actions such as dressing with no thought of 'reward' actually do experience reinforcement for it; second, that Charlie was getting no such reinforcement; third, that when reinforcement was provided he dressed himself very well. The difference was that for Charlie the reinforcement had to be deliberately decided on and given if he was to achieve the same as other children.

So, when a programme quickly results in a child successfully performing the kind of behaviour we want of him we should not assume that he could 'do it all the time', that the programme is redundant, and that if we put a stop to it he will automatically continue to do what we want. Instead we should realize that we have found the key to this kind of behaviour for the child, and rejoice in his success: it is also ours.

How to end a token programme

A few children may need to go on getting and exchanging tokens for a long time if they are to go on doing the things that we want them to, but for most the token programme need not last for ever.

Sometimes it just fades away: the child continues doing the things we want without apparently needing tokens or reinforcers. This happened with Philip (page 105) who seemed just to lose interest in his stars and the toys for which he used to exchange them, but continued sleeping through the night in his own bed. Where this happens, however, it is 'the effect of good luck, not to be reckoned on'.

In other cases the tokens can be faded out because other reinforcers take over. In some of the happiest instances social reinforcers become effective, and the child continues his good behaviour because of the attention and appreciation his efforts receive. Or the activity itself may become reinforcing – the child finds he likes having a tidy bedroom, or enjoys reading for its own sake – so the tokens become unnecessary.

In other cases the good behaviour becomes part of the child's everyday life, and he does it as a matter of habit, but continues to need the extra pleasure he had been getting from his reinforcers. Here there is usually little difficulty in finding another skill or activity for which the child can get his tokens – the world is full of things for him to learn. Ann's mother went on, when disobedience and swearing were no longer a problem, to teach Ann simple cooking, knitting and housewifery, and Ann enjoyed getting tokens for mastering these new tasks.

In other cases, again, we may need to stretch the schedule of reinforcement, giving it more and more infrequently until we are giving it only very occasionally, but not doing away with it altogether. It may then be possible to stop giving the tokens and give only the reinforcer in this way. Had Philip needed more help his mother might sometimes have said to him what a splendid boy he was to sleep all night in his own bed, how pleased and proud of him she and his father were; while on a very few occasions she might have added that a boy who was able to do this was so grown-up that he could probably use a few pence more in pocket-money (or something).

One last way of ending the tokens is to say to the child that he has made such good progress that it seems that he no longer needs them: that the exchange reinforcers which he has been earning will now be freely available – so long as the good behaviour continues satisfactorily. If it falls off too much then we may have to set up the programme again. For example, once her temper tantrums had nearly disappeared Mandy was allowed her special biscuits every day for tea: at one time she went through a bad patch, so for a short time she had again to earn tokens and exchange them for the biscuits: the tantrums once more decreased, and after this tokens were again discontinued and have not been heard of since, and Mandy will have the biscuits every day for tea as long as she wants them.

The main points

1. Tokens, points, stars (money) are all generalized reinforcers.

2. Although not reinforcing in themselves, they can become so by being paired with other reinforcers – the exchange reinforcers.

3. Tokens can be earned for good behaviour and later exchanged for the reinforcers.

4. Tokens are especially useful for older children who are

interested in larger reinforcers, or those that cannot be given immediately following a good behaviour.

5. Tokens can also be used with younger or more handicapped children to save interrupting work sessions.

6. Younger and more handicapped children may need to be taught what the tokens stand for.

7. In setting up a programme we have to decide on:
   (a) the good and bad behaviour and define them
   (b) the schedule of reinforcement
   (c) the exchange reinforcer
   (d) the exchange rate of tokens for reinforcers: making sure that the child has a good chance of being able to get the reinforcers.

8. Tokens can be taken away as a punishment for 'bad' behaviour.

9. We may need to adjust the programme because the child is able to get either too little reinforcement or too much.

10. We can adjust the programme by changing the number of tokens the child is given, or the number that he has to give for his reinforcer.

11. We should not 'cheat' by refusing to give the child reinforcement when he begins to earn it successfully.

12. Token programmes can fade out:
   (a) when other reinforcers take over
   (b) when the activity itself becomes reinforcing
   (c) by moving the child on to learning and being reinforced for new skills
   (d) by stretching the schedule of reinforcement until the reinforcement is infrequently but still occasionally given
   (e) by making the reinforcement freely available to the child so long as the good behaviour continues.

Some practice problems

1. Can you think of something that anyone in your family, over the age of sixteen, does that you might want and be able to change using a token programme?

2. Which of these would be a good exchange reinforcer for you:
   breakfast in bed on Sunday
   an air ticket to Majorca
   a day off once a month
   one meal a week cooked by somebody else
   a ticket for a theatre/ballet/stock car racing/Test match/ Celtic v. Rangers (or equivalent).

   Choose any two – or any two others you like. Which of your tiresome kinds of behaviour would you be prepared to modify in order to earn them?

*3. A child constantly mislays her tokens. What would you do?

*4. If you were running a token programme on a desert island what would you use for tokens?

*5. People sometimes run token programmes on themselves to help them lose weight. These programmes are often unsuccessful. Why do you think that is?

*6. Charlie's programme laid down that he would get a token for each garment that he put on by himself – vest, pants, two socks, shirt, sweater and trousers; seven tokens, each one to be exchanged for a sweet. On the first morning he earned all the tokens and got all the sweets. Supposing you were Charlie's parent, and you felt he was earning the sweets too easily: what would you do?

5. Teaching by Guiding

If a child knows how to do something but is not keen on doing it, we can encourage him to do it more often by reinforcing him every time he does. However, if we want the child to learn a new activity that he has never done before, reinforcement alone is not enough – there is nothing there yet to reinforce. We need different methods to teach new skills. This chapter and the next are concerned with these methods.

What to teach and how to teach it

When setting out to teach a child something new it is important to be as sure as possible that what we are aiming to teach is something that he is capable of doing; that it is not physically impossible, or very difficult for him. No one would try to teach a child who only feeds from a bottle to feed himself with a knife and fork, or one who cannot speak to talk in sentences. A good

general guideline is to teach the child something that is only just beyond him – the next step up the ladder. The order in which normal children learn things can often give an idea of what this next logical step would be. Sometimes, however, it is quite hard to decide whether a skill is really the right one to teach. One boy, for example, who did not talk, had also failed to learn a system of hand-signs (Paget-Gorman Sign System, see page 198). His teacher was uncertain whether this meant that neither speech nor sign language was a suitable communication system for him, or whether he was at that time not capable of communicating in any systematic way. She decided to go for the first possibility, that the two previous methods had not been suitable for him, and to try out a third alternative, a picture language – this he picked up quickly. The golden rule is: if in doubt, try it out – systematically and keeping careful records. You will soon see whether you're trying to teach something too hard for the child and will be able to try something else that may suit him better.

In this chapter I shall be discussing four main teaching methods: shaping; prompting; breaking down the activity; and backward chaining.

Shaping

Shaping means reinforcing the child for doing something which is not at first precisely what we want but which comes gradually closer and closer to it. Suppose we want to teach a 5-year-old to respond when he is told to 'Sit down' and decide to do this using shaping (there are other methods we could choose which will be discussed later). Our baseline observations show that Kevin never sits down when he's told to but clearly he is not deliberately being naughty – he just doesn't understand. We cannot reinforce him for sitting down when he is told to – it never happens, but he does, however, stay in the room with us (if only because the door is locked). Our observations show that sometimes when we say 'Sit down' he is at the other end of the room, quite often standing quite near the chair. We decide that if he stands or moves to within three feet of the chair when we say 'Sit down' we will reinforce him. In time Kevin spends more and more of his time within three feet of the chair. Then we decide he will only be reinforced if he is within two feet of the chair, then within one foot of it, then almost touching it, then touching it, then standing with his back to it and touching it; then he is only reinforced if he is standing with his back to the chair, touching it and slightly bending his knees. And so on. By reinforcing actions that gradually come closer and closer to what we actually want we should finally reach the point where we can reinforce him for sitting down when we tell him to.

Shaping is one way of teaching a child to do new things, but does have some serious drawbacks. First, although we choose to reinforce something that the child already does pretty often, we are at first dependent on his doing it of his own accord. It would be quite possible, for example, for Kevin to lie on the floor in the far corner of the room while we monotonously chant 'Sit down' at him for the entire session. If this happened we would back down on what he had to do to get reinforcement until we reached something he might do even while lying in the far corner. For example, he might be reinforced at first for looking towards the chair. This, however, would lengthen the programme a good deal, and that brings us to the second of the drawbacks. On its own shaping tends to be extremely slow as a teaching method, though it can be usefully combined with other methods and is often used in, for example, language programmes (see chapter 13). It would probably work very much better to teach Kevin to sit down by using prompting.

Prompting

Prompting means helping the child to do the action – guiding him through it, then reinforcing him so that he will be more willing to try to do the action himself. This perhaps highlights the difference between reinforcement and reward. A reward is usually given for a virtuous action whereas reinforcement is given for an action that we want to encourage. If we help a child to do something we may feel he hardly deserves a reward since he was hardly responsible for the action; but reinforcement is given so that he will be more likely to try to do it another time.

There are three kinds of prompts: the first, and most important, is *physical* prompting, the second prompting by *gesture*, the third *verbal* prompting.

1. *Physical prompts*

In physical prompting we guide the child, using our hands to move his limbs, to do the action we want him to learn. In this way he himself will begin to feel, through the movements of his own body, how he should do the action; and because he is reinforced for the completed action he is the more eager to do it the next time.

It is obviously desirable for a handicapped child to learn to feed himself and prompting is a very suitable method to use to teach him. Christine enjoys her food and can feed herself with her fingers, but she cannot manage a spoon and up till now has had to be fed all her meals. Christine is sat at the table, wearing an enveloping bib, with her plate in front of her, a suitable-sized spoon on the right-hand side (she is right-handed). Some food that she loves is put on her plate and a spoonful of it is ready in the spoon. We put her hand round the handle of the spoon and, holding our hand round hers, guide the spoon to her mouth, into it, tip the food off the spoon into her mouth and guide the spoon out of her mouth and back on to the plate. Since the food is something she likes the food itself is the reinforcer. When she has finished that mouthful we try again with another spoonful.

To use prompting to teach Kevin to sit down when he is told to we would first arm ourselves with a supply of whatever is reinforcing for him – say, pieces of apple and cornflakes. We break these up into small bits (each apple quarter would be cut into about six pieces) and take them and Kevin to a chair which he can sit down on easily. We stand him with his back to it, say, 'Sit down Kevin', gently push him down to sit on the chair, and immediately, as soon as his bottom hits the chair seat, praise him – 'Clever boy, Kevin! That *is* good!' and at the same time pop a piece of apple or cornflake into his mouth. In a few moments, when he has finished chewing and swallowing, we stand him up and do it again. Gradually we should find him becoming more ready to sit down of his own accord when we ask him to.

Teaching an action to a child in this way is not at all the same as just 'doing it for him'. Although at this point we are making the action happen, the child is also going through it, and is feeling the pattern of the movement in his own body, which leads on to his doing it eventually without help.

Physical prompting may be used on any moveable part of the child's body – head, arms, legs, shoulders – or to move the whole child from one place to another (for example in teaching him to respond to the words 'Come here'). Prompting can also be used on smaller parts such as the mouth, jaw or fingers, though this is more awkward and fiddly.

2. *Prompting by gesture*

Gestures can help children to understand what we want them to do, especially children who are attentive to other people. We often use gestures along with words, to make our meaning clearer. For instance, we would point to the chair, or pat the seat, at the same time telling Kevin to 'Sit down'. Later on we may have to be careful not to use too many gestures, if we want to be sure that the child really understands what we say: quite often children who have been thought to understand everything said to them are found to be responding more to the gestures that have always accompanied them than to the words themselves.

Most gestures are made with the hand and arm, like pointing, but effective gestures can also be made with a jerk of the head or with 'eye-pointing' – glancing at or looking towards an object. These, especially, are the kind of gestures we may make without realizing it.

3. *Verbal prompts*

Verbal prompts tell the child in words what to do. Obviously they can only be useful with children who understand the mes-

sage the words convey. Verbal prompts may be very general –
'Get dressed'; or, if this does not result in the action we hoped
for it may be helpful to break down the sequence implied in that
single instruction into a series of prompts: 'Open the cupboard;
now get out your vest; put on your vest; now get out your
pants', and so on.

These last two, gestural and verbal prompts, are often referred
to as *cues*, because their function is more to indicate or hint to
the child as to what he should do, rather than to produce it
willy-nilly from him, as is the case with physical prompts.
However, they all three perform a similar task in helping the
child to do the action we want him to learn.

Fading the prompts

This is so important and so tricky it deserves a heading of its
own.

As the child begins to learn what he has to do, through being
prompted through the action, so he begins to take part in it,
begins to put some effort into it and to take over the performance of some of the action. As he does so, his teacher *fades*
out his prompt – the amount he is contributing to the action –
by just enough to allow the child to do as much as he can and
will, but still ensuring that the action is successfully completed.
This is amazingly difficult. It demands constant alertness and
sensitivity on our part to the changing pattern of the child's
response, so that we neither persist with iron grip in pushing
him through movements which he could to some extent do on
his own; nor make the opposite mistake of relaxing and releasing
our prompts before the child has really taken over the action, so
that the spoon (or whatever) clatters to the floor and the action
grinds to a halt half-way through.

Fading physical prompts means that a prompt that was initially
given firmly is given a little more lightly, then more lightly still,
then more lightly again and so on until we are not actually
touching the child but still keep our hands over and very close
to him; at the slightest sign of hesitation or difficulty we are
there to help the action to completion. This method of keeping

our hands very close to the child but not touching him is called *shadowing*.

Fading gestural and verbal prompts goes in much the same way. Gestures become less emphatic, and shorter; what was a rigidly pointing finger becomes a casual wave, and then less even than that. Verbal prompts, instructions or words, become shorter – 'Say Good morning' becomes 'Say Good morn' . . .' then 'Say Good mor' . . .' until it is only 'Say G' . . .' – or it can become fainter, being said in a quieter and quieter voice until it is hardly a whisper.

The eventual aim of all prompting is that the child shall be able to do the action independently. This is achieved by very gradual fading of the prompts, and by never fading them so quickly that the child fails to complete the action. If in spite of all our efforts the child does falter this shows that we have been trying to fade the prompts too quickly, and that the child is not yet ready to take over so much of the action. We should at once go back, not necessarily to the beginning but to the level of prompt we were using just before the child faltered. And we should remember to fade the prompt more slowly this time.

Most problems seem to come from prompts being faded too quickly. On the other hand we should always be on the alert to notice whether the child is able to do just a little more himself.

Breaking down an activity into small steps

When setting out to teach a child an activity he finds rather complicated it is usually best to break it down into a series of very small steps and teach one step at a time. If you think about Christine learning to spoon-feed herself, this involves picking up the spoon, pushing it into the food so that some food goes into it, raising it to her lips without turning it upside down, putting the bowl of the spoon into her mouth, tipping or scraping the food off the bowl of the spoon into her mouth, taking the spoon out of her mouth and returning it to her plate. Seven steps, and tipping up the plate to scrape the food together hasn't been included.

The important point is to make sure that the steps are really small enough. It is easy for us, because we are so used to doing these tasks, to underestimate how difficult they are for somebody who is learning them for the first time. I never realized what a complicated task it was to put on a cardigan until I saw my small daughter struggling with it. Tying a single knot seemed a simple process until I started teaching Philip (see page 104) to do it. So we break the task into as small steps as we possibly can. No harm is done if they are too small – the child just whizzes through a couple at a time – but if they are too large he may fail to learn and everyone gets discouraged. If your teaching stops working and the child fails to learn there are two questions you should first ask yourself: one, are the reinforcers really effective? two, are the steps in the task small enough?

When the task has been broken down the child can be taught first one step, then another, and then the two steps can be *chained* (or joined) together. *Forward chaining* involves teaching the child the first step first, and then chaining that to the second step, and so on.

Backward chaining

We often, however, prefer to use backward chaining which means teaching the *last* step *first*. This may sound odd, but the point is that the child becomes skilled first at the step that leads immediately to the completion of the task and so to reinforcement. When he has learnt this and does it easily, we then teach the preceding step that leads on to the last which he has already mastered, and then rapidly to reinforcement. In every case the likelihood of reinforcement is clearly before him, and this seems to help him to learn.

In the case of Christine learning to feed herself, if we taught her by forward chaining we would first teach her to pick up the spoon: there would then be quite a long gap before she received the reinforcement of eating the food. If we used backward chaining we would prompt her, without making any demands on her, right through the task until she got to the point where the food should be tipped into her mouth: we would relax the prompt at that point first, expecting that as she would be eager to get the food she would now be most willing to put in some effort of her own. When she was able to do this part of the task we would next relax the prompt just as the spoon reached her lips, so that now Christine would have to do some of the new step of putting the spoon into her mouth, following this with the familiar and well-learnt step of tipping the food into her mouth and enjoying the reinforcement – the food.

At this point it may occur to you that on page 73 I spoke of returning the spoon to the plate, not tipping the food into Christine's mouth, as the last step. But as the food is the reinforcer, tipping it into the mouth is the step preceding reinforcement and it is the one we have to teach first. In fact it is often quite difficult to teach children, who learn pretty well to take the spoon to their mouth, to return the spoon to the plate, presumably because the reinforcement – the next mouthful – is at that time so far away. They will often simply drop the spoon unless we are there to control it. It may be that taking the spoon to the mouth and returning it to the plate should be regarded as two separate tasks, and separate reinforcements could be earned for each. Feeding is discussed in greater detail in chapter 12.

Setting the scene

Up till now we have been discussing ways in which we can, by our own actions, help the child to do something new. Another way to help is by reorganizing or rearranging the surroundings. For example, if Christine found it very difficult, as many children do, to scoop the food onto her spoon we could give her a special guard to fix onto the outside of her plate to make the scooping easier for her. Jack, who was learning to dress himself, was very much distracted by the sight of people walking up and down the corridor on the other side of his glass bedroom door: when a screen was put across he learned more quickly. Another boy, Timmy, who refused to drink out of a cup and always drank in small sips out of a spoon, gradually came round to drinking from a cup by being given, over a period of months, a series of spoons which gradually became deeper and the handle more curved until it was a cup. In these cases the children were helped to learn by changes in the objects around them. Here again the need for very small steps applies – each of Timmy's spoons was only fractionally different from the one before it – and for fading, so that eventually Christine will be able to manage without the plate-guard, as Jack was able to do without the screen.

The main points

1. We set out to teach the child something only just beyond what he is doing now.

2. Shaping involves reinforcing the child for doing something that gradually gets closer and closer to what we want him to learn.

3. Prompting means helping the child to perform the action and then reinforcing him for his part in the completed action.

4. There are three kinds of prompts: physical prompts, gestures and words (the last two are also often referred to as *cues*).

5. Prompts should be minimal – only as much as is needed to ensure that the child performs the action.

6. Prompts should be very gradually faded as the child learns the task and takes it over.

7. A complicated task is easier to learn if it is broken down into very small steps, which are taught separately and then chained together.

8. Backward chaining – teaching the last step first and moving backwards in the chain – is a good way of teaching.

9. Setting the scene can help a child to learn.

Some practice problems

1. Try prompting another member of the family to do something – wash their hands, peel a potato, slice bread, kick a football, knit, anything.

2. Pretend that you are unable to do something, and get somebody else to prompt you to do it. (Don't forget the reinforcers!)

In each case try gradually fading the prompts.

3. Take some small, everyday task and break it down into small steps. Would it be best taught by forward or backward chaining?

6. Imitation: Learning by Copying

Young children learn a good deal by imitating what they see other people do, and it is a particularly useful way of learning complicated skills. However, the ability to imitate is one that many mentally handicapped children lack, so we teach it to them.

To teach imitation we use methods discussed in the previous chapters, plus the new one of *modelling*. We ourselves do – model – the action to be imitated, *prompt* the child to do it, and *reinforce* him for his prompted response. Gradually, as he begins to be more ready to reproduce the modelled action, we *fade* the prompts until eventually the child will imitate the model without any prompting.

After taking a baseline, and finding that he imitates very little or not at all we start by teaching the child to imitate large, simple movements such as putting a brick in a cup, or raising arms out sideways: the reason for choosing these actions is chiefly that they are easy ones to prompt. If there is another person available it is very helpful to have him or her stand behind the child and act as prompter. The teacher stands (or sits) directly in front of the child, says, 'Do this', and models the action – for example, arms out sideways; the prompter then lifts the child's arms out to the side and the teacher instantly reinforces him. Then they try again, and after a few attempts the teacher waits for the child to hold the position himself for a moment before giving the reinforcement; later the prompter uses gradually less and less energy, as he feels the child doing more himself, until a light touch is all that is needed. Finally, when the teacher models the movement and says, 'Do this' the child produces a fair copy of the movement.

When the teacher is satisfied that the child can imitate one movement he moves on to another. This is an important step, because up till now we cannot be sure that the child understands that the words 'Do this' mean 'Do whatever I do'; he may at this stage understand it to mean 'Do this particular action' (in this example, 'Raise your arms sideways'). Not until the child will attend to the modelled action, whatever it is, and then reproduce it, is it clear that he understands that he should imitate, not just that he should perform a particular action. This is rather different from responding to particular words, as discussed in the previous chapter, when the words 'Sit down' always meant, 'Carry out the particular action of sitting'. Now what is meant is, 'Be ready to do whatever you see done in front of you'. Again, because we are teaching the child to imitate, if he spontaneously, without being told 'Do this', raises his arms sideways, we do not reinforce him. We are not trying to teach him to raise his arms sideways: we are trying to teach him to do, when told, whatever he sees done. For the same reason it does not matter that the actions we ask him to do are ones which are not very useful like raising his arms out sideways; at the moment we are not trying to teach him a useful action, we are trying to teach him to imitate.

Having taught the child to imitate one movement, we teach him another: preferably a quite different one, like stepping on a box. Then we ask him to imitate the two movements whenever we make them, in a mixed-up order. Then we may teach another movement, and include it in with the others, and so on. As the child learns to imitate several movements we usually find that he needs less and less teaching on each one, until eventually he imitates without prompting the first time we do a new movement. When this happens the child has developed a *set* to imitate.

The development of an *imitative set* is of immense value for teaching a child actions that are difficult to prompt. When he has learned to imitate several large movements we go on to more complex ones (pick up a waste-paper basket and carry it across the room), or smaller movements, say, of the hands; then, especially if our eventual aim is to teach him to speak, to mouth movements. All of these can be prompted, to some extent – we can push the child's mouth into an 'o' shape, press

his lips together for 'm' or stretch them sideways for 'ee'. But small movements are more difficult to prompt than larger ones, and some things (speech, for instance) are impossible to prompt. So it is useful to get the child to the stage of imitating whatever we ask him to do without the need for prompting, before we go on to sound imitation. Clearly, the more the child gets the idea of doing what we do – the set to imitate – the easier it is to teach him to imitate these complex actions. An imitative set is pretty essential if we want him eventually to imitate such unpromptable sounds as 'l' or 'k'.

When the child will imitate mouth movements we may move on to sounds. This again is a big jump as the production of sounds cannot be prompted. So if the child cannot imitate sounds we may have to start with blowing: blowing on our own hand, then on his, then getting him to blow on his own hand; blowing a feather, a piece of fluff, a candle; gradually the blowing becomes hoarser and harder until it becomes a sound. Then we teach imitation of different sounds. Obviously, if the child already makes some sounds himself we may use shaping (discussed in chapter 5, pages 68–9) to encourage him still further to produce the sounds we want. When he will imitate one sound we teach him another; then we teach him to join the sounds into a word: m – u – m – mum.

Speech training is discussed in greater detail in chapter 13.

Once a child has learned to imitate he can learn many things more easily: washing and drying dishes, how to behave in public, mouth-washing and gargling, road safety, table-top games, and so on. For children who may be helped by learning one of the sign systems (this applies to those children who may develop speech as well as those who, because of some special handicap such as deafness, may never do so) the ability to imitate is extremely important; we can prompt hands and fingers into the shape needed for making signs but teaching this is very much easier if the child himself can try to imitate the shape he sees.

Who to imitate

It has been found that people are more ready to imitate someone whom they admire and feel sympathy with – a warm, loving friend whose actions bring him success rather than a cold unsympathetic teacher who apparently gets little fun out of anything. Parents, of course, have many of the qualifications of a good model. However, it may be a good idea to try using as the model someone more like the child we are teaching – another child, a favourite sister perhaps. Because the model is nearer his own age, and a child like himself, the child may be more inclined to imitate what he sees this model do. We may then have a few trial runs in which the child-model is asked to imitate something, and is reinforced for what she does. This will help the child-pupil to realize that imitating other people's actions brings reinforcement, and may sharpen up his interest and willingness to take part.

Imitation is one way a child can learn to do something new. He may then need to learn one of two things connected with his new skill: either *generalization* or *discrimination*. I will discuss each of these in turn.

Generalization

The child may need to learn that a piece of behaviour learnt in one place, in the company of one person, working with one object, may apply equally well in another place, with another person, and another object; or in a number of places, with many people, and with a wide variety of objects. In this way he learns to *generalize* the action.

Supposing David's mother teaches him to drink from a cup. She always uses a particular yellow plastic cup that is David's own, and because at the beginning he was likely to make rather a mess she has always carried out her teaching in the kitchen with its lino floor. When David has learnt the task his mother may find to her dismay that he will only drink in the kitchen, from the yellow cup, when she is there. He won't drink in his bedroom, or from a blue china mug, or when his uncle offers him a drink. This is a somewhat exaggerated example: it is unusual for a child to be quite so specific as to how he will drink. Nevertheless, there are plenty of examples in which a piece of behaviour which has been quite well learnt is so limited in its application as to be positively embarrassing. Simon, for example, learnt to use the toilet in his home, but that was the only one he would use; so his mother could never take him out for a day, or even for part of a day, because he adamantly refused to use any toilet but the one at home.

So the child must be taught to generalize what he learns. What we have to teach him, in fact, is that a piece of behaviour that is reinforced in one situation is likely to be reinforced in another. David must learn that if he enjoys a pleasant liquid and a caress from his mother when he drinks in the kitchen he is equally likely to get both enjoyments if he drinks in the bedroom or dining-room; if he gets them from drinking from a yellow plastic cup he will also get them from drinking from a pink plastic cup or a yellow china cup. He may, of course, learn this or some of this of his own accord – many children do. But it is a good principle, when teaching a mentally handicapped child, not to bank on his doing so. To be on the safe side, we should build generalization into our teaching programme.

For a start, it is always a good idea to teach the child in the place where, and with the people with whom, he is most likely to be. This is why it is no longer thought best for children to be taught, as a rule, by specially trained psychologists or teachers, in special laboratories, the things that they will mostly need to use at home (although there may be cases where this is necessary). They usually make better progress if they are taught at home. Even this however may not be enough, as we saw in the case of Simon and the toilet. We may need to ensure that the skill can be generalized to occur in different parts of the home or outside the home, in the presence of people other than his original teacher, and with a variety of suitable objects.

There are two ways we can make sure that this generalization takes place. We may teach the child in the normal way, expecting that he will have little difficulty in generalizing what he has learnt; then, if he does show some difficulty in other situations, we can be ready to help him re-learn it. Many children will have relatively little difficulty in re-learning, or learning to generalize, a skill. If, however, we realize that the child is likely to have difficulty in generalizing we should deliberately include it as part of his training. This happened with Simon. The difficulty Simon had had in generalizing from one toilet to another was taken into account when he was taught a new skill – buttoning; his teacher took care to vary the teaching situation from the start. She taught him buttoning in his bedroom, another child's bedroom, the bathroom or the passage; she, his mother and his father all took part in the teaching; he buttoned his pyjama jacket, an anorak, a coat belonging to another child, and his own shirt. In this way Simon learnt to do up buttons in many different circumstances; once he had learnt it he was able to do it whenever he needed to and not just in one particular set of conditions.

Discrimination

This is the other side of the coin. If a child must learn that some kinds of behaviour which are reinforced in one situation are also reinforced in others, he must also learn that there are some other kinds of behaviour which are reinforced only in certain specific situations; and he must learn to *discriminate* between these situations.

For instance, he must learn that it is all right to throw a ball but not all right to throw a pot plant or occasional table; it is all right to undress when he is going to bed, or to have a bath or a swim but not if he is in the supermarket; it is all right to hug and kiss a member of his family when they meet, but not the policeman; he should clean his teeth with *his* toothbrush but not with anyone else's.

To teach discrimination we use the same methods discussed before: prompting if necessary, reinforcing the right responses and not reinforcing the wrong ones. In addition, we try to help the child to pick out and attend to the signals, the *cues,* that tell him whether or not reinforcement is likely. These cues, telling the child what sort of behaviour is expected of him (and therefore likely to be reinforced), may consist of a variety of things – a place, a person, something happening, a word or a sentence may all act as cues for a piece of behaviour. A red traffic light is a cue to stop, a green light one to go ahead. A strict teacher may be a cue to a child to behave sedately, an indulgent grandmother a cue to kick over the traces. A nearby chair plus a few friendly words from an adult may be a cue to a child to sit down (which is why we should be cautious about believing that he knows the meaning of the words 'Sit down'; if a chair were in the vicinity he might, if we said, 'Go to bed', sit down just the same – the chair itself may be an important cue). The ringing of a gong may be a cue to go to the dining-room, and the words 'Dinner is ready' may serve the same purpose.

Many of the cues to which we respond are complex and subtle: a slight chilliness in someone's manner can deter you from speaking to them, a person in a blue uniform with a yellow band

round his hat walking along a pavement may cause you to park the car elsewhere. These sorts of cues are often difficult for the mentally handicapped child to pick up. He may at times fail to make the right response, not because he does not know how to do it, but because he didn't understand what was expected of him. We can help him to produce the kind of behaviour we want by making the cues very clear.

If we are teaching him the names of two objects, for instance, the things should differ strikingly from each other, not only in what they *are* – a ball and a cup for example – but also in as many other ways as we can manage – size, colour, texture and so on. In the same way we would, at least early on, choose to teach recognition or naming of objects whose names are very different – ball and cup would be fine, ball and bell would not (though this could come later). Again, the cues which the child should attend to should be very distinct from the background against which he perceives them: so it might help to have a blue ball and a red cup resting on a white, and not a blue or a red, table top. More important perhaps in this respect is the background against which he hears important word-cues: so we don't say to him, 'That's-a-good-boy-Tony-come-and-sit-down-that's-nice-where's-the-oh-here-it-is-no-don't-do-that-sit-down-sit-down-I-said-do-I-have-to-tell-you-everything-twenty-times-that's-better-now-give-me-the-ball-no-not-throw-it-I-said-give-me- . . .' Instead we wait until Tony is settled and he is paying full attention and then say, 'Tony; give – me – the *ball*'. Just that.

Another important area in which we should make the cues very clear is that of the approval and disapproval that we show the child. A normal child may get the message from a barely-perceptible shake of the head or a murmured 'Good'; for the mentally handicapped child the message needs to be made more distinct. Again, we use as many different ways as we can think of to get the message across – words, voice, facial expression, the way we use our hands. A thumbs-up sign, plus a delighted voice saying 'Tony that's *terrific*', plus a wide smile and a pat on the back all emphasize that we are pleased. Tony is left in no doubt that he has done the right thing. Here, too, it is important for the approval-cue, and in its turn the disapproval cue, to be quite distinct from their background. If you look back at the 'verbal garbage' above you will see that there are in it three approval-cues and two disapproval-cues: but I doubt you noticed them.

Nor would Tony.

The main points

1. When we teach a child to imitate:
   say, 'Do this'
   model the action
   prompt the child
   reinforce him for the prompted response.

2. As the child begins to do some of the action, we gradually *fade* our prompt.

3. We start by teaching large simple movements.

4. It may help to have one person as model and reinforcer, a second person as prompter.

5. When one action has been learned we teach another: then give them in a mixed-up order.

6. From large simple movements we go on to more complex, or to finer movements (hands and fingers) and movements of the face and mouth.

7. Imitation is useful for children learning language, either speech or a sign system.

8. Generalization means that a child who has learnt to do something in one situation can apply it in other situations.

9. Generalization may need to be taught by reinforcing what the child learns in many different situations.

10. Discrimination means that a child learns that he should do something in certain situations, not in others.

11. We teach discrimination by reinforcing these things in the appropriate situations and not reinforcing them in others.

12. The cues that tell a child that his actions are likely to be reinforced should be very clear.

Some practice problems

*1. Can you think of two or three things that you or any member of your family have learned by imitation?

*2. Is there any other way you might have been taught these things?

*3. Can you think of any behaviour of a non-handicapped child (of your own or someone else's) which was learnt in a very specific situation and did not easily generalize?

4. How was this difficulty got over?

*5. What are the cues that tell us to:
    (a) Put on a mackintosh
    (b) Drive on a certain side of a road
    (c) Raise our voices
    (d) Give over money
    (e) Get out of bed
    (There may be more than one possible cue to each action.)

7. Learning Not To

There are two groups of things we may want to teach a child to do: first, to increase the number of times he does the things we want him to – his good behaviours (this has been discussed in chapters 3 to 6); and second, to decrease the number of times he does things that we would rather he didn't – his bad behaviours.

Decreasing a child's bad behaviours is important for several reasons. The first is that these behaviours upset other people's lives – interfering with belongings, disturbing the peace, making it difficult to get on with everyday life, messing up the surroundings and making a lot of extra work, and so on. The second, and important, reason is that the bad behaviours may hinder the child himself in the learning of new skills that would be useful to him – for instance, if a child spends much of his time rocking it may be difficult to teach him more useful things such as dressing or language until he stops rocking enough to pay attention to what he is being taught. These two reasons – the disturbance of other people and the disadvantages to the child himself – can also interact, as when the child, through his bad behaviour, puts people right off him, so that they are unwilling to spend time with him and teach him. Finally, children whose bad behaviour is that of injuring themselves may do real damage to themselves, crippling themselves, or in some cases actually endangering life. For all these reasons the child needs to be taught that there are some things he should not do. This chapter is concerned with ways of teaching this.

When a normal child does something very wrong he may be punished, and the punishment will usually consist in the child's receiving something that is seen as unpleasant – a spanking, docking of pocket-money, not being allowed out to play, or whatever else is thought of as unpleasant. For many people 'punishment' automatically includes, amongst other things, retribution – it is felt that the child should himself suffer to some extent for the wrong he has done. In behaviour modification the word 'punishment', like some other words, is used differently. *Punishment is defined as: anything which when it consistently follows a kind of behaviour results in that kind of behaviour occurring less often in the future.*

You can see that this definition is the exact opposite of the definition of reinforcement on page 36. You can see, too, that it says nothing at all about what might be used as a punisher. No assumptions can be made about that. Indeed, some things that we might think of as very unpleasant, like a spanking, may not reduce the kind of behaviour at all, while some other action that seems very mild, like putting the child in his toy-strewn bedroom, may succeed in doing so (see the example of Tim on page 94). As with reinforcement the crucial question for behaviour modification is: what effect does the method we are using have on the child's behaviour? We are not at all concerned to make him suffer for his misdeeds: the only concern is to see his bad behaviour lessen.

There are two main ways in which we can set about teaching a child not to do things. When he does one of these bad kinds of behaviour we can either take something pleasant, that we think that he likes, away from him; or we can give him something unpleasant, that we think he doesn't like. In each case we look to see whether what we are doing is resulting in a decrease in the bad behaviour.

A. Taking away something pleasant

1. *Time-out from positive reinforcement*

When this method is used the child is ordinarily in a very enjoyable situation, getting a lot of reinforcement, until he behaves badly; then the reinforcement suddenly disappears. After a short time the reinforcement becomes available to him again, and only disappears if he again produces the bad behaviour.

Let's take an example. Alice is a severely mentally handicapped little girl who had a habit of smearing her own saliva on her hands and rubbing it all over her face. This doesn't sound very bad but it made Alice smell unpleasant so that people tended to avoid coming near her. Her teacher decided to try to stop her smearing her face. Alice loved being tickled, so tickling was used as the reinforcement. The teacher ran sessions in which she tickled Alice continuously: as soon as Alice smeared saliva over her face the teacher stopped the tickling and only began it again five seconds after Alice had stopped smearing. In time Alice smeared her face less, she smelled more pleasant, and people were more willing to do things with her.

Time-out can be used whenever the reinforcer is one that other people can control. Time-out cannot be used where the reinforcer is impossible for another person to control, such as the reinforcement gained from the feeling of tongue-rolling or lip-smacking; luckily this sort of reinforcer is pretty unusual. If a child is fond of one particular toy time-out might mean removing the toy for a time whenever he behaved badly. TV was used as a reinforcer with a little boy who sucked his fingers until they were raw, especially when he was watching TV: every time his fingers went to his mouth the TV set was switched off for ten seconds. Another boy, Don, who at 12 years old was both mentally and physically severely handicapped, was very fond of music and his mother used to switch on the radio when she went into his bedroom in the morning. She complained that day after day he was very difficult to dress as he would become silly and giggly and deliberately stiffen his arms and legs as she was trying to get them through the sleeves and legs of his clothes. So it was decided that when he did this he would be timed-out from his reinforcement – the radio was switched off for fifteen seconds. So long as Don cooperated in the dressing process the music-reinforcer was always there; as soon as he became difficult he lost it. Don learnt that it was more fun for him – he was able to listen to the music he loved without interruption – if he cooperated and his mother found him progressively easier to dress.

Misbehaviour at meal-times can be treated by time-out from the meal – if the child is very keen on his food; we would not get far if we timed him out from a meal he didn't want much anyway. Trevor was very, very fond of his food and would eat practically anything. So anxious was he to get his food that he would gulp it down, cramming one mouthful in on top of another and using his fingers to eat with instead of his knife and fork. So each of these things was treated by time-out from the meal – his plate was taken away for thirty seconds each time one of them occurred. He quite quickly learnt to swallow one mouthful before putting in another and not to use his fingers.

Time-out can be used effectively where the reinforcers are social ones – attention, praise, smiles, hugs and kisses, or the social situation of being with other people. Here the time-out may be given in different ways, depending on what exactly is the social reinforcer. If the child very much enjoys an adult's attention, time-out may consist of the adult turning his back on the child, or even just turning away his head. Where the child enjoys social situations, such as being with several people, or enjoys the activities going on in a classroom, or the attention he gets from several people at once, time-out may mean removing the child from the reinforcers (this being easier than removing all of them from him) and, often, removing the child to a 'time-out room'. An important thing about a time-out room is that when he is put in it, the child should not only lose the reinforcers that he was getting before his bad behaviour but also should not find in the time-out room any fresh ones to console himself with. If Patsy enjoyed company but tended to throw things a great deal, her father might decide to treat this by putting her in a time-out room each time she threw something. He would make sure that he did not put her in her bedroom where she had her dolls, picture books and the transistor radio which she enjoys. Instead he would either make sure that the bedroom had previously been cleared of favourite toys; or would make use of a downstairs cloakroom or a bathroom – if necessary first removing everything breakable and firmly turning off all the taps (in one child's programme the taps were chained up during the day to make sure he could not spend his time-out enjoying a really satisfying flood). Whichever room Patsy's father decided to use, he would put Patsy in it and leave her there for a certain fixed length of time (say, two minutes, or five minutes – see page 95). During this time he would ignore Patsy's howls and sobs, and would take Patsy out only when the time was up. In addition, when the time was up he would take her out only if she were quiet. It would be a great mistake for Patsy to get the idea that her howling and sobbing resulted in her release from time-out: much better if she realized that only quietness (plus the passage of time) made for her release.

Sometimes a child makes so much noise and for so long that we may begin to wonder whether we are ever going to be able to get her out of the time-out room. If she understands speech the problem is not too difficult. Nanette could understand pretty well what was said to her, so towards the end of her five minutes her teacher positioned herself outside the door of the room and said, 'Nanette, can you hear me?'

The sobs died away.

'You can come out when you are quiet. You aren't coming out while you make all that noise.'

Silence reigned while the teacher counted ten. Then she opened the door and let Nanette out. The next time that Nanette was naughty and had to go in the room the teacher only had to say to her, 'Now be quiet!'. After that, on the few occasions that Nanette had to go to the room, it was not necessary to say anything at all.

If the child does not understand speech then we may have at first to seize on the slightest pause in the noise, or even on a lowering of the volume, to take her out. We do not leave her in there for long periods, of fifteen minutes or more.

Whether a time-out room can be used in the home depends on the home and on the child's behaviour. If the home does not have a usable room, or if the child is so aggressive or destructive that he would wreck any room he was in, then the use of a time-out room may not be possible and we may have to think of something else. At the other extreme, with some children it may be possible to use a very ordinary unmodified room as a time-out room. Tim's mother decided to use time-out for his tantrums; when he screamed and hit and kicked at her she put him in his bedroom, pausing only to remove his tape-recorder. Over the weeks in which this treatment was put into effect the record of Tim's tantrums went steadily down: so it seemed likely that the most important reinforcers for Tim were those that he lost when he was put in his room – perhaps his mother's company? perhaps the freedom to run about the house? – and that the other things in his bedroom were not sufficiently enjoyable to him to upset the effect of time-out. Once again we could really only find out what was effective by trying out our chosen method and keeping very careful records of what happened. If the tantrums were not getting less frequent we should have to think again.

At this point perhaps a question which is often raised should be dealt with: if the child's bedroom is used as a time-out room will he come to hate it, and be afraid or unwilling to sleep in it? This seems to me an entirely reasonable worry; I can only say that neither I nor the other workers whom I have consulted have ever known this to happen. It may help to understand this if we realize that what we are doing is not punishing the child by putting him *in* a nasty place – his bedroom does not become a cold damp cellar nor a small dark cupboard; instead, we are taking him *away* from a pleasurable situation. So going to his bedroom is not a matter of going to a horrid place, but of an interruption of whatever enjoyable things had been going on. So his bedroom is not frightening, and at bedtime is still, to him, his normal place for sleeping.

Just as positive reinforcement should be given immediately after the child's good behaviour, so also any of the methods I am discussing here should follow immediately after the bad behaviour. For this reason, if Patsy's father decided to use her bedroom as a time-out room he would clear it of all the enjoyable toys well ahead of time; it would probably lessen the effectiveness of the time-out procedure if, having taken Patsy to her room, he had to spend time removing the toys before Patsy could be put in it.

How long time-out should last depends, first, on the child (how old he is, how he behaves during time-out, and so on) and secondly on the kind of time-out being used. Where the kind of time-out is like that described on page 92 and consists of the adult turning away from the child, the time-out is usually fairly short, varying between fifteen and thirty seconds. Where a time-out room is used the time the child spends there may be a little longer, say, about five to ten minutes. It is especially important that the length of time should not be set too long at first: if we give a child a long period of time-out, such as ten minutes, and then, overcome by remorse, feel this is too long and too unkind to him and *reduce* the time-out period the child's bad behaviour is likely to *increase*; if on the other hand we start with a short period and later decide to *lengthen* it a bit the bad behaviour is likely to get *less*. So it seems better to start with a fairly short period like five minutes (and indeed this is often sufficient anyway).

It is important not to use very long periods of time-out, like half an hour or an hour. First of all it may just be too much and too unkind. Secondly, it may actually work less well because the child after a time seems to forget what it was he was taken away from (remember that it is 'time-out from positive reinforcement'). If the time-out is fairly short, then the interruption of the enjoyable time he was having seems more noticeable.

Time-out should never be used as an excuse for a bit of peace and quiet for us.

2. Extinction

Extinction means that the child finds that the reinforcement, which has usually followed what he did, no longer does so. Chrissie was a bright little 6-year-old who tyrannized her entire family by crying. She cried a great deal of every day, especially when she had to go to school (although she enjoyed school), at any time when her mother had to leave her, when her father returned from work, when visitors came, when she went to a party, if she didn't go to a party. Her parents had consulted numerous doctors and psychiatrists who had said Chrissie was 'deeply disturbed'. Chrissie continued to cry and her parents were at their wits' end. Careful observation showed that when Chrissie cried her concerned and loving parents showered her with attention, asked her what was the matter, begged her to tell them if anything unpleasant had happened, and so on and so on. The psychologist discussed with them the fact that Chrissie seemed to be getting reinforcement (attention) when she cried. They agreed that in future they would take no notice of her when she cried. We should not underestimate the difficulty for the parents in carrying out this programme: you can perhaps imagine for yourself how hard it would be to turn your back on your pathetically sobbing little 6-year-old when every fibre of your being is crying out to scoop her up and comfort her. However (perhaps because Chrissie's crying was wrecking family life and they were desperate), Chrissie's parents faithfully carried out the programme and ignored her crying. At the same time they strongly reinforced Chrissie – gave her a great deal of warm, loving attention – whenever she was *not* crying (this is known as DRO, or Differential Reinforcement of Other ways of behaving, which will be discussed further on page 104).

What followed was fairly typical of what happens when extinction is used. To begin with, Chrissie's crying got worse.

Finding that she could no longer get her mother's attention by just crying Chrissie first cried harder, then screamed distressingly; when her mother still did not turn round to her Chrissie beat her mother on the bottom with her fists; finally as the time for school approached, Chrissie rushed up into the bathroom and made herself sick. At this point Chrissie's mother rang up the psychologist, and it was decided that, as Chrissie did not seem to be ill, she was to be taken calmly to school. Chrissie found that in spite of her intensified efforts she did not manage to get the reinforcement she had previously been accustomed to get for her crying, and she began to cry less and less until, about three months later, she was a very different, cheerful, self-reliant, little girl who went happily off to school in the morning.

That her mother did not give in when Chrissie intensified her crying, and never attended to her crying once the programme was under way, was of enormous importance for the success of the project. If her mother had given in Chrissie would have learnt that, even if 'normal' crying no longer brought her reinforcement, she could still get the attention she craved by crying longer or harder. Once she had learnt this it would have been very much more difficult to treat the crying by extinction as Chrissie would have got the idea that, even if the present level of her crying did not bring the reinforcement, she only had to do it a little bit more – and a little bit more – and a little bit more – and sooner or later the adults would crack and reinforcement would be hers. If Chrissie successfully learnt this lesson she might learn to persist with, or to intensify, her crying to the point where it became impossible for her parents to hold out any longer.

So it is an important rule that, where a bad behaviour is being treated by extinction, it must *never* be reinforced.

As we have seen when Chrissie's mother first embarked on her extinction programme, and withdrew the reinforcement – attention – that Chrissie had been used to get for her crying, Chrissie cried harder. It is quite usual for a child's behaviour to get worse before it gets better when it is treated by extinction. Obviously it is important for parents to know this, before they start on the programme. If her mother had not known beforehand that Chrissie would probably cry harder at first she would have been quite likely to drop the programme like a hot potato saying, 'I tried that and it made her worse.' As it was, she knew that this worsening of Chrissie's behaviour was to be expected, and she was prepared to persist.

In Chrissie's case, where the problem was crying, and in the case of many other undesirable but fairly harmless behaviours, extinction is a useful treatment method. In some cases however, as when the bad behaviour consists of serious self-injury, or aggression to other children, extinction may not be a good method, simply because of the fact that the behaviour can be expected to get worse before it improves. We would not be justified in allowing a child to do serious damage either to himself or to other children, even if we felt confident that later the damaging behaviour would lessen. By that time irreparable harm might have been done. In these cases other kinds of treatment must be found.

Extinction can be used to treat problem behaviours by withholding almost any kind of reinforcement (except those the child makes within himself, see page 91). It is especially suitable for those children who enjoy provoking adults, and who seem to get reinforcement from the upset they cause, and from the distress, irritation or anger of the adults around them (see page 42).*

Once we realize that anger does not necessarily discourage the child's bad behaviour, but actually increases it, a programme can be worked out in which we will no longer react angrily, or will not, probably, react at all, to the child's bad behaviour. How easy it will be to carry out this programme is another matter: it is not always easy to remain unflinchingly calm while

---

* That scolding may be a reinforcer and, if it is withheld, the unacceptable behaviour may die out (extinguish) is not an entirely new idea. Here, in a passage written in 1815, the couple, who have just got engaged to each other, are a man, and a girl half his age.

'Mr Knightley. You always called me Mr Knightley.'

'I remember once calling you "George", in one of my amiable fits, about ten years ago. I did it because I thought it would offend you; but as you made no objection, I never did it again.'

Emma, Jane Austen, chapter 17.

a child spits accurately in your eye or pushes over every item of furniture in the room. However, once again, if we decide to apply extinction it is most important that we should be consistent about it: if, goaded beyond endurance, we eventually vent on the child all the anger he has been working for he will realize that persistence pays dividends and be encouraged to persist even more.

Extinction is a powerful method of getting rid of patterns of behaviour. It is important to realize that it can work on good as well as on bad behaviour. If we have been reinforcing a child for something we want him to do, and then stop reinforcing him for it, that piece of behaviour is likely to die out eventually. This is particularly likely to happen if we change suddenly from giving a lot of reinforcement to giving none at all. So in the case of good behaviour we need to guard against the possibility of extinction by going from a continuous to a variable schedule of reinforcement (see page 44): the reinforcement can become more and more infrequent – from VR3 to VR8 to VR15 right up to VR200 perhaps – but we should try to make sure that we continue to reinforce the good behaviour, at least occasionally. There is an exception to this – where what the child is learning is in itself reinforcing: for instance, if you teach a child to read, or to ride a bicycle, once he has learnt the activity thoroughly the Smarties and expressions of delight will not be needed; the child enjoys reading and cycling for their own sakes. But with other activities that are not in themselves reinforcing we need to be careful not to allow them to extinguish for want of occasional reinforcement.

3. Fining

The child finds that, when he shows his bad behaviour, something he values is taken away from him. The thing or things taken can vary from privileges to money, but usually in the programmes outlined in this book refer to points, stars or tokens, which have been earned for good behaviour (see page 48). Fining is a method often used with normal children, or with people who are mildly mentally handicapped, but is less often used with severely handicapped children. When it is used it is important to make sure that the child does not lose so many tokens (or stars, or whatever is being used) that he has no more to lose: when this happens the possibility of positive reinforcement disappears and with it the incentive to demonstrate the good behaviour. With severely handicapped children fining programmes sometimes fail because taking away what the child values upsets him so much that he again behaves badly, leading to a further loss until at last his token supply is exhausted. All this makes a fining programme tricky to apply, but sometimes such a programme can be used successfully.

There is more discussion of fines on page 57.

B. Giving something unpleasant

Although, as a general rule, many of the other ways of dealing with bad behaviour seem preferable to those I'm going to discuss now, we may sometimes want to tackle the bad behaviour itself.

To many of us as children, serious naughtiness was followed by a smack. Smacking has gone up and down in popularity over the years. The Victorians used the expression 'Spare the rod and spoil the child', and some of them seemed even to think that corporal punishment was good for a child's soul. Later smacking became much more unpopular, and some people now feel that any smacking is wrong. Probably few would now be in favour of cold-blooded beating though the occasional wild slap by a goaded parent does not seem such a crime (if it is a crime I was guilty, though my children tell me I was not much good at it – I used sometimes to try to slap them, but tended, they say, to miss). I personally feel that parents should not feel so inhibited that they can never slap an irritating child – and there we have it: the slap, in my view, is more a way of relieving the parents' feelings than of doing anything to improve the child's behaviour. There is not much evidence that smacking makes children good. Some parents of handicapped children have found this out for themselves.

'It stops her at the time, but whether she really understands what it's for I don't know.'

'It works for the moment but it doesn't really alter his behaviour.'*

So for myself I do not feel that smacking is the most useful way to change a child's behaviour, and I do not propose to discuss it here. Instead there are two methods that I will discuss – brief restraint and restitution.

1. *Brief restraint*

Children who are active and enjoy their freedom (this can apply even to children who cannot walk) may find it unpleasant to have their freedom to move around interrupted by having their limbs firmly held down. This is usually done by holding the child's hands down firmly to his sides for a count of, say, twenty. After this we release him in order to get back to normal activities. If, when we release him, the child again shows the bad behaviour, we again hold him down for a count of twenty and repeat this until when we release him he does not misbehave.

Andy's misbehaviour consisted of, amongst other things, kicking and hitting adults, and it was decided to try treating this with restraint. The next time he hit an adult his arms were calmly and firmly held down. When he was released he hit out again and was held down again, and this sequence was carried out four times altogether before he behaved quietly when he was released. After two or three sessions like this Andy needed only one period of restraint following his misbehaviour – with that particular adult. Andy did not readily generalize his learning and had to learn afresh with several different people that whenever he hit or kicked his arms would be held down.

One possible complication of using restraint that we have to watch out for is that for some children it may be reinforcing. Just as anger, slaps, shouts and so on may be reinforcing so, too, to a child who very much enjoys adult attention and closeness, restraint may be enjoyable. We can try to guard against this by giving as little attention as possible to the child while we restrain him, turning our head away and not speaking to him. Here again the important thing is what our records show. If the

* *Young Children with Down's Syndrome*, Janet Carr, Butterworth, 1975.

number of times the bad behaviour occurs goes up, then it is likely that, in spite of our efforts, the child is finding the restraint reinforcing. We had better look for something else.

2. Restitution and over-correction

When a child deliberately throws things on the floor it is quite usual for people around him to make him pick them up again: this is restitution and is seen as a suitable way for him to put right what he first put wrong. In some cases this may be enough to stop the child doing it again – it just isn't worth the trouble it brings him. In other cases making him pick the object up is not enough; so we may use over-correction, in which the child not only picks up the object he has thrown but also anything else that is lying around *and* straightens the furniture *and* empties the waste-paper basket *and* sweeps or even polishes the floor. In other words, he not only puts right the damage he has done to his surroundings, he goes on to make them better than they were before he started. One theory behind this form of treatment is that the child supposedly will learn a better way of treating his surroundings. Another explanation is that, if it works, it may do so by boring the pants off the child who is made to go through an unenjoyable routine when he would rather be doing something else. We go about it in the same way as we apply restraint: calmly and neutrally, not talking to the child apart from the first instruction, 'Clear it up', prompting him physically just as much as is needed to make sure that he works really hard. To be effective over-correction usually has to last for more than just a few seconds: five minutes is probably the minimum, while with one determined furniture-thrower the teacher used over-correction for twenty-five minutes for the throwing of a single chair (the child gave up throwing, at least while that teacher was around). With children who need a lot of physical prompting over-correction is an exhausting business for the adult, and how long it lasts may depend, at least partly, on how long the adult can keep going.

Restitution and over-correction can be used to discourage

most sorts of bad behaviour; spilt liquids can be mopped up; a child who wets his pants may wash them, going through the washing performance even if the things need to be washed properly afterwards; a child who hits or bites another may (in theory at least) be made to 'apologize' by stroking his victim; and so on. All that is needed is a little ingenuity in working out what is the appropriate kind of restitution for the particular kind of bad behaviour.

Plus, as before, careful assessment beforehand to see whether the treatment is likely to work *and* careful record-keeping so that we can see whether or not it has. Once again, as with restraint, we have to be aware of the possibility that restitution or over-correction may be reinforcing to the child, usually because it means that he gets a lot of adult attention. If this is the case we shall find the bad behaviour increasing and will have to change our treatment.

Schedules

In chapter 3 (pages 44–5) we saw how different schedules of positive reinforcement may be useful for different purposes. For example, when we begin to teach the child something new a *continuous* schedule (giving the child reinforcement every time he does what we want) is best: once he becomes a bit more skilful an *intermittent*, every-now-and-again, schedule is best for keeping it up. When we are trying to get rid of bad behaviour a continuous schedule seems the best. That is, the bad behaviour seems to die away most quickly when the method used (time-out, restraint, restitution) is given every time the bad behaviour occurs. Using these methods on an intermittent (every-now-and-again) schedule is not so effective, though it may still work so long as we do not stretch the schedule too much; if more than two or three misbehaviours in succession regularly go unchecked we may not succeed in getting rid of them. (But see page 15, 'Getting Started', on dealing with the bad behaviour in certain situations only.)

Where we decide to use extinction we should be very careful to use a continuous schedule: then it is very important *never* to reinforce the misbehaviours, or they may come back more strongly than before and be much more difficult to get rid of.

Now we come to two other methods of trying to get rid of bad behaviours, which are different because the concern is not with a corrective follow-up but with prevention.

Differential Reinforcement of Other behaviours – DRO

This is one of the most hopeful ways of trying to reduce a child's bad behaviour. This is done not by attacking the bad behaviour itself but by building up other, good behaviours. If possible we build up other kinds of behaviour which, while the child is doing them, make the bad behaviour impossible to carry out. For instance, Carol, a nearly-blind girl, was further damaging her sight by constantly poking her fingers in her eyes. As she was very fond of loud squeaky sounds she was given a switch to press which turned on a tape of these sounds as long as she pressed it. Carol loved this, but found that she could press with one hand and poke her eyes with the other. So she was given two switches that had to be pressed at the same time to produce the sound. After a bit Carol learnt to operate one of the switches with her elbow, so that she could still get the sound and poke her eyes. Finally the switches were built into a board in such a way that they would only work if Carol pressed them with the fingertips of both hands and this made it impossible for her to poke at the same time. After this, although Carol did not altogether stop eye-poking, at least when she was pressing the switches and getting the sounds she loved she was not at that time able to poke her eyes.

In many cases DRO is a much simpler affair: if a child has a particular bad behaviour that we want to get rid of, we may reinforce him just for not doing it. Chrissie's parents reinforced her whenever she was *not* crying, and Andy (page 101) was also regularly reinforced whenever he was not hitting adults. In another case Philip's parents asked for help with his habit of coming into their bed every night: it was suggested to them that he should be firmly returned to his own bed whenever that happened, but, in addition, for every night that he did not come in Philip should receive a star to put on a chart, four stars to be exchangeable for a new toy. This programme resulted in an immediate and dramatic lessening of interrupted nights for his parents.

Whenever we set out to decrease a child's bad behaviour we should always try to combine this with building up a good behaviour: first, to make sure that the child has the chance of getting the enjoyment he needs, and of which he may to some extent be deprived by our method of treating his bad behaviour; second, that he makes progress in positive things as well as learning not to do the bad things; and third, that concentration on what he should do as well as on what he shouldn't will help to speed up the reduction in his present misbehaviour and, which is very important, make it less likely that new ones will appear in the future.

Changing the surroundings

Lastly, it may be possible to help prevent a child's bad behaviour by altering the surroundings he lives in. For instance, many parents of young children deal with the children's tendency to break small objects and ornaments by clearing these away to the attic until the children are old enough not to break them so easily. In the same way Paul, who would pull the hair of any child he sat next to, was sat well away from other children in the classroom. Of course this didn't teach Paul not to pull other children's hair; but it did allow him to learn other things and to be reinforced for what he did, whereas previously there had been little opportunity for this as so much of his time had been taken up with hair pulling. As Paul began to enjoy what he was learning and the reinforcement he was getting for it, it was possible to move him gradually nearer to the other children without his pulling their hair.

Changing the surroundings can allow other kinds of behaviours to emerge but it does not actually teach them to the child; so it is often combined with other methods, such as prompting or shaping, or, in Paul's case, DRO.

Some special problems: swearing, masturbation and self-injury

When using behaviour modification great stress is laid on careful observation of each child, so that it is possible to judge what particular methods are likely to work with this particular child; we take care not to say, 'For *that* problem use *this* method' – what we do depends on what our observations tell us of the individual child. However, there are two quite common problems which I think I can suggest particular ways of dealing with: swearing and masturbation. This is because the reinforcers for each of these problems are nearly always the same. Self-injury, which is quite different, is discussed later.

1. *Swearing*

Many people find swearing unpleasant and especially embarrassing in public – which is when it often happens. We may try telling the child not to use such words, that we don't like it, and neither do other people, scold him sharply when he uses the words – and find his swearing goes on unabated. The reinforcement for swearing seems to be, almost always, the attention that it brings (though there may be exceptions to this that I don't know of). So the method worth trying first is extinction. When the swear words are used, we just don't react. We don't start back, look horrified, tell the child to be quiet, or say anything about it at all. We behave as if we had heard nothing, and continue talking pleasantly of the weather, the neighbour's dog and the price of fish. It is not always easy to do this, especially since, as in other cases where we might use extinction, the child is likely to redouble his efforts at first and produce longer, louder and more appalling swear-words. We may have to take friends into our confidence, tell them what we plan to do and ask them to cooperate. If the swearing happens in a really public place we may have to beat a dignified and discreet retreat before the general public's shock becomes reinforcing to the child. But if we stick to our guns, it nearly always works. We may, of course, combine extinction with DRO – offer something nice, or tokens to exchange for something bigger, for times when the child does not swear – one token for every half hour or hour, or even half day, when the child does not swear – and this too may help things along. Swearing was one of Ann's problems, as well as disobedience (see page 54). Ann's mother used these two methods, extinction and DRO, as a result of which Ann took to saying 'Oh blow' instead of the things she had said before; and everyone was happy.

2. *Masturbation*

Masturbation can be a problem with either boys or girls though it often seems more intense, more embarrassing and more difficult to control in boys, especially during adolescence. It is another habit which is very embarrassing especially when done in public. In addition a child who masturbates may be unwilling to do anything else, and his masturbation may seriously interfere with his learning of other useful things. So it must be controlled, although we may not want to stop it altogether – after all it may offer the only form of sexual pleasure the child will ever experience.

Once again, you can be pretty sure what the reinforcer is. But in this case the reinforcer lies within the activity itself – the pleasure the child gets from masturbating. So we cannot ensure that he does not get this reinforcement but we may be able to ensure that he only masturbates at certain times, and only in private. We make it clear to him (or her) that he may not masturbate in the streets or the shops or the classroom or the living-room, but he may when he is alone and private in his bedroom. If the child understands speech well it may be enough to tell him this and to remind him. If he does not understand speech then it may help to put him in special clothing, like high-sided dungarees, which make it less likely that he will slip his hands into his trousers. One boy was also given a cricketer's box to wear which prevented accidental contact and rubbing of his penis, and this also helped to lessen his urge to masturbate and allowed him to concentrate more easily on other things. These measures will not teach the child not to masturbate (which is not really the aim), and usually the minute the clothing is removed the child will return to masturbating; but at least it may be controlled so that it doesn't interfere too much with the rest of his life, or cause too much embarrassment to those around him.

3. *Self-injury*

Lastly, a problem that is quite different from the other two in that there is no straight-forward way of tackling it: self-injury. There are a number of children who hurt themselves, not accidentally but deliberately; and in some cases sufficiently severely to cause bruises or open wounds, occasionally even endangering their lives, so that, for their own protection, some children have spent their days and nights spread-eagled on a bed, hands and feet tied to the four corners of the bed.

Why some children deliberately damage themselves – by banging their heads, poking at their eyes, slapping, pinching, scratching or biting themselves – is uncertain. Many theories have been put forward: some people have thought that children injure themselves because they feel unloved; others that they do it to gain attention; with some children it has seemed that they were more likely to do it if they were unoccupied, others when they were over-excited; some children, it has been suggested, may injure themselves because they actually enjoy the sensation it gives them.

All these ideas have been put to the test in attempts to treat self-injuring children. All have had some success – except the first: if children are given extra love and attention when they injure themselves their rate of self-injury increases (as you might expect from what you know of reinforcement); extra love and attention given when they are not self-injuring does not have this effect but neither does it, by itself, usually result in a lessening of the self-injury. Ignoring the child when he injures himself can, if done rigorously enough, result in a lessening of the self-injury, but is very difficult to do, and may take so long that the child hurts himself seriously in the process. Brief restraint (discussed on page 101) and forced exercise (making the child go through a series of arm exercises every time he hits himself) and *facial screening* (dropping a light cloth briefly over the child's face every time he hits his head) have been used successfully with a few children. So has mild electric shock – enough to cause an unpleasant tingling feeling but not enough to do any harm to the child – which at one time was in considerable vogue and appeared to have resulted in some dramatic 'cures'. The crucial point about self-injury, however, is that, unlike swearing and masturbation, the reinforcers for this kind of behaviour may be quite different for different children; so it is impossible here to lay down a routine method of attempting to deal with it. What works with one child may not work with another. We must observe the child carefully, looking particularly for the reinforcers that work for him, and at what seems to make him begin injuring himself – in what sort of situations, with which people, at what times of day he is more likely to do it, whether he is more likely to do it when he is ill, well, happy, cross, lively, tired, and so on and so on. Then we select a method from amongst those described earlier in this chapter (or any other method we can think of) that seems promising for this particular child, and try it out, keeping careful records in order to be able to see how useful is the method we have chosen. Because these kinds of behaviour are so distressing and difficult it may be a good idea to ask for professional help if any problems arise, or even right from the start (see page 19 for where to go for help).

There is one routine method that I can suggest you try. If the child has only just begun to injure himself, and if the injury is not very severe – light slapping for example – it may be worth, as a first move, studiously ignoring it. With many children, paying attention to them when they injure themselves has the effect of increasing the number of times they do it. So, for a start, we would not comment on what the child was doing, not watch him, not pull his hands down. We would turn away from him, and only turn back to him and give him our full attention when he had stopped injuring himself. And if this resulted, in a few days or so, in a lessening of the number of times he injured himself we would breathe a sigh of gratitude; if not, we would go on to make a more careful study of the problem and, if at all possible, ask for professional help.

There is one particular professional who may be able to give very special help: the occupational therapist. An occupational therapist may be able to devise ways of protecting the child from his efforts to injure himself, which may make it possible for us to use whatever seems the best method of tackling the problem. For instance, we may think extinction (see page 96) would be the most effective method we could use. We may have noticed when observing the child that there was something that appeared to be reinforcing his self-injuring, and have felt that he was hurting himself 'so as to get' something or other. I have already mentioned adult attention as a possible reinforcer: other children who dislike doing certain things find that, if when they are asked to do the task they begin hitting their heads or biting their hands, the task quickly disappears from the scene. They find they can avoid the task by hurting themselves; their self-injuring is reinforced by their being able to get out of the task they dislike. Brian disliked being taken to the toilet. He learnt that if he banged his face with his fists when he was being taken to the toilet he would be left alone to wet his pants. Soon his parents gave up the struggle to toilet train him and left him in nappies. Brian then went on to bang his face when he was asked to do other things he did not like – move out of his favourite chair, have a strange person in the room with him. His life, and the lives of his parents, became more and more restricted.

When we use extinction we make sure that the reinforcer does not follow on the piece of behaviour we want to lessen. In Brian's case this meant that he should not be able to avoid going to the toilet but should be firmly taken there, despite all his face-bangs. But Brian had his parents in a cleft stick. If they did not allow him to avoid going to the toilet he would bang himself so badly that he opened up big bleeding wounds on his face; if they held his hands so that he could not hit his face with them he would bring his knee up sharply to his chin or hit his face on the corner of a table. The injury he caused himself was so bad that they could not allow him to do it; extinction, it seemed, was impossible to use.

At this point Brian's parents were put in touch with a hospital whose staff included an occupational therapist. She made a Plastazote helmet for Brian in such a way that all the parts of his face that he banged were covered and cushioned. Now when he banged his face it had very little effect, and certainly he was not able to open up the wounds as he had once done. Now it *was* possible to use extinction, Brian *was* firmly taken to the toilet, his face-banging was no longer followed by avoiding going to the toilet. In time he learnt that going to the toilet was not so bad – indeed it became positively pleasant as he was rewarded for going – and he banged his face less and less.

The helmet was not, of course, very pretty, and Brian's parents didn't much like taking him out in it, but it did help them to get over the really horrid hump of Brian's self-injuring episode. Later the occupational therapist was able to make smaller and less conspicuous helmets, until finally Brian was able to do without one altogether.

There are other possible forms of protection besides helmets – splints, gloves and so on – and occupational therapists are inventive and skilful in finding the best way to protect a particular child while still leaving him, as far as possible, free to do other things. Most large general hospitals have occupational therapy departments which may be able to help, or if you have any difficulty contact the Disabled Living Foundation (see 'Aids and Equipment', Appendix 4, page 266) who can give information and advice on where to go for help.

The main points

1. A child's 'bad' behaviours should be decreased because:
   they can disturb the lives of people around him
   they can reduce his opportunities for learning.

2. There are two main methods we can use to decrease bad

behaviour: by taking away something pleasant, or by giving something unpleasant, when the bad behaviour occurs.

3. Time-out from positive reinforcement means that the child, who is in a highly reinforcing situation, has the reinforcement interrupted when the bad behaviour occurs.

4. It is better to start with a short period of time-out, and increase it if necessary, than to start with a long period and then reduce it.

5. Extinction means that where a child has been used to getting reinforcement following a piece of behaviour, he now finds the reinforcement no longer follows and the piece of behaviour occurs less often.

6. At the beginning of an extinction programme we can expect the piece of behaviour to increase (to get worse, if it is a bad behaviour).

7. Once a kind of behaviour has begun to be treated by extinction it should *never* be reinforced.

8. We should be very wary of using extinction programmes for self-injurious or aggressive kinds of behaviour.

9. Extinction can work to decrease either bad or good behaviours.

10. When using fines we remove from the child something he values, following his bad behaviour.

11. Restraint involves preventing the child, for a short time, from moving freely.

12. Restitution, and over-correction, mean that the child has to restore the situation or make it better than it was before his bad behaviour occurred.

13. Methods of lessening bad behaviours work best when they are given on a continuous schedule.

14. We can further help to reduce the child's bad behaviour by DRO – Differential Reinforcement of Other kinds of behaviour (building up other, good behaviours in the place of the bad ones).

15. Changing the surroundings can help to avert a child's bad behaviour.

Some practice problems

*1. Think of any public figure you don't care for (TV or pop star, politician, sporting personality, etc.). How would you use *(a)* extinction, *(b)* time-out to eliminate one or more of this person's bad behaviours?

*2. Which of the methods discussed – time-out, extinction, fining, restraint, restitution, DRO or changing the surroundings – might you use for the following:

(a) A neighbour who often calls with a gift of fruit or flowers from her garden and then stays to tell you about her illnesses over the last twenty years.

(b) Your teenage sons who, in spite of being asked politely not to do so, enjoy throwing their sweet papers at the waste-paper basket, and miss.

(c) Your three-year-old who, when you are out shopping, interrupts every conversation you attempt with your friends with demands to be taken to the lavatory.

(d) Your ageing mother who asks at the end of every meal she has cooked for you: 'Well, did you enjoy that?'

(e) Your elderly cat who has suddenly taken to stealing butter.

Are there any of these for which none of these methods would be appropriate? What else would you do? Would you just put up with it?

8. Records and Graphs

In chapter 2 we saw how helpful written records can be in showing exactly what happened, what worked and what didn't, and, especially, the progress the child has made over time. Record-keeping is a chore, but records help you to see what is going on and to plan what to do next, and looking back over them can be very rewarding. So you may want to try keeping some records; but it is not always so easy to know how or what to record. Again, the purpose of the records is to show you whether your treatment is doing what you hoped it would – producing more of the good and less of the bad behaviours – and it helps to see this if you can make graphs from your records; but it is not always easy to record things in such a way that they can easily be put on a graph. For example, a record might look like this:

Mon Did well today, worked hard and seemed interested.
Tues Quite good but needed a lot of prompting.
Wed Poor concentration today.
Thur Out to tea, no session.
Fri Prompted most of the time but did a good deal.

This is a method which many people use when they first start to keep records. It is quite time-consuming to write, and as you can see there is nothing there – no solid facts – that could be put on a graph to show whether or not any progress is being made. So, we might think about ways to make our records more useful, and how to make graphs out of our recordings.

Records

Recording a bad kind of behaviour is usually quite simple – we just record every time it happens or how long it lasts. The main difficulty here is that the bad behaviour may happen anywhere, any time, and you do not want to have to rush all over the house looking for pencil and paper to write it down. So you could keep a piece of paper and a pencil, stuck on the wall perhaps with the invaluable Blu-tack, in several places – kitchen, living-room, bathroom, hall, garden shed – or perhaps just in those places where you know you are most likely to need them. Then at the end of the day, or the week, you can, if you like, transfer your records to your main record sheet (more about record sheets in a moment, see page 119) and, if you like, put them on a graph (see page 120).

Recording teaching sessions

This is where most of the difficulties arise. There are three main ways of recording teaching sessions:
1. Grading prompts
2. Counting the number of things achieved
3. Probes

1. *Grading prompts*

Much of our teaching involves prompting the child through actions that are new to him (see pages 69–73). We may do this when we teach him to feed or dress himself, to play with a toy or do a puzzle, to imitate what we do, to understand or to use language, and a myriad of other things. At first we have to prompt the child a good deal, but later when he gets more skilful we fade the prompts as he takes over more of the action. So, in order to see how much progress he is making, we can record how much prompting he needed on each task on each occasion. To do this we grade the prompts, and give scores to each grade, like this:

> Full prompt: score 0
> Partial prompt: score 1
> No prompt: score 2

We could, if we wanted to, grade the prompts more finely than this, with scores going up to 5 or 6. This would give us a better feeling of the progress the child is making – he is liable to stay for quite a long time on a score of 1 – but it can get tricky deciding which level of prompt has been used, and on the whole I think it is easier to stick to only three grades.

When you have recorded the amount of prompting you used in your session you can add up the scores for the session. For example, supposing Joanna is learning to feed herself, and as she is only just beginning to learn this she is only asked to feed herself the first three spoonfuls of her pudding. Supposing today she needed full prompts for the first spoonful, full prompts for the second, but only a partial prompt for the third. Her score would be 0 for the first and 0 for the second and 1 for the third spoonful: her score for today would be 1. Then as the sessions go on you may see the total gradually rising in which case you can carry on your teaching; or you may see it not rising, or possibly actually falling, in which case you may think about changing what you are doing. Another example of using graded prompts in recording is given on page 121.

2. Counting the number of things achieved

This is a good method for a child who is making quite rapid progress, or for records kept over a long time. We simply count the number of things the child has mastered in his teaching sessions: the movements he can imitate, the words he says or understands, the garments he can put on without help. We record this not at every teaching session but perhaps once a week, once a fortnight or once a month. Again we should as time goes on see the total gradually rising.

The snag about this kind of record is that it may show rather slow improvement, especially at first, and so may not be very encouraging. On the other hand it is an easy method, and saves us from having to make the recordings during the teaching sessions.

3. *Probes*

A probe is something inserted to discover what is going on. When we use a probe to discover what effect our teaching is having a 'discovering session' is inserted in between our teaching sessions. This means that we do not have to do recording in the teaching sessions themselves. We begin as usual by taking a baseline – a record of how much the child can do before we start to teach him. Then we embark on our teaching. Every now and again, once a week or once a month or whatever suits us, we set up things exactly as they were in the baseline and see how much he can do now, and compare it with what he did in the baseline. This is another method which has the advantage of separating the recording from the teaching sessions.

For example, if we wanted to teach Clive to understand the words 'ball', 'car', 'pencil' and 'shoe' we would take the baseline by putting each object in turn in front of him (always paired with another object) and asking him to give it to us, like this:

Ball and shoe on the table in front of Clive.

Teacher : 'Clive, give me the *shoe*'

Teacher gives no help (not pointing or even looking towards the shoe), but simply records whether or not Clive hands over the shoe. Then the other objects are tested in the same way, and each object is tested several times – say, about five times each. Then his teacher counts up how many times each object was handed over. This is the baseline score.

After a week or so of teaching, by prompting and reinforcing the right responses, the teacher carries out the probe – repeating the baseline exactly as on the first occasion, and recording how many times Clive now hands over the object he is asked for.

What the probe should tell us is how much further along the road towards full competence in this activity the child has gone; how much nearer he is to being able to do it entirely on his own, without any help. So, strictly speaking, whatever the child does in these probe sessions should not be reinforced. It seems to me that it is asking too much of human nature not to look and sound pleased when the child succeeds – and these signs of pleasure may be reinforcing to him. It seems to me, too, that we may be unwilling to discourage the child by suddenly stopping his reinforcement. In this case we need to be clear that the conditions in which we are doing the probes are similar to the baseline conditions *except* for the important difference that the child is receiving reinforcement: whereas, in the long term, we are aiming for him to be able to do his task without special reinforcement. Another way to get over this problem is to continue to give reinforcement in the probe sessions, but to give it randomly. Instead of giving the reinforcement as we do in our teaching sessions, following on the child's successes, in the probe sessions we can give the reinforcement quite arbitrarily, at any time, whether he has succeeded or not. In this way the child continues to have the fun of getting what he enjoys but as this is not closely tied up with what he does we are not, strictly speaking, just carrying out another teaching session. In this case our probe does tell us what the child is now able to do, whether or not this is followed by reinforcement.

An example of the use of probes to measure progress is given by Paula's programme. Paula dribbled constantly and her mother wanted to teach her not to do so. In her baseline her mother, using time-sampling (see page 27), recorded at the end of each quarter of an hour whether Paula's chin was at that moment wet or dry. She recorded this from 4 to 6 p.m. for five days, giving her a total of forty recordings. In all forty Paula's chin was wet. Paula's mother then went to work with her treatment, encouraging Paula to keep her mouth closed and reinforcing her for doing so. After a few weeks Paula's mother did a probe. On one day she once again recorded at the end of each quarter of an hour from 4 to 6 p.m. whether Paula's chin was wet or dry. During this time she did not encourage Paula to keep her mouth closed. At the end of one of the eight fifteen-minute intervals Paula's chin was dry. After another few weeks Paula's mother did another probe in the same way. This time Paula's chin was dry at the end of two of the intervals. So her mother was able to record that Paula's success rate had risen from none to one to two of the eight intervals, or from nought to twelve to twenty-five per cent. It was a slow start, but the result of the probes suggested that the method Paula's mother was using was having some effect.

Probes are a useful way of measuring progress when the problem being worked on is concentration. The aim is to teach the child to continue with one activity for longer and longer periods, but inevitably as time goes on he has to move on to new activities as he grows out of the old ones and it becomes difficult to compare one activity with another. So, in our baseline we may record how long he persists with a number of different activities: then we would focus the teaching on other activities and toys – reinforcing the child for sticking with these for longer and longer times – and then return to the original baseline activities for the probes.

Each of these three recording methods may be useful in different circumstances: or we could use all three at once, to measure different kinds of progress. Scoring prompts will measure day-to-day progress; counting the number of things achieved in sessions gives a longer-term view; while probes will give the overall picture of the child's progress towards final success.

Record sheets

You can, if it suits you, keep your records on any bit of paper you have handy. Timmy's mother, when she was recording how many tantrums he had, used the back of an old calendar which she stuck up on the kitchen wall: each day she wrote down the day and date on it and then every time Timmy threw a tantrum she put a tick under that day. In many cases, though, it is a good deal easier if we make out a record sheet in advance, especially if we are teaching the child something; then we can arrange the record so that in the middle of the teaching session we only have to put a tick when the child performs the task or a cross when he does not, or something else simple.

Supposing we wanted to teach Adrian to imitate, and we had picked six different movements to work on – stand up, put ball in box, clap, touch table, blow, hands on head. Our record sheet might look like this:

Adrian – *Imitation*

Full prompt = 0
Partial ″ = 1
No   ″ = 2

Date	Trial no.	Stand up	Put ball in box	Clap	Touch table	Blow	Hands on head	Total score

If we only tried to get Adrian to imitate each action once each day we would use only one line of the record sheet per day. But if we were giving him two or more trials of each action then we would use two or more lines of the record sheet each day.

Graphs

The next step is to transfer your graphable data to a more readily readable graph.

Constructing the graph

The graph can be drawn on any piece of paper but it is much easier to use graph paper. This usually consists of tiny squares set in groups of ten, 100 tiny squares to the square inch, and can be bought from most stationers.

We draw a line across the bottom of the page: along this line (the horizontal axis) will go time (days or weeks) or sessions.

We draw another line down the left hand side (the vertical axis):
along that line will go the child's scores. We write in the figures
of possible scores, put the child's name at the top and the task
we are working on.

Let's look at some scores and see how we could put them on a
graph. Supposing Adrian's prompt scores – how much prompting he needed to imitate the six actions – over two weeks went
like this (X means no session run that day):

	Sun	Mon	Tues	Wed	Thurs	Fri	Sat	Total
Week 1	0	0	1	0	2	2	X	5
Week 2	X	3	0	3	2	3	X	11

The highest score Adrian can possibly get, if he imitates all
six actions without any prompting and getting a score of 2 for
each, is 12; so we set our scale on the vertical axis from 0–12.
We then put (plot) each of the scores on the graph and join
them up. (I always use a pencil to plot and join up scores, at
least at first. It is horribly easy to get it wrong, and if they are
wrong in ink you are faced with either a messy graph or drawing
up a new one. If you do it in pencil first you can always go over
it in ink later, when you are sure it is right.) We will ignore the
two days missed out and join up the scores for Friday and
Monday. If there were a longer gap, say of a week, it would be
better to leave a break in the line, to show that there had been a
break in Adrian's teaching.

It is important to get the right scale on the graph, leaving
room for scores to go far enough up or down, from the beginning; because we cannot, absolutely cannot, change the scale in
the middle. This would give a false picture of what had happened.
If we find we have got it wrong and not left enough room for,
say, higher scores then we have to re-draw the graph, this time
leaving enough room, and re-plot all the scores.

Not only must we not change the *scale* of what we are graphing
but we must also not change *what* it is that we are graphing. So
if we began by recording how many toys Ivor threw in five
minutes when he had ten toys within reach; and if during our

Graph 1: **Adrian** – *Imitation*

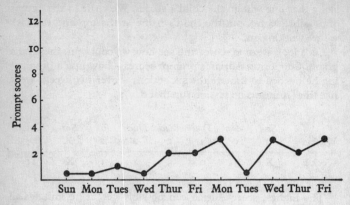

teaching it seemed more convenient to record how many times he threw one particular toy; then we should not plot these new records and join them up to the first – it would be like joining up a record of numbers of oranges with a record of numbers of elephants. Instead we should start a new graph for the new records. The only disadvantage is that we cannot compare the two graphs, since they are telling us about different things. If we want to get over this we can turn again to the probe: from time to time we could once again surround Ivor with the ten toys and once again record how many he threw in five minutes, and plot this on our first graph. Now we would have some later records to compare with the very early one.

It is quite difficult to pick the right recording method from the start, because we cannot be sure how things will change as teaching progresses, so we should not be afraid to change it if necessary and start a new graph.

Average scores

Adrian's graph is fine, but you can see that it is going to use up the graph paper rather quickly if we plot a score for each day or for each session. To get a more compact and manageable graph we can combine the figures over a period – say, a week – and find the average figure for that period. Let's take as an example Adrian's scores on page 121, taking one week at a time. To get the average scores for Week 1 we:

(a) Add up all the figures recorded. These come to: 5
(b) Count up the number of recordings made. These were for one week minus Saturday: 6
(c) Divided the total (a) by the number of recordings (b).

This can be written like this: $\dfrac{5}{6} = 0.8$

or like this: 6)5 (0.8

So for week 1 the *average score* is 0.8. On the graph this will be plotted on the nearest half-number: so this will be plotted as 1.

Similarly for Week 2 we:

(a) Add up all the figures recorded. These come to: 11
(b) Count up the number of recordings made. These were for one week minus Saturday and Sunday: 5
(c) Divide the total (a) by the number of recordings (b),

written like this: $\dfrac{11}{5} = 2.2$

or like this: 5)11 (2.2

So for Week 2 the *average score* is 2.2.

We can then draw up a new graph on which to plot these figures. Not only will this graph take up less space but it will also give a better idea of the general trend of progress over a long time. In addition, since individual variations are ironed out, it lessens the despair we may feel over the occasional disastrous session. Another big advantage of using average, rather than total, scores is that it does not matter so much if we do not always run the same number of sessions, or if we don't collect the same number of records each week. Supposing we had two more weeks' records for Adrian, like this:

	Sun	Mon	Tues	Wed	Thurs	Fri	Sat	Total
Week 3	2	3	2	3	3	3	2	18
Week 4	3	Adrian staying with Gran				4	4	11

If we plotted the totals for the four weeks – 5, 11, 18, 11 – it would look as though Adrian had done worse in the fourth week; whereas actually he has done better, but over fewer sessions. If instead of using totals we work out the *average* scores for weeks 3 and 4 $\left(\dfrac{18}{7} = 2.6 \text{ and } \dfrac{11}{3} = 3.7\right)$ and use these we can see more accurately on Graph 2 the progress he is making. (The averages for weeks 3 and 4 are plotted as 2.5 and 3.5 respectively.)

Graph 2: **Adrian** – *Imitation*

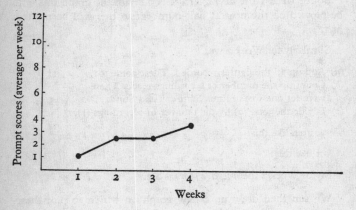

Percentages

We can use percentages in much the same way as we use averages, working out the child's scores as a percentage of the highest score he could possibly make.

In Adrian's case the highest possible score he could make each day, if he imitated all six actions without any prompting and got a score of 2 for each, is 12. Then we work out the percentage scores like this: we

(*a*) Add up all the figures recorded. These come to: 5
(*b*) Count up the number of recordings made. These were: 6

(c) Take the highest possible score he could make each
day. This is 12 (if all 6 actions were scored 2):   12

(d) Divide the total (a), by the number of recordings
(b) multiplied by the highest possible score (c).

This can be written like this: $\dfrac{5}{6 \times 12}$ $\dfrac{5}{72}$

(e) Multiply the whole thing by 100, like this: $\dfrac{5 \times 100}{72}$

This can be written: $72\overline{)500}$ (6.9

$\underline{432}$

680

$\underline{648}$

So for Week 1 Adrian's percentage score was 6.9. On the graph
this would be plotted as 7.

In the other three weeks his totals were:

Week 2: 11   Week 3: 18   Week 4: 11

and the number of recordings made were:

Week 2: 5   Week 3: 7   Week 4: 3

The highest possible score stays the same – 12: so does multiplying by 100. So for the other three weeks the percentages are
worked out like this:

Week 2: $\dfrac{11}{5 \times 12} \times 100 = \dfrac{11}{60} \times 100 = \dfrac{1100}{60}$

$= 18.3$ per cent (plotted as 18 per cent)

Week 3: $\dfrac{18}{7 \times 12} \times 100 = \dfrac{18}{84} \times 100 = \dfrac{1800}{84}$

$= 21.4$ per cent (plotted as 21 per cent)

Week 4: $\dfrac{11}{3 \times 12} \times 100 = \dfrac{11}{36} \times 100 = \dfrac{1100}{36}$

$= 30.5$ per cent (plotted as 30 per cent)

An advantage of using percentage scores is that the highest
possible score is always 100: Adrian cannot possibly score more
than 100 per cent, no matter how high his scores go, or less than
0 per cent; so with the scale on our graph going from 0–100
we will never run out of space.

Another advantage of using percentage scores is that we can if we like put the scores for two or three different kinds of teaching on the same graph. (More than three tends to be messy and confusing.) Supposing, for example, we were teaching Adrian not only imitation but also to use a potty. We could work out the number of times that he used his potty as a percentage of the number of times he needed to use it – the times when he wetted either in the pot or in his pants. Divide the figure for 'Used pot' by the figure for 'Wetted anywhere': multiplied by 100 this gives us the percentage of his success in using his pot.

Supposing the figures for the first week went like this:

	Mon	Tues	Wed	Thurs	Fri	Sat	Sun	Total
Used pot	1	0	0	0	1	0	0	2
Wet pants	6	8	7	8	5	7	7	48
Total – Wet anywhere	7	8	7	8	6	7	7	50

We work out: $\dfrac{\text{Total used pot}}{\text{Total wetted anywhere}} \times 100$

That is: $\dfrac{2}{50} \times 100$

$= \dfrac{200}{50} = 4$

So for the first week Adrian used his pot 4 per cent of all the times he needed to use it.

Supposing we had more figures for his success with the pot, we could plot both sets of figures, those for imitation and those for his success on the potty, on the one graph. We would use different kinds of marks and lines for the two sets of figures, and label them clearly, so that it was easy to see which was which. Suppose there was an interruption for Christmas and then we have the records for four more weeks after that (Graph 3).

You can see that the graphs are pretty variable, especially the toiletting one – Adrian had a disastrous week number 8 as far as using the potty went. Well, it can be like that at times. Luckily Adrian's parents were not discouraged and kept going and, as you can see, things improved.

Graph 3: **Adrian**

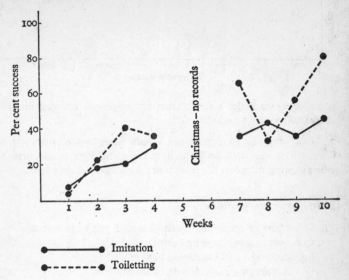

● ———— ● Imitation
●- - - - - ● Toiletting

The main points

1. If we keep records that can be put into figures we can see more clearly the progress we are making.

2. Bad behaviours can usually be quite simply recorded each time they happen.

3. The results of teaching sessions can be recorded by:
   (a) grading prompts
   (b) counting things mastered
   (c) probes.

4. It is easier to record teaching sessions if we make out a record sheet beforehand.

5. When we draw a graph time, or number of sessions, usually goes along the horizontal axis and scores along the vertical axis:

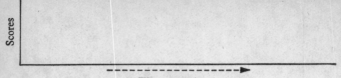

Time or sessions

6. In order to make a more compact graph we can combines scores taken over a period.

7. Using average or percentage scores saves space, irons out fluctuations in scores, and gets over the difficulty that can arise when varying numbers of sessions are done in different weeks.

Some practice problems

*1. What sort of recording method would you expect to use if you were working on these projects:
    (a) teaching a child to thread beads
    (b) encouraging playing with other children
    (c) discouraging throwing toys over the garden fence
    (d) teaching recognition of letters.

*2. Try making a graph of these records of projects with Henry.

Week	Dry bed training Dry nights	Cooperation Requests made	Obeyed
1	2	27	4
2	1	30	12
3	3	31	18
4	4	28	12
5	5	30	17
6	4	29	25
7	3	24	19
8	6	34	31
9	7	28	26

Part 2: Some Things to Teach

Where Part 1 is concerned with general principles of behaviour modification, with ways of teaching and of dealing with difficult behaviour, in Part 2 I shall be looking more closely at some particular things that children need to learn, and of particular ways in which we can help them to do so.

There may be people who, eager to get on with the job of teaching their children, skip the first part of this book and turn straight away to the second part. If you do so you may find that some of the words and terms in Part 2 are unfamiliar and that the teaching methods are not explained. All this is dealt with in Part 1. So if Part 2 on its own seems difficult, go back and have a look through Part 1.

9. Dressing and Undressing

For the mentally handicapped child, clothes to be put on in the morning and taken off again in the evening (to say nothing of all the shoes, plimsolls, gumboots, cardigans, jackets and coats that have to be donned and doffed during the day) are just a few more hurdles in a life already full of difficulties and frustrations. Many children master these tasks quite easily but for some children their parents feel that they are so complex as to be hardly worth attempting. Dressing, too, takes place in the morning when time tends to be short: 'We're always in a hurry and he's got to be on that coach so it's easier to dress him myself.' Nevertheless if the child *can* learn to dress himself it will ease the morning rush for his parents, while he himself will have the satisfaction of having mastered another interesting skill.

To teach dressing we use the methods already discussed – reinforcement: prompting and fading: and breaking down the task into small steps (see chapters 3–5). This last seems particularly important. We are so accustomed to putting on our clothes, and put them on so automatically, that it is difficult to realize what a complicated process it is. It is quite an eye-opener to try to analyse exactly what we do, and how we do it, when we (for instance) put on a sock. For a handicapped child such a task may be too much to tackle all at one go; if he tries it he may fail. But if we break down the task into small steps the child can cope with learning just one step; then he can learn the next step; and so on, until finally he manages to do the whole task. In this way, learning only a very small part at a time, a child can master tasks which before seemed completely beyond him.

Backward chaining (pages 74–5) also figures largely, because it seems a satisfactory way of teaching dressing: but if forward chaining (breaking the sequence down into small steps, teaching the first step first, then teaching the second step and joining – chaining – it to the first, and so on) appeals to you more for any reason, go ahead and use it. (To do this you could usually reverse the backward chaining scales given.)

Looking at the problem

Before we begin to teach a child to dress himself it is often helpful to get clear in our minds exactly how much he can and can't do for himself. Jack, who was mentioned on page 75, was taught to dress himself after years of being encouraged, cajoled, chivvied, prompted, helped and downright dressed. When his teacher decided to set about teaching him systematically to dress himself, she was not really sure how much of this jumbled process Jack did on his own, and how much, in the event, was done for him. So for four mornings when he dressed she watched carefully to see how much he could do by himself, and how much help he really needed. She noted down how many garments he could put on without any help and whether it made any difference if his clothes were arranged on his bed in the right order, or if they were then handed to him one at a time. At the end of the four days his teacher found that Jack had never succeeded in putting on his socks; he had managed his vest, pants and shoes once each, his cardigan twice and trousers three times, while his greatest success was with his shirt which he had managed to put on ten times, although he could not button it up. Out of 128 opportunities to put on garments Jack had been successful 18 times; he had managed to put on garments only when they were handed to him in the right order. By now his teacher had a much clearer idea of what Jack was able to do, and of how to set about teaching him.

In the same way we can look at how much a child is able to do in undressing himself. We take him to his room, or the bathroom, or wherever he normally gets undressed, and say, 'Get undressed Bobby', and see how much he can do without any help at all. We look at:

1. What garments he can manage – vest, pants, socks, shoes, shirt, jumper, trousers, tie, cardigan. And/or, if Bobby is Roberta, dress, skirt, bra, petticoat, tights.

2. Whether he can undo zips, laces, buckles, poppers or hooks and eyes.

3. Whether he drops the clothes on the floor, puts them on a chair or hangs them up.

It is usually helpful to set a limit on how long the child will be left to struggle on his own, either depending on time or on the child's behaviour. For example, when we tell Bobby to get undressed we might decide to let him try to get out of his sweater for between thirty seconds and a minute, or until he clearly gives up. We would then remove the sweater for him and then let him try on his own with the next garment.

One minor variation of this preliminary analysis of what the child can and cannot do is to try the effect of incentives. Philip (see page 104) never undressed himself at home, although his parents had heard that he did so at his nursery school. After they had attended a course in behaviour modification his parents offered Philip a jelly-tot for every garment he removed without help: within a short space of time Philip became, unaided, stark naked. In this case he did not need to be taught the skills to undress himself but he did need the motivation to use the skills he in fact already possessed.

Teaching dressing

A. *Putting on pants – backward chaining scale*

Supposing it is decided that Bobby should begin to learn to put on his pants. His teacher sits him down, on a chair or on the floor, wherever he is most comfortable: she puts his feet through each of the leg openings of his pants, pulls them up to his knees (or thereabouts), stands Bobby up, and pulls the pants up to about three inches below his waist. The she guides his hands to the waistband, holds them on to it, says 'Pull your pants up Bobby', and prompts him to pull them up to his waist. Then she reinforces him.

Bobby can of course be taught to do this step in pulling up his pants not only when he is being dressed in the morning but also every time he goes to the toilet. As he begins to do some of the action himself his teacher fades her prompts, until Bobby is able to pull his pants up the last three inches by himself. Next his teacher pulls up his pants to about three inches lower still – about six inches from his waist – and again Bobby is prompted as much as he needs to be to pull them up. After this the sequence may go as follows (the whole sequence is given for convenience):

Done by adult	*Done by child*
1. Pants pulled up to mid-hips	1. Pulls up to waist
2. Pants pulled up to lower hips	2. Pulls up to waist
3. Pants pulled up to mid-thigh (between thigh and knee)	3. Pulls up to waist
4. Pants pulled up to knees	4. Pulls up to waist
5. Pants pulled up to mid-calf	5. Pulls up to waist
6. Pants put on over both feet to ankles	6. Pulls up to waist
7. One of child's feet put into leg opening	7. Holds waistband, puts other foot in leg opening, pulls pants to waist
8. Pants held spread out in front of child's toes	8. Holds waistband, puts in first one then other foot, pulls pants to waist
9. Pants handed to child right way round	9. Puts on pants and pulls them up
*10. Pants handed to child any way round	10. Gets pants the right way round, puts them on and pulls them up
11. Pants laid out on bed or chair	11. Takes pants, puts them on and pulls them up

* Step 10 may require special teaching – see 'Back-to-front and inside-out', page 138.

How much to teach?

How far the programme goes depends on the child's age, and how well he gets on. With a young or very handicapped child we might think it enough, for the time being anyway, to stop at step 9, and reckon that he was doing a good job if he could put on his pants when they were handed to him the right way round. On the other hand with a more capable child we might want to go beyond step 11, and teach the child to take his own pants from the wardrobe or drawer, pick out the right ones to put on, and so on. If our eventual aim is that the child should be able to dress himself entirely without help we must make sure that our training goes far enough for him to be able to do so. When Simon learnt to do up buttons (see page 83) his delighted teacher told her colleagues that he was able now to button up his shirt without any help from her. However, when she arranged for Simon to demonstrate his newly learnt skill her colleagues found that, although Simon could successfully manipulate the buttons through the buttonholes, he waited before each one for his teacher to start him off by wagging her finger at him and saying 'one', 'two', and so on. So then she had to fade out these prompts until Simon would do up all his buttons on being told 'Do your buttons up'. Eventually he should learn to do them up without any instruction at all, as a natural consequence of putting on his shirt in the morning.

Putting on trousers can be taught in much the same way as putting on pants. Although they are a larger, more complicated garment some children find trousers easier than pants because there is less chance of getting two feet into one leg-opening. Some children however find trousers more difficult because when they are expected to put a foot into the trouser leg they try to shove the foot in flat, without pointing their toes to the ground, so the foot gets stuck in the trouser leg. In this case it may help to have 3 extra steps, between 6 and 7, like this:

Done by adult	*Done by child*
6(*a*) Trousers put on over both feet to ankles	6(*a*) Pulls up to waist
6(*b*) One of child's feet put into trouser leg to ankle, other foot put two-thirds of the way in, with foot pointing to floor	6(*b*) Pushes second foot all the way through, pulls up from ankles to waist

| 6(c) | As 6(b), but second foot put half-way in, pointing to floor | 6(c) | Pushes second foot through, pulls to waist |
| 6(d) | As 6(b) but second foot put quarter way in, pointing to floor | 6(d) | Pushes second foot through, pulls to waist |

During steps 6(b), 6(c) and 6(d) the adult will at first prompt the child to point his foot down the trouser leg, and will gradually fade this prompt so that the child learns to do it for himself. If necessary the same process is carried out with the second foot between steps 7 and 8.

Again, if the trousers don't have an elastic waistband, but an opening at the waist with zip and button it seems best to treat putting on the trousers and doing them up as two separate tasks to be taught separately (see section on 'Fastenings', pages 145–8).

Other garments can be taught in much the same way. You will find examples of backward chaining scales for teaching putting on different garments, to go over the head (vest/jumper/petticoat/dress) or round the back (shirt/cardigan/jacket/coat), for socks and for fastenings at the end of the chapter (pages 142–4). (See also 'Making your own adaptations of the scales', page 136.)

Note: I recommend that you do not try to read through all the backward chaining scales as literature: only read them if you want to use them, or read one or two to see how they work. They do work, but they are mind-boggling to read cold.

Teaching undressing

Undressing is usually easier for children than dressing, and some children undress enthusiastically all day long. Nevertheless, if a child can't undress himself it may be worth taking the trouble to teach him how to do it. The steps in a backward chaining scale to teach taking off a jumper might be as follows:

B. *Taking off jumper/dress/vest/petticoat*

Done by adult	*Done by child*
1. Removes jumper completely, leaving child holding it	1. Puts jumper on to chair
2. Pulls jumper up over child's head, takes one arm out of sleeve	2. Grasps other sleeve and pulls off, puts jumper on chair
3. Pulls jumper over child's head, leaving both arms in sleeves	3. Grasps one sleeve and pulls off, then the other and completes
4. Pulls jumper up to and just over child's shoulders	*4. Pulls jumper over head and completes
5. Pulls jumper up to just below child's shoulders	*5. Pulls jumper over head from shoulders and completes
6. Pulls jumper up to rib level	*6. Pulls jumper over head from rib level and completes
	*7. Pulls jumper over head from waist level and completes

*Steps 4 to 7 may be done by the child in one of two ways: either the child crosses his arms in front of him and grasps the right side of his jumper with his left hand and the left side of his jumper with his right hand to pull the jumper over his head; or he puts his arms straight back over his shoulders and grasps the jumper at about shoulder level to pull it off. For some reason women seem to favour the first, and men the second method.

On the whole undressing involves fewer steps than dressing, probably because garments fall off us more easily than they fall on to us. For this reason I have not given backward chaining scales for taking off other garments – they are fairly easy to devise yourself if you want them.

Making your own adaptations of the scales

The backward chaining scales given here are intended only as a guide, and are not meant to be taken as a sacred text. You may find that some different way of putting on a garment suits your child, or you, better than the one given; you can then work out and teach the steps that make up the method you have chosen.

For example, some people do not take a jumper off in the way I have described on page 136, first pulling it over the head and then taking the arms out; they prefer to take their arms out first and then pull it over their heads. If this is how you would prefer to do it it should be fairly easy to adapt the scale. Again, you may find you need extra steps in a scale; to go back to taking off a jumper, the scale on page 136 assumes that the child can learn to pull the jumper over his head all in one step (3 to 4 on this scale). If he finds this very difficult we could insert extra steps: getting the jumper almost but not quite over his head, then getting it half-way over, then pulling it up to his ears, before expecting him to move on to step 4 and pull it right over his head.

You may find, too, that different kinds of garments require slightly different methods. For example, although vest, petticoat, jumper and dress have been grouped as garments that go over the head, they are not quite the same – vests and petticoats don't usually have sleeves, for one thing. Again, the crucial step of finding the second armhole may be more difficult with a soft floppy cardigan than it is with a firm jacket. Whenever a particular difficulty arises, the important thing is to work out exactly what the difficulty is: once you have done that it is usually easier to see how it can be got over.

For example, Jack had a particular difficulty at step 2 in learning to put on his sock (see page 144). He managed step 1, pulling up the socks from his ankle, quite easily, but when his teacher moved on to step 2 Jack pulled and tugged at his sock without being able to get it over his heel. His teacher saw that the problem lay in the position in which Jack sat to put on his socks. He would sit on his bed, cross one leg over the other, resting the heel of the crossed-over leg on the other knee and attempt to pull up the sock on that foot. When he had to pull the sock up over the heel it was virtually impossible to get the sock past the barrier formed by his heel resting heavily on his knee, and Jack got very frustrated. His teacher tried to make him keep his foot on the floor and bend down to put the sock on, but Jack refused to do this, and in fact was rather too stout to do so comfortably. In the end his teacher brought in a small chair, and made Jack put his sockless foot on it. She then put the sock over his toe and up to his heel, and by resting his toe on the chair Jack could pull the sock up over his heel. When he moved on to step 5, when the sock was put only over his toes, he first rested his heel on the chair, pulled the sock up to his heel, then rocked his foot to rest his toes on the chair and pulled the sock all the way up.

Again, with some children we find that, with garments like pants, the child successfully achieves the first step – pulling them up to his waist – but manages to pull them up either at the front or at the back, but not both; so that somewhere there is a sagging gap. (The same sort of thing can happen with pulling down jumpers or vest.) So we may have to insert an extra step here, and make sure that the child learns to get the garment pulled straight at front *and* back.

Back-to-front and inside-out

If a child is going to learn to dress himself properly without help he will have to learn to put his clothes on the right way round. To help him learn which is the front and which the back part of his garments it is a good idea to sew a label, or a clearly sewn thread mark, into the back of jumpers, vests, pants, trousers without a front opening, petticoats and dresses. The child can then be taught to begin putting on the garment by placing it on his bed or chair front side down and with the label uppermost: when he picks it up to put it on, it is facing the same way as he is. Socks seem to be more easily managed if the mark is put on the front.

Which shoe should go on which foot can cause difficulty. Philip (see page 132) would go on and on asking his mother whether he had got them right, even after he was told he had. So his mother made a template for him: she put his shoes down on a piece of cardboard, side by side and slightly apart, and drew round them with a red felt tip. Philip was delighted with this, and kept the template in his bedroom with his shoes resting on it. When he wanted to put on his shoes he went up to them as they stood with their heels towards him on the template, and, standing behind them, put each one on the corresponding foot.

He no longer had to ask whether they were right.

Which is the outside of the garment and which the inside can be taught by showing the child the seams on the inside, and rubbing his thumb along them. If the seams are not obvious, as for instance with socks, or on a garment with raised seams on the outside, again a label on the inside may help. In this case the label on the back of, say, a jumper may be enough but if the child still has difficulty it may be better to sew another label right inside, perhaps on the shoulder. Then the child can be encouraged always to make sure that the garment has the label, or the seams, inside before he starts to put it on.

Organizing the teaching

When we begin teaching a child to dress or undress it is much easier if the clothes are loose, easy ones to get on and off – especially around the neck; there is something alarming as well as frustrating about having your head stuck half-way inside a constricting woolly tube. Once the child is skilful with these easy garments he will be able to move on to managing more awkward ones.

At first we use garments that are as simply constructed as possible – trousers with elasticated waistbands, slip-on shoes, jackets without buttons at the cuffs. People sometimes ask, why try to teach a child to go beyond these simple garments: why, for instance, when someone can quite well wear slip-on shoes all his life, should he ever have to bother with learning to tie shoe laces? Of course, he needn't. But if he can learn to deal with extras such as buttons, laces and straps many more garments will be available to him (the invaluable bumper boots don't come in slip-on form) which may be more like those that normal people wear (normal men don't wear trousers with elasticated waist bands). So if he is capable of learning to manage zips, hooks and eyes and so on, it may be worth teaching him to do so.

We like to teach activities to a child at the time of day at which those activities normally take place. But many people find early mornings, the normal time for dressing, a rush without adding to them extra things to be done; it may take too much of the available time to teach a child the rather slow process of dressing himself. In that case we may keep the lessons for the weekend; or we may decide that if we can't teach all the garments together we can at least teach them one at a time – we teach the child to put on his pants, for instance, and dress him in all his other garments ourselves. Then when he has mastered pants and can quickly put them on himself we go on to teach him to put on his vest, and so on. He will learn more slowly, but he will learn.

Finally, don't forget the reinforcement.

The main points

1. To teach dressing, we use prompting, fading, breaking down the activity into small steps, backward chaining, and reinforcement.

2. Forward chaining can be used if preferred.

3. Before starting to teach a child to dress we look to see just how much he can do already and how much he needs to learn.

4. Examples of backward chaining scales are given. These may be altered or adapted as required.

5. Where problems arise it helps to see how to overcome them if we work out exactly what the difficulty is.

6. Teaching a child to know the back and front of garments is made easier by sewing a label in the back.

7. Teaching the inside and outside of garments can be done by showing the child the seams, or a label, on the inside.

8. Begin teaching dressing with loose, easy, simply constructed garments.

9. If a child can learn to cope with buttons, laces etc. he will be able to wear a wide variety of clothing.

10. Lessons in dressing are better carried out occasionally, or on one garment at a time, than not at all.

Some practice problems

*1. What steps would you have in a backward chaining scale to teach putting on:

    (a) mitts
    (b) a woolly hat
    (c) Wellington boots.

*2. Children differ in what they find the most difficult step, but which would you *expect* to find the most difficult in teaching putting on:

    (a) jumper
    (b) shirt
    (c) tying a bow.

*3. Can you think of any garment which it might be harder to teach a child to take off than to put on?

Backward chaining scales

A. *Putting on pants, trousers* : pages 134–5
B. *Taking off jumper/dress/vest/petticoat* : page 136
C. *Putting on vest/jumper/dress/petticoat*

Done by adult	*Done by child*
1. Vest put over child's head, arms pulled through armholes, vest pulled down to rib level	1. Pulls vest all the way down
2. Vest put over child's head, one arm pulled right through armhole, second arm put half-way through armhole	2. Pushes second arm right through armhole, pulls vest down
3. Vest put over child's head, one arm pulled right through armhole, second hand put to armhole	3. Pushes second arm into and right through armhole, pulls vest down
4. Vest put over child's head, one arm pulled right through armhole, second hand doubled up under vest against ribs	4. Finds armhole with second hand, pushes arm right through and pulls vest down
5. Vest put over child's head, one arm pulled right through	5. Puts second arm into and through armhole, pulls vest down

Done by adult	*Done by child*
6. Vest put over child's head, one arm put half-way through armhole	6. Pushes arm right through armhole, puts second arm through armhole and pulls vest down
7. Vest put over child's head, one hand put to armhole	7. Pushes first arm into and through armhole, puts second arm through armhole and pulls vest down
8. Vest put over child's head, one arm doubled up under vest against ribs	*8. Holds bottom of vest with second hand Finds armhole with first hand, pushes arm right through; puts second arm into and through armhole and pulls vest down
9. Vest put over child's head	9. Puts each arm through armhole and pulls vest down
10. Vest handed to child rolled up and ready to go over head	10. Puts vest over head, puts each arm through armhole and pulls vest down
11. Vest handed to child the right way round	11. Puts vest on
†12. Vest laid out on bed	12. Puts vest on

D. *Putting on shirt/cardigan/jacket/coat*

Done by adult	*Done by child*
1. Both arms put into shirt, one shoulder of shirt pulled up onto child's shoulder	1. Pulls other shoulder of shirt onto own shoulders
2. Both arms put into shirt	2. Pulls shoulders of shirt onto own shoulders
3. One arm put into sleeve, other arm put half in	3. Pushes second arm right in and pulls shirt on
4. One arm put in sleeve, other arm put to armhole	4. Pushes second arm into armhole and through sleeve, pulls shirt on

* This part of the step can be included earlier if it would help.
† May require special training – see 'Back-to-front and inside-out', p.138.

Done by adult	Done by child
5. One arm put in sleeve, other arm put near armhole	5. Finds second armhole, pushes arm through and pulls shirt on
6. One arm put in sleeve	6. Finds second armhole, puts arm through and pulls shirt on
7. One arm put partly in	7. Holds shirt by collar. pushes first arm right in, puts second arm in and pulls shirt on
8. Shirt handed in right position, with first armhole in right place	8. Holds shirt by collar, puts first arm in, puts second arm in, pulls shirt on
9. Shirt put on bed/chair in right position (shirt fronts uppermost)	9. Picks up shirt right way and puts on
10. Shirt put out in any position	10. Finds correct sleeve for first arm, puts shirt on

E. Putting on socks (each one in turn)

Done by adult	Done by child
1. Sock put on up to ankle	1. Pulls up sock from ankle
2. Sock put on foot and half over heel	2. Pulls sock over rest of heel and up
3. Sock put on foot just to heel	3. Pulls sock right over heel and up
4. Sock put on to instep	4. Pulls sock from instep and up
5. Sock put over toes	5. Pulls sock up from toes
6. Sock rolled right down to toe and handed to child	6. Puts foot in sock and pulls sock up
7. Sock rolled down to heel and handed to child	7. Puts foot in sock and pulls sock up
8. Sock handed to child	*8. Puts foot in sock right way round and pulls sock up
9. Socks put out on bed or chair	9. Takes socks in turn and puts them on

NB: Teaching putting on tights is partly like teaching putting on trousers, partly like teaching putting on socks.

* May need special teaching – see 'Back-to-front and inside-out', p.138.

F. *Fastenings*

Tying single knot (on a shoe with black lace on right-hand side and white lace on left-hand side, when toe furthest away from child. Assumes child is right handed.)

Done by adult	*Done by child*
1. Pick up white lace, lay it diagonally towards toe of shoe: pick up black lace, lay it across white: pick up tips of both laces, pass black behind white and bring tip of black lace under white, bring through	1. Picks up both laces and pulls tight
2. Cross laces as in (1): pick up tips of both laces straight up in air, keep white lace taut, slacken tension on black lace, pass black behind white and leave tip of black just through crossing of laces	2. Pulls black lace through and pulls both laces tight
3. Cross laces as in (1)	3. Picks up tips of both laces straight up in air, keeps white lace taut, slackens tension on black lace, passes black behind and under white, pulls tight
4. Pick up white lace and lay diagonally towards toe of shoe	4. Picks up black lace, lays it across white: picks up tips of both laces straight up in air, keeps white lace taut, slackens tension on black lace, passes black behind and under white, pulls tight
5. Hands shoe to child	5. Picks up white lace, lays it diagonally towards toe of shoe: picks up black lace, lays it across white: picks up tips of both laces straight up in air, keeps white lace taut, slackens tension on black lace, passes black behind and under white and pulls tight

Tying a bow (on a shoe with one black and one white lace, as above. Assumes single knot already tied.)

1. Pick up white lace in the middle, pinch it together to form loop, pass black lace round white loop, push through and pull out black loop

2. Make loop with white lace, pass black lace round white loop, push black loop just through

3. Make loop with white lace, pass black lace round white

4. Make loop with white lace, give middle of black lace to child

5. Make loop with white lace

6. Gives middle of white lace to child

1. Holds white loop with left hand, black loop with right hand and pulls tight

2. Pinches looped tip of black lace, pulls through and pulls both loops tight

3. With first finger of left hand pushes black lace under white loop against right thumb, pulls through and pulls both loops tight

4. Wraps black lace round white loop, pushes through and pulls both loops tight

5. Picks up black lace in middle, wraps round white loop, pushes through and pulls both loops tight

6. With right hand pinches white lace to form loop, wraps black lace round white loop, pushes through and pulls both loops tight

7. With right hand picks up white lace in the middle, makes a loop, wraps round black lace, pushes through and pulls both loops tight

Zips

N.B. Most zips need to be held and straightened from the bottom, but men usually straighten trouser zips from the top.

Done by adult	*Done by child*
1. Hold bottom (or top) of zip (to straighten it), pull zip all the way up.	1. Turns tag of zip down and presses it flat
2. Pull zip three-quarters up	2. Holds top (or bottom) of zip with one hand, pulls up the last quarter, turns tag down
3. Pull zip half up	3. Holds top/bottom of zip, pulls up last half, turns tag down
4. Pull zip quarter up	4. Holds top/bottom of zip, pulls up last three-quarters, turns tag down
	5. Holds top/bottom of zip, pulls it right up, turns tag down

These steps are suitable for zips that are fixed at the bottom, for instance those in skirts or trousers.

If the zip is one that comes completely apart, as in an anorak, three further steps will be needed. In this case the straightening hand has to be at the bottom of the zip.

5. Seats slide part of zip closure in holder part	
6. Puts slide part of zip closure partly in holder	6. Seats slide part of zip closure fully in holder part and pulls up
7. Puts slide and holder parts of zip closure side by side	7. Seats slide part of closure in holder part and pulls up
	8. Closes bottom of zip and pulls up

Buttons

It is best to start with large buttons and fairly loose buttonholes, as for instance on pyjamas. This is better than teaching buttoning on a special button frame, or on a garment that is laid out in front of the child, as this is rather different from buttoning garments on his own body. Later the child can learn to do up smaller buttons.

The instructions given are for a girl: for boys reverse the indications for left and right hand.

Done by adult

1. Push button three-quarters through the buttonhole

2. Push button half through buttonhole

3. Push button quarter way through buttonhole

4. Put edge of button to button-hole

5. Put button opposite appropriate buttonhole

Done by child

1. Holds edge of buttonhole band in left hand, side of button in right, pulls button through

2. Holds buttonhole band and button as above, pulls button through

3. Holds buttonhole band with left hand, pushes button with thumb of that hand, holds button with right hand and pulls through

4. Holds button with left hand, buttonhole band with right hand hear buttonhole: pushes button half-way through, transfers button to right hand, band to left hand, and pulls through

5. Inserts edge of button into buttonhole with left hand, transfers to right and pulls through

6. Feels upwards from the bottom to find the button and buttonhole opposite each other and does up the button

10. Washing

To teach a child to wash himself we use prompting, fading and, as always, reinforcement. Very important, too, are backward chaining and breaking down each activity into small steps. So for each one I have given a backward chaining scale; as before (page 136) you should only take these as rough guides, and should make your own adaptations of them where you want to, or where you think some other method would suit you, or your child, better than the one given.

Teaching a child to wash himself can include teaching him to:

wash his hands
wash his face
clean his nails
dry his hands and face
clean his teeth
bath himself
wash his hair
know when he needs to wash.

Washing hands

For a child to wash his hands by himself he must be able to:

1. Go to the basin
2. Put in the plug
3. Turn on the cold tap
4. Turn on the hot tap
5. When sufficient water in the basin turn off the hot tap
6. Turn off the cold tap
7. Take the soap
8. Put hands and soap in the water
9. Take soap and hands out of the water, rub soap between hands

10. Put soap down
11. Rub palms and fingers together
12. Rub hands together, interlacing fingers
13. Rub palm and fingers of right hand over back and fingers of left hand
14. Rub palm and fingers of left hand over back and fingers of right hand
15. Rinse hands in water
16. Pull out plug.

We can teach the child to wash his hands by prompting him right through the process, fading our prompts first on step 11, and reinforcing him for completing the washing. When he is able to pull out the plug by himself we begin fading the prompts on rinsing, and so on.

Sometimes children get quite skilful at some earlier parts of the process – for example, turning on the taps – before they have mastered later steps such as taking the soap. There seems no point in insisting on prompts where they are not necessary – we let the child do as much and as independently as he can. But we would continue concentrating our teaching at the end of the scale, with the main reinforcement at the end (there is nothing to stop us giving squeals of delight at anything the child can do along the way).

Washing face

Faces can be washed with or without soap, with or without a cloth. How we teach the child to wash his face depends on what sort of a face-wash we are after but probably the easiest way is to teach a child to wash his face with a cloth and without soap. The sequence might be:

1. Go to the basin
2. Take his face-cloth
3. Turn on tap
4. Wet face-cloth
5. Turn off tap
6. Bend over basin

7. Rub cloth all over face
8. Turn on tap
9. Rinse cloth
10. Turn off tap
11. Squeeze out cloth
12. Put cloth away.

It will help him to find his own face-cloth if it is quite different from everyone else's. If he is washing his face at the same time as his hands he can miss out steps 1, 3, 5, 8 and 10.

Cleaning nails

This is fairly advanced (and some of us may feel, judging by the fingernails of our children, that we aren't very good at teaching it). However it can be taught. The sequence for a child who has already got a basinful of water for washing his hands could be:

1. Pick up nailbrush
2. Wet nailbrush in water
3. Rub nailbrush on soap
4. Brush fingernails of left hand
5. Brush thumbnail of left hand
6. Rinse nailbrush in water
7. Rub nailbrush on soap
8. Brush fingernails of right hand
9. Brush thumbnail of right hand
10. Rinse nailbrush
11. Put nailbrush down
12. Rinse hands.

A fairly soft, unspiky nailbrush will help prevent him from being frightened of being hurt. He will also have to be encouraged to continue the brushing (steps 4, 5, 8 and 9) until his nails are clean: it may be worth having a little extra reinforcement for the completion of each of these steps and deliberately withholding it until all the dirt has gone.

Drying hands and face

The child should:

1. Take his towel
2. Hold it in one hand and rub the towel over the palm and back of the other
3. Hold the towel in the other hand and rub it over the palm and back of the first
4. Rub the towel all over his face
5. Put the towel back.

The main problem here is to make sure that the child dries his hands and face thoroughly. This might be dealt with by having extra reinforcement for these steps and not giving it until he is really dry, as with the fingernails.

Cleaning teeth

This is one of the most important of the washing tasks, one of the most difficult to teach, and probably the one which it is most difficult to ensure has been done properly. Again, a not-too-tough brush is advisable (get your dentist's advice on this, as well as on the best size and shape of toothbrush to use) plus a toothpaste the child likes.

Then the steps might be:

1. Takes the toothpaste
2. Unscrews the cap from the toothpaste
3. Puts the cap down
4. Takes his own toothbrush
5. Squeezes out half an inch of toothpaste onto the toothbrush
6. Puts toothbrush down
7. Puts cap back on toothpaste
8. Takes toothbrush
9. Brushes downwards on outer surfaces of all upper teeth
10. Brushes upwards on outer surfaces of all lower teeth

11. Brushes downwards on inner surfaces of all upper teeth
12. Brushes upwards on inner surfaces of all lower teeth
13. Brushes to and fro on biting surfaces of upper and lower teeth
14. Puts down brush
15. Takes tooth-mug
16. Turns on tap
17. Fills mug with water
18. Turns off tap
19. Rinses mouth and spits out three times
20. Rinses toothbrush
21. Puts toothbrush away
22. Wipes mouth on towel.

The particular difficulty here is likely to be brushing the inner surfaces of the teeth, which is awkward. If steps 9, 10, 11 and 12 are too big and the child has difficulty in learning them, each one could be broken down into three – brushes front, brushes left side, brushes right side.

Bathing

This again is a complicated activity, and normal children do not as a rule bath themselves completely independently until they are about 8 or 9. The whole process includes running the bath and getting the temperature right, washing in the bath, getting out, letting out the bath water, drying all over and putting on pyjamas or other clothes.

Since scalding water is extremely dangerous we should continue to supervise the running of the bath until we are quite sure that the child can test the temperature safely. Washing and drying are taught in much the same way as washing hands and face, except that a wider area is covered and the washing may be done with a cloth.

Some children develop fears of bathing, and refuse to get into a bath. This happened with Simon (pages 82 and 134): he had no baths at all between the ages of five and eleven. To get over this his teacher used *graded practice* (see page 219). At first she encouraged him to play with favourite toys in the bathroom, gradually moving them nearer and nearer the bath: then she put some toys on the edge and later into the (empty) bath, so that Simon had to lean over the edge of the bath to play with them. When Simon was quite happy about this she popped him into the bath to play, and later began taking off some of his clothes while he sat in the bath. When Simon was happy to play in the bath with no clothes on she ran a few drops of water into the bath, and when this became more than just a few drops she put in some bubble bath that Simon enjoyed playing with. Gradually the bath was made deeper and the water was gently stroked over Simon's legs, his arms, his back, his front and finally his neck and face. Simon now baths regularly like anyone else.

Hair washing

This is most easily taught in the bath. Since shampoos are mostly made of detergent it is best if the child washes his hair first with the shampoo, rinses it, and then washes the rest of himself with soap afterwards. The sequence might be:

1. Wets his hair in the bath (either by dipping his head in the bath or by pouring bath water over it)
2. Unscrews the cap of the shampoo bottle
3. Pours a little shampoo in his hand
4. Puts down the shampoo bottle
5. Rubs the shampoo into a lather all over his hair
6. Rinses his hair by wetting it as in (1) above.

The most common difficulty is that the child may be scared of having water run down over his face and getting soap in his eyes. A non-stinging shampoo, and a shampoo shield to hold the water back from his face (see Appendix 4, 'Aids and Equipment') may help.

After he has washed his hair, the child should be taught to dry it with a towel, or, with careful supervision, an electric hair dryer.

Knowing when a wash is needed

Most children are used to the routine of a regular bath. Once they have learnt to wash their hands it should not be too difficult to teach them to wash them before meals and after going to the toilet. It may be rather more difficult to teach a child to recognize

and deal with dirty hands or face in between times – when he is going shopping or to visit friends, or if he comes indoors very, very dirty. If he does not seem to notice that he needs a wash we might ask, 'Do you want a wash?', prompt him to look at his hands, and if necessary point out the dirt on them. Later the question and the prompt might be gradually faded, much in the same way as spontaneous language is encouraged (see pages 193–5) until eventually he is able to see for himself when his hands are dirty and need a wash.

The main points

1. We may want to teach a child to wash and dry his hands and face, clean his nails, clean his teeth, wash his hair, and to know when he should wash.

2. In each case the process is broken down into small steps and taught by backward chaining.

3. Prompting, fading and reinforcement are also used.

4. A face-cloth, towel and toothbrush that are clearly different from everyone else's will help the child to pick out his own.

5. Some important steps, such as getting all the dirt off, or drying thoroughly, may need to be reinforced separately.

6. If a child is frightened of the bath this may be tackled by using graded practice – getting the child from a situation quite different from bathing gradually nearer and nearer real bathing, making sure that he is always happy and relaxed.

Some practice problems

*1. How would you set about teaching Bobby to get the bath-water temperature right?
*2. How dirty is dirty? or, How do *you* decide your hands need washing?

11. Dry Pants, Dry Bed

Toilet training is an important part of all children's early learning, and even modern parents, who are not too fussed about early training, are usually pleased to see an end to the washing of nappies and knickers. Some children may become trained as young as one year old but for many it is a much longer process: in one large study only just over half of the normal 4-year-olds were reliably toilet trained.* So it is not surprising if it seems rather a slow business for handicapped children.

Training

Most children become toilet trained through a combination of imitation, parental pleasure and displeasure, and luck. When a child is not making progress in the normal way something more systematic must be tried. The methods we use are likely to rely mainly on reinforcement of the proper use of the toilet and withholding reinforcement from, or in some cases, mildly punishing wetting and soiling in places other than the toilet.

With even quite small babies some mothers become very skilful at knowing when their babies are likely to wet or soil, and are able to 'catch' them on the pot. They often say that it is not the babies who are trained but they themselves, and this is probably right. Nevertheless a mother who can 'catch' her child in this way has a lot going for her; the child can be reinforced for performing on the pot, even if it is the mother's effort and not his that has brought this about. If the child is consistently reinforced for performing on the pot he will, if he is old enough, gradually come to realize the association between what he does and the reinforcement, and become more ready to

* *Four Years Old in an Urban Community*, J. & E. Newson, George Allen & Unwin, 1968, Penguin Books, 1970.

perform of his own accord. So 'catching' and reinforcing are good ways to begin training. With an older child we can often do much the same; observing him carefully to see when he is most likely to wet or soil, and putting him on the toilet at these times.

Some children however are not so regular in their habits. Six-year-old Julie had been so unpredictable that her mother had given up trying to catch her, and Julie was in nappies night and day. When her mother decided to make a big effort to toilet train her she first of all had to take her out of nappies. She put Julie into trainer pants, made of terry towelling, which absorbed a good deal if Julie had an accident but, like ordinary pants, were easy and quick to take off and put on. She decided she would put Julie on the pot every half hour, and would keep her there until she performed, or for at least two minutes. In this way there was a good chance that occasionally Julie would perform on the pot; when that happened Julie's mother seized the chance to shower her with reinforcement.

As Julie wasn't keen on staying on the pot for two minutes her mother stayed beside her, putting her back whenever she tried to get off. A potty chair can help a child to feel safe on the pot and straps can be fitted to put round the child which will encourage him to stay on the pot (see Appendix 4, 'Aids and Equipment'). Julie was also given one or two toys or favourite belongings to play with, especially at first, when her mother wanted the whole business of potting to be a pleasant and rewarding one for Julie. Later when Julie had accepted the routine of sitting on the pot her mother began to fade out the toys a bit, to encourage Julie to concentrate on what she was supposed to be doing.

Julie's mother kept a record of how the training went: she recorded for each half hour whether Julie's pants were wet or dry when she was taken to the pot and whether or not she used the pot. If her mother had found that Julie was almost always wet, and that she hardly ever used the pot she might have thought it worth while, for a time at least, putting Julie on the pot every fifteen minutes in the hope of 'catching' her, and of getting the opportunity to reinforce her. Once Julie began to realize that using the pot was followed by reinforcement, and began to use it more often, her mother could gradually space out the times Julie was put on the pot.

All sorts of things may contribute towards the decision to embark on toilet training – what stage the child seems to be at, how much time his mother has to spare just then, ups and downs in the rest of the family, and so on. Everything else being equal many mothers prefer to start in the summer, when the child will be wearing thinner and fewer clothes, so accidents can be spotted more quickly and changing is easier; and puddles and damp clothes seem somehow less important in the summer – Nature is on our side where drying is concerned.

Accidents

During her training Julie naturally had a good many accidents, when she wet or soiled her pants. Her pants then had to be changed, and her mother soon realized that this pants-changing was in many ways a very enjoyable time for Julie. She loved attention, and here she had her mother all to herself for ten minutes or so; in addition her mother used at these times to talk to her a great deal, scolding her, commenting on what was going on, praising her for pulling up her pants, and so on. If Julie was soiled her mother often used to give her a warm bath, as this seemed the quickest way to get her cleaned up, and then

Julie would play in the water and enjoy being hugged dry in the towel. Once her mother realized that the whole business of changing pants was a rewarding one for Julie she decided to make it rather different. Now when she was changing her Julie's mother remained very neutral, not scolding, not praising, indeed talking very little. When Julie was soiled she was cleaned up with cool water from a basin. However, when she managed to go for a whole day without being soiled her mother gave her an extra long enjoyable bath and extra towel-hugging in the evening: she did not want Julie to lose this pleasure, only for it to follow her good rather than her bad kinds of behaviour.

Wiping up

A child who is to be completely independent for toiletting needs to learn to wipe his bottom after defecating. This is quite an advanced skill, which we probably would not attempt to teach unless the child was physically fairly skilful, and also quite confident and secure on the toilet seat. Then we teach him by physical prompting – putting the toilet paper in his hand, closing our hand round his and making the necessary movements to wipe his bottom and drop the paper into the toilet. One difficulty is knowing when to stop wiping: so we prompt the child to look at the paper which he has just used, and if it is dirty to take another piece, only stopping when the piece he has just wiped himself with is clean or almost clean.

Girls should be taught to wipe themselves from front to back, as wiping in the opposite direction can cause urinary infections. Boys, for whom it is less important, are apparently likely to wipe from front to back anyway.

'I want to go!'

When a child has learnt to keep himself dry and to use the toilet appropriately it may be helpful to him if he can let people know when he wants to go: if for instance he is away from home, or can't open doors, or needs help with his clothes or with getting on and off the toilet. So, right from the early stages of the

training, it is a good idea to begin to teach him to use some
signal whenever he is taken to the toilet. If he can talk we can
when taking him always say 'Toilet' (or any other word normally used); if he does not talk we can use the word plus the
'Toilet' sign from one of the signing systems (see pages 197–9):
or the word plus any kind of sign the child himself tends to use,
such as clutching at the front of his trousers. (Even if this last is a
bit unlovely it may be worth using it to teach him to indicate his
wants – if he learns it we can later, in the same way, pair it
with and teach him a more sophisticated sign.) After a few days
of always using the signal when we take him to the toilet we can
go on to prompting him to imitate the signal; later still, fade the
prompts, and then go on to using a question instead of only
modelling the response – 'What do you want? Say, "Toilet" ';
or 'What do you want? Do "Toilet" ', plus whatever sign he
knows or is learning. Later again we fade this too (see page 193,
'Using words spontaneously') until the child is able to ask for
the toilet when he wants it.

Help from the surroundings

Julie's toilet training was begun on a pot, as happens with most
small children, and a special potty chair to help her sit more
securely, and perhaps a musical potty which plays a tune when
she uses it, might help (see Appendix 4, 'Aids and Equipment').
In time, however, she will need to learn to use an ordinary toilet,
as part of becoming more grown-up and also to make it easier
for her to go to the toilet when she is away from home. Many
small children find the big toilet alarming, with its big opening
through which a small person might slide. Trainer seats, which
fit on to the ordinary toilet seat and make a smaller seat for the
child to sit on, can be a help. These are obtainable from most
large chemists. Children often find it difficult to climb up on to
the high seat; a firm box that they can climb on to first, and on
which they can rest their feet while sitting on the toilet, makes
it easier and adds to the child's feeling of security. For a child
who is very nervous of sitting on the toilet seat it may be worth
fixing a handle to the wall beside the toilet for him to hold on to.

Where to keep the toilet paper can be a problem: it must be available for the child to use, but sometimes a child gets the idea that it is hilarious to unwind yards of paper and push it down the toilet. In this case it may be a good idea to put the main roll or packet of paper on a high shelf out of reach of the child and keep a few pieces, to be replaced as necessary, at toilet-seat height for legitimate use.

Intensive programmes

If, in spite of putting into practice the ideas discussed above, a child still makes little progress with his toilet training we may have to resort to more drastic methods, along the lines of programmes devised by Drs Nathan Azrin and Robert Foxx in America. These programmes concentrate full-time on toiletting, and include very frequent regular checks on pants, extra liquids for the child to drink, frequent trips to the toilet, massive reinforcement for success and some mild punishment for accidents. Lennie was 9 years old and had never been clean and dry, although there seemed no real reason why he should not be. His teacher decided to try an intensive programme with him. First she set up the toilet area with a table, two chairs, some toys, a cup, a bottle of Lennie's favourite orange squash, several spare pairs of pants, a kitchen timer, several bars of Lennie's favourite milk flake chocolate and a record sheet. She planned to carry out Lennie's programme from 9.30 in the morning till 12, when he would go to lunch, and again from 12.30 to 3.30 in the afternoon. Lennie was taken to the toilet area at 9.30, and his teacher felt his pants: for a wonder, they were dry. *'Good boy Lennie, you've got dry pants!'* she said in a tone of voice doubt-less used by somebody conveying to Wellington the result of the battle of Waterloo. She put his hand to his pants and made him feel them himself, once again saying 'Good boy, *dry* pants', and she broke off a little bit of chocolate flake and gave it to him. When he had, delightedly, eaten it she filled the cup with diluted orange squash and gave him as much as he would drink – two cups. The point of these extra fluids is to increase the number of times Lennie will want to pass water, hopefully into the toile so that he can be reinforced for his success, but even if the result is sometimes wet pants this, too, can be used as part of the teaching process. His teacher waited for about a minute after he had had his drink and then said, 'Go to the toilet Lennie'. Lennie didn't budge from his chair, so she gently prompted him to go to the toilet, pull down his pants and sit on the toilet. She set the kitchen timer to twenty minutes: Lennie was to sit on the toilet for twenty minutes or until he used it. After a few moments Lennie had had enough of sitting on the toilet and he tried to get off it, but his teacher pushed him back, and pushed him back every time he tried to stand up, until eventually he gave up and just sat there.

Seventeen minutes went by, and then came the welcome sound of splashing. The reaction Lennie got now was like that customarily reserved for the liberator of a beleaguered city – arms flung round him, kisses showered on him, his praises sung to the skies, and a generous wodge of chocolate flake popped in his mouth. Then his teacher allowed him to stand up, she prompted him to pull up his pants, and led him back to the table. For the next five minutes they played with the toys. His teacher then felt, and prompted him to feel, his pants. They were dry, both then and at the following five minute check, so each time Lennie was praised and given a small piece of chocolate flake. By now it was 10 o'clock and time to start the whole process again. Lennie was again given as much diluted orange squash as he would take – a cupful – and as before he was prompted to go to the toilet, but this time he didn't use it. At the end of twenty minutes his teacher stood him up without comment, and they returned to the toys. At the next five-minute pants check, Lennie's pants were damp. His teacher made him feel them, shook her head and said sadly and with emphasis, 'That's *bad*, Lennie, your pants are *wet*.' She picked up a piece of chocolate and showed it to him, shook her head again and said 'No chocolate, your pants are *wet*,' and put the piece down again. Now she made Lennie take off his pants, put on a clean pair and rinse his pants out in cold water. (This is the mild punishment.) She did not praise him for any of this. They then returned to the table, but Lennie's teacher did not play with him or talk to him for the next five minutes but made him sit quietly in the chair. At the next pants check his pants were dry: she praised him, but did not give him any chocolate flake, and, when he was next due for fluids, he had plain water instead of orange squash. (She had decided that when he had wet his pants he should miss out on the foods for a time, to help to impress on him that it was not a good idea to wet his pants. The next time he got the enjoyable food and drinks was after the next time he

Name: Lennie
Date: 6.7.72

Time	9.30	10	10.30	11	11.30	
Fluids given	✓	✓	water	✓	✓	
Amount taken	2 cups	1 cup	$\frac{1}{3}$ cup	1 cup	1$\frac{1}{2}$ cups	
Waited 1 minute	✓	✓	✓	✓	✓	
Child goes to toilet without prompting	−	−	−	−	✓	
Sent to toilet	✓	✓	✓	✓		
Used toilet: Yes	✓	−	✓	✓	✓	
Time taken	17′	−	11′	12′	2′	
Reinf. given	✓	−	✓	✓	✓ + + !	
No		✓				
Five-min. checks	✓ ✓	✓ ✓	✓ ✓ ✓	✓ ✓ ✓	✓ ✓ ✓ ✓	
Dry	✓ ✓	✓	✓ ✓ ✓	✓ ✓ ✓	✓ ✓ ✓ ✓	
Edible reinf. given	✓ ✓	X	✓ ✓ ✓	✓ ✓ ✓	✓ ✓ ✓ ✓	
Wet		✓				
Restituted		✓				
Comments	Loves reinforcer	Upset at not getting reinforcer	Sits better	Seems to know what he needs to do to get reinforcer	Triumph	

used the toilet, at about 10.42 a.m. If he had not used the toilet at this time he would have got the chocolate the next time after this that his pants were dry.)

So the morning wore on – rather slowly, it must be admitted, for Lennie's teacher. Her reward however was at hand. At 11.30 a.m., after he had had his drink, Lennie took himself, unprompted, to the toilet, and used it after only two minutes. After nine years of incontinence he had cottoned on to the fact that it was worth his while to use the toilet and to keep his pants dry.

Opposite is the record that Lennie's teacher kept of his first morning of the intensive programme.

Maintaining progress

Lennie responded unusually quickly to the intensive toilet training programme – it can take several days for children to reach the stage that he got to in one morning. His teacher kept up the programme for another three days, to make sure that his success was not accidental; Lennie continued using the toilet, having dry pants, and enjoying the reinforcement he was given. Next, his teacher began to fade out the intensive programme: first the table and chairs were put outside the toilet area, then further up the corridor, then into his normal classroom. The pants checks took place now every ten minutes, then every fifteen, then on the half hour. The extra liquids were dropped. Lennie continued to get food reinforcers every time he used the toilet but only now and again for dry pants, though he was always praised. He was always reinforced if he went of his own accord and used the toilet, and now he was only told to go if he had not been for an hour. If he wet his pants, as he did with less and less frequency, he was told that was bad, made to change his pants and wash them out, and did not receive the food the next time that that was due.

After two weeks of this 'faded' programme Lennie returned to normal work in his classroom. He went to the toilet at the normal times – before and after meals, and so on – with the other children, and his pants were occasionally checked at these times.

Every now and again as well as the praise that all the children got for using the toilet Lennie got a piece of his chocolate flake. Later still even the pants checks and the chocolate were discontinued. Lennie was back to his former routine with the one difference – he was no longer wet, smelly and uncomfortable.

Variations in intensive programmes

Lennie's teacher set up his intensive programme on an all-day basis because she thought this would be the quickest way to get results, and because she was able to do so – she had enough staff working with her who could be with the other children while she was with Lennie. If this had not been possible she might have run the programme in the mornings only, or even just for a couple of hours each day – progress would be likely to be slower but better than if there were no programme at all. Again, if Lennie's teacher had not been able herself to devote the whole day to the programme she might well have enlisted the help of others, to take half-hour shifts; in this case it would be important that everybody was aware of all the details of the programme, and carried it out in exactly the same way as everyone else. The shift system does have the advantage of lessening the tedium for the teacher.

Night-time training

Learning not to wet the bed is harder for most children than learning not to wet their pants, because when they are asleep they have less control over what is going on. However, there are some ideas we can try out to help the child become dry at night.

First, a couple of things that hardly ever help. Punishment is said to be almost always ineffective (and seldom used by parents nowadays), and limiting drinks in the evening to be disappointing. Many mothers of bed-wetters do try cutting down the amount the child drinks in the evening but perhaps should not be too surprised if it doesn't have much effect.

Now to go on to some ideas that may help.

Medical help

A very few children may have some medical condition which makes it difficult for them not to wet the bed; it is rare, but may be worth checking. Drugs, too, help a small number of children, so it may be worth taking a child to the doctor and asking his advice about bed-wetting.

Potties and night-lights

A child may be put off getting up at night if he has to go out of his room to the toilet; so, if he has not already got one, it may be worth giving him a potty by his bed. Again, he may dislike getting up in the dark, so an electric night-light, or a light left on on the landing, may help. (In our family we only gave up having the landing light on all night when our youngest was sixteen – admittedly it had become a habit and we had forgotten why we left it on.)

Lifting

Many parents lift the child late at night and put him on the pot, and this may help a child to go through the night without wetting his bed earlier than he otherwise would have done. If, when he is lifted, he is regularly already wet, it may be worth lifting him progressively earlier in the evening until you find a time when he is regularly dry. He can then be rewarded for being dry at this time. After a week or so you can begin lifting him very slightly later, advancing the time at which he is lifted, by, say, five minutes at a time. The idea is that, although he will still be dry, he will begin to associate the lifting with a gradually more and more full bladder, so that eventually the full bladder itself will wake him.

Star charts

Some children respond well to a star chart with a star to stick on for every dry night. For some, just seeing the star go on to the chart and the praise and attention that goes with it seems to be reinforcement enough, but for others it may be more effective if there are exchange reinforcers, so many stars to be exchanged for the reinforcer (see chapter 4).

Bell and pad

Most children learn, in due course, to wake up when their bladders are full, to get out of bed and go to the toilet. For bed-wetters the full bladder is not enough to wake them and they may need to learn to associate the feeling of a full bladder with waking. This is where the bell and pad apparatus comes in. The pad is put on the bed and covered with a drawsheet: when the child begins to wet a few drops of liquid (urine) are enough to close an electrical circuit which sets off the ringing of the bell, which wakes the child, who then goes to the toilet. (The apparatus is so constructed that there is no chance of the child getting an electric shock.) As he has passed only a few drops of urine before he is woken he gradually begins to associate the feeling of fullness of his bladder with waking up: after which he no longer needs the bell and pad.

This way of treating bed-wetting is said to be by far the most effective, and success rates of 60 to 100 per cent have been reported. It does have its complications. If the bed-wetter sleeps in a room with other children the bell may wake them as well, and cause disruption to the family. With normal children it is usually not recommended where the child is under seven years old, as he may get in a muddle when he wakes, not go to the toilet properly or not remake the bed adequately afterwards. All this may apply to a mentally handicapped child, too. However, the apparatus can be used slightly differently, for instance by putting the bell in the parents' room instead of in the child's, so that when it rings one or other parent wakes and goes quickly to him and lifts and organizes him. If this causes too much disruption of the parents' nights it may be worth while to connect up the apparatus, and make use of it, in the evenings only, when they are awake anyway, switching it off when they themselves go to bed. A lot depends on how desperate they are for the child to stop wetting the bed.

The apparatus can be obtained on loan from hospitals, through the family doctor.

The main points

1. A good way to start training a child is to see when he is most likely to wet or soil, and 'catch' him on the pot.

2. If the child's habits are not regular enough for this, half-hour toiletting can be tried.

3. Trainer pants are easier to manage than nappies.

4. It is probably best to clean a child up neutrally after a toiletting accident, especially if he likes attention.

5. The child can be taught to wipe his bottom by prompting him to do it.

6. It is helpful to teach the child to indicate, either by a word or a sign, when he wants to go to the toilet.

7. A potty chair with straps, a toilet seat, a step up to the toilet, a handrail, can all help the child to feel more secure: keeping most of the toilet paper out of reach avoids having it stuffed down the toilet.

8. An intensive toilet programme includes: full-time concentration on toiletting, frequent pants checks, extra fluids, massive reinforcement for success and mild punishment for accidents.

9. The programme should be gradually faded out.

10. If an intensive programme all day is not possible a partial one is probably better than nothing.

11. Night-time training:
    (a) punishment and restricting fluids do not usually help much
    (b) it is worth asking the child's doctor whether he can help
    (c) a potty by the bed, or a night-light, may be useful

(d) it may be worth lifting the child and potting him some time after he has gone to sleep. If a time can be found when the child is dry he can be lifted then; gradually the time at which he is lifted can be advanced

(e) star charts for dry beds work for some children

(f) the bell and pad apparatus may help a child to learn not to wet the bed.

Some practice problems

*1. In what ways do you think toilet training a child and house training a pet are similar? How are they different?

*2. What would you do if the child you were training always wet two minutes after he came off the toilet, even if he had been sitting there for half an hour?

12. Eating and Table-manners

Teaching a child to feed himself is often one of our most enjoyable tasks. Most children like their food, so the reinforcer for them is the food itself, and they are usually willing to make an effort to learn this interesting skill. Once again, teaching relies mainly on backward chaining, prompting and fading – this last, fading, seems particularly important in teaching feeding.

A list of aids to teaching feeding, together with the names and addresses of suppliers, can be found under 'Aids and Equipment' in Appendix 4.

Sitting in a good position

Before starting to teach a child to feed himself we make sure he is sitting in a good position. He should be sitting securely in the chair, supported by arms or straps if necessary. His feet should be flat on the floor, or, if this is not possible, resting on a box. Most importantly, the table should be at the level of his waist, so that he can comfortably rest his elbows on the table. A child who can hardly see over the edge of the table is going to have a tough time learning to feed himself.

Feeding himself

Teaching a child to feed himself is done most easily if the teacher stands behind the child: what is lost in face-to-face contact is made up for in the natural flow of the teacher's movements guiding the child's hand.

In general it seems best to start teaching the child to feed himself with foods that he is very, very fond of. If he loves pudding but only tolerates meat and vegetables, we feed him his first course as usual and start the teaching with the pudding.

If the food he is really mad about is ice-cream then we have ice-cream for pudding for a few days. When he begins to get the hang of feeding himself he can go on to foods that he likes but which are not his first favourite.

1. *Finger feeding*

To teach this we take a suitable food that the child likes and cut it up into pieces or lengths: apple, banana, biscuits, bread and butter or toast and spreads, celery, carrot, fried bread, sweets such as barley sugar, rusks, are all possible. Standing behind the child, we close his fingers round a piece and move his hand up to his mouth. We encourage him to smell the food, touch it with his lips and tongue, to put it into his mouth and taste it. Gradually as he begins to hold and move the food to his mouth himself we relax our pressure.

2. *Using a spoon*

Sometimes a child is slow in learning to feed himself because it doesn't occur to his family to let him try to feed himself: in other cases he actively resists the process. With some children it may be helpful to put a tiny blob of a favourite food – jam, syrup, melted chocolate, a smear of Marmite – onto the tip of the spoon, give the child a taste of it, and then let him try by himself taking the spoon to his mouth. Later he may be willing to take the spoon with tiny portions of dinner on it to his mouth.

Other children, however, will not take the spoon to their mouths at all. Karen was one of these; she was pleased to get her food as long as her mother fed it to her, but as soon as she was given a spoon she would open her hand and drop it, and if her mother returned it to her she got cross and threw it away. When Karen was four, and obviously perfectly capable of feeding herself, her mother decided it was time for her to begin doing so. For the first attempt her mother made her favourite dinner – sausage, mashed potatoes and carrots. She cut the sausage and carrots up into small pieces and poured over some

of Karen's favourite gravy. She popped Karen into her high chair and put on a good sized plastic bib. She put the plate in front of Karen, loaded the spoon with a small quantity of sausage and potato, and, standing behind the high chair, put Karen's hand round the handle of the spoon: with her own hand round Karen's she guided the spoon to Karen's mouth. Karen resisted holding the spoon, but as her mother's hand held hers firmly round the handle she could not drop it, and she was really pleased to get such a nice mouthful of food. Her mother guided the spoon back to the plate, gave Karen a little hug and said to her 'What a clever girl! You did it yourself!' Then she scooped up another small spoonful of food and, when Karen had finished her mouthful, they were ready to start again.

As Karen was so resistant her mother did not at first insist on her feeding herself the whole meal. Instead she stopped after the first three mouthfuls, and fed Karen the rest of the meal as she had always done. They went on like this for three or four meals, and then Karen's mother increased the number of spoonfuls Karen 'fed herself' to four, later to six, eight, eleven, and so on, until eventually Karen was expected to help with the whole course. This was the normal way of things, but her mother would not insist on Karen doing so much if she were unwell or upset or if the meal were something she was not so keen on. Never again however did Karen get away with having the whole meal fed to her.

As Karen began to be more skilful at using her spoon her mother began to fade out the help she was giving her. At first she slightly released her hold just as the spoon reached Karen's lips, so that Karen did more of the action of putting the bowl of the spoon into her mouth; she did not let go of Karen's hand entirely, and it was just as well she did not because when Karen had got the mouthful of food she forthwith lost interest in holding the spoon and would have dropped it if her mother had not made sure that she replaced it decorously on the plate. Later on her mother was able to release Karen's hand earlier and earlier in the process of taking the spoon from the plate to her mouth, and eventually gradually to release her hold of Karen's hand, until she was not actually touching Karen's hand at all. The first time she let go altogether of Karen's hand she was so delighted that she stood back to enjoy the sight of her daughter feeding herself – whereupon Karen dropped the spoon. Karen's mother retrieved the spoon from the floor, gave it a wash, and decided that she should not be quite so precipitate next time; when she next let go of Karen's hand she kept her hand hovering just above Karen's, shadowing her movements, so that if Karen showed any sign of making a mistake her mother was right there to help.

Karen made good progress with learning to take the spoonful of food to her mouth – probably because she liked the food; the reinforcement was there for her at the end of the spoon-lifting process. It was more difficult to teach her to put the spoon back on her plate – probably because there was not much reinforcement in that. Her mother decided that Karen would be more likely to learn to put down her spoon properly if she were reinforced for doing so. As her mouth was always full with her last spoonful of food her mother could not use a food reinforcer; instead, when the spoon reached the plate her mother would praise her and gently stroke her cheek which Karen loved. With this and the gradual fading of her mother's prompts she learnt to return her spoon to the plate.

Another difficult task was loading the spoon. Her mother did not start teaching this until Karen was well on the way to being able to take the spoon to her mouth. Then her mother collected the food to one side of the plate before giving the spoon to Karen, putting her hand round Karen's and helping her to scoop up a spoonful of food. Later, when Karen was beginning to be able to do the scooping her mother prompted her to scrape the food together.

3. Using a fork

When Karen was able to use a spoon with little help her mother put a fork into her left hand and prompted her to use it to push the food into the spoon. Her mother thought that, occupying her left hand, the fork would help to discourage Karen from using her fingers. Occasionally in the past Karen would use her fingers to push food on to the spoon, so here the fork was of practical help as well as socially more acceptable.

Once again Karen's mother gradually faded out her prompts, taking care not to go too quickly, until Karen could manage the fork by herself.

4. Using a knife

When her mother wanted to teach Karen to cut with a knife she began teaching her as part of a game, which they played in play-time, quite apart from meal times. Together they cut plasticine, clay and dough, with her mother prompting Karen to hold and move the knife with her right hand and to hold whatever she was cutting with her left hand. Later they started cutting bread with the crusts off at tea-time: at the same time, and using the same methods of prompting and fading, her mother taught Karen to spread soft butter and jam on the bread.

A good deal later, when Karen had for some months been able to use a spoon and fork quite by herself, her mother began to teach her to cut foods such as bananas, fish fingers, soft buns, cooked carrots, pears, tinned peaches and so on with a knife while holding the food steady with a fork. She then encouraged

Karen to put the food into her mouth with the fork. (This was quite a big change for Karen as up to now she had taken the food to her mouth in a spoon held in her right hand, whereas the fork now was in her left hand.) Her mother made a point of showing Karen how to cut the food with a forward and backward movement of the knife; so when she came to use her knife at dinner she could cut her meat instead of trying to wrench it apart sideways.

5. Drinking from a cup

When we want to teach a child to drink by himself the kind of cup we use depends on what he finds easiest. Some children do best with a beaker without handles, for others a two-handled cup is good (see 'Aids and Equipment', Appendix). For the very young children the Teacher Beakers are excellent and save spilling. Whichever kind of cup you choose, fill it with a drink the child likes and about half full – more and it is likely to slop about, less and the child has to tip it so far to get anything as to make the task extra difficult. We put the child's hands on to the cup: even if he is using a one-handled cup the hand on the other side will help to steady it. We help him to pick the cup up to his lips, tip it so that he gets a little of the drink, and then put the cup down again. Gradually, as he begins to be able to do some of the task himself we fade the prompts.

Once again, as with the spoon, the most difficult part to teach is putting the cup back on the table, and it may help if we reinforce this part of the task separately. We shadow the child's hands carefully at this stage so that he can't drop the cup or spill the drink. Later on, when he is quite good at drinking by himself, if he seems often to drop or spill the drink on purpose, we may make him clear it up, or may use over-correction – make him wipe it up *and* dry the table *and* polish it *and* sweep the floor. And so on. (See page 102.) Once again, if we use over-correction it is worth keeping records to see whether the deliberate spilling becomes less frequent. If it doesn't we shall have to think again.

Managing and taking foods

1. *Chewing*

It is difficult to teach this, especially with an older child. Try offering, or getting him to take to his mouth, long pieces of food, to encourage him to bite them, hopefully to bite them off, with his front teeth. Try any of the foods listed under 'Finger feeding' (page 172). To teach chewing with his back teeth, gently move his jaw up and down; put his hand on your jaw while you make chewing movements: then put his hand on his own jaw while you move it up and down, saying to him, 'Chew'. Let him watch himself in a mirror if you think it will help.

It doesn't often work but you never know, it might. We have to try.

2. *Going from smooth to thicker to lumpy foods*

This problem often goes with the last. Children who can't chew will only take very smooth liquidized food – or else it is that children who will only take smooth foods never learn to chew. Whichever way round, the time comes when the child should get on to thicker foods as a first step towards ordinary foods. Carol (page 104) at the age of 10 would take only liquid food and only out of a bottle. She was a big girl, and quite active, and it looked absolutely ridiculous for her to be sitting up at table drinking from a bottle, and so her teacher decided to try to teach her to take more normal food. First, Carol had to be persuaded to drink out of a cup. Next her favourite milk drink was made very slightly thicker by adding a little cornflour to it. When she would take that well it was made a little thicker still. At the same time she began to have other foods, meat, fish and vegetables, at first liquidized to a consistency of thin cream but later becoming rather thicker by leaving out some of the liquid.

When her teacher wanted Carol to begin to take lumpy foods she started off by introducing very tiny lumps – half grains of cooked rice – into the milk drinks. She also began to teach Carol to eat from a spoon, giving her the first two or three mouthfuls from a spoon before allowing her to have the rest from a cup. This programme is still going on. The most difficult part is with the lumps: as soon as Carol finds a lump larger than a cooked grain of rice she spits it out. So it looks as if it is going to be a long job to get her to eat ordinary food like anyone else.

Since it is so difficult to persuade older children to accept foods of different textures, especially if they have always been used to a smooth liquid diet, it is important to introduce thicker lumpy foods to children while they are young – if possible under a year. This difficulty with food textures seems to occur particularly with children with visual handicaps, though we don't know why.

3. *Taking new or disliked foods*

If a child is suspicious of trying new foods we offer him a very small amount of it at first, following it up with a spoonful of something he does like. Much the same approach can be tried if a child particularly dislikes a food which it is important that he should eat – one or two food fads are permissible, dozens are not. Simon (page 83) would eat only potato, toast, fish fingers, mince, milk, baked beans, mousse and ice-cream. He would not eat eggs, meat (apart from mince), fruit, vegetables or salads, and suffered badly from constipation. His teacher decided to try to teach him to take a variety of foods. At first he had to touch a piece of, say, carrot with his tongue: later he had to touch it with his lips, then take it into his mouth, then chew, and later still swallow it, in order to gain his reinforcement – a piece of Smartie. It sounds weird, giving a child sweets in the middle of his dinner, rewarding him with chocolate for swallowing a piece of cauliflower, and many people said it would never work: but it did. You couldn't really say that Simon now eats a normal diet but he eats a great many things – eggs, bacon, meat, and some vegetables – that he never did before.

In the same way if a child loves his pudding and dislikes his first course it may be worth rewarding him with a spoonful of the pudding for taking a spoonful of the first course. Later he may have to take two spoonfuls of the first course, then three, and so on, in order to get his spoonful of pudding. And if the idea of toad-in-the-hole alternating with chocolate blancmange makes you shudder, but it works, then you should, as my son said on a quite different occasion, try not to think about it.

Table-manners

Besides teaching a child how to feed himself we may also want to teach him good table-manners. This may make all the difference between people being pleased to have him at meals with them and not being willing to sit down at table with him. For Owen it meant the difference between being taken on family excursions and being left behind. 'Before, he was so awful we didn't dare take him to a restaurant, but now – well we had lunch in a restaurant on Friday and he was fine, and we all enjoyed it.'

We teach table-manners by prompting the good behaviour, where necessary; reinforcing it by praise and by allowing him to continue eating; and sometimes mildly punishing the bad behaviour by, for instance, interrupting his eating. It is important to be very consistent in our teaching so that the child does not learn that he can occasionally get away with bad manners. Later we have to fade out the supervision while still making sure he does not slip back into bad habits.

1. *Using fingers*

Some foods, like biscuits and sandwiches, can and should be eaten with fingers: others like stew, mashed potato and jelly, should not. Sometimes children prefer to use their fingers, especially when they are not very skilful with a spoon and can get the food more easily with their fingers. To avoid this we try to keep the hand not holding the spoon busy, prompting it to hold a fork, or the side of the plate, or perhaps just to stay on the child's lap. If the child does use his fingers we say 'No' and remove his plate for thirty seconds. Then we wipe his fingers if they are messy, give him back his spoon, re-occupy his other hand, and try again.

2. *Troughing or pigging*

These picturesque terms refer to eating straight from the plate
with the mouth, without benefit of fingers or cutlery. Again, we
say 'No' and remove the plate. Before we give it back again we
make sure the child is sitting up straight, lifting his chin with
our hand if necessary. His seating position is important here;
a child whose chin is only just over the table top is more likely
to lapse into troughing than one whose position puts him at the
proper height above the table.

3. *Bolting food*

Sometimes a child will gobble down his food, perhaps without
chewing it. If telling him to eat more slowly does not have any
effect we may try taking his plate away between mouthfuls.
Another method, used with Trevor (page 92), was to take away
the plate for thirty seconds every time he tried to put in another
mouthful before he had swallowed the last. Another method to
try is to hold down the child's arm when he tries to gobble –
this, like taking away the plate for thirty seconds, means that he
gets his food more slowly than if he were eating properly: so he
learns that he actually gets more food in a shorter time if he eats
properly.

4. *Snatching food from somebody else's plate*

We try not to let the child benefit from his snatching – that is,
we try to get the food he snatched away from him before he can
eat it. Then we take away his plate, if there is anything on it, for
thirty seconds. If his plate is empty we hand round something –
more food, a sweet, or lavish praise – to everyone present,
pointedly leaving out the snatcher.

5. *Throwing food and tipping over plates*

Sometimes a child seems to do this when he has had enough to
eat but is urged to take some more. In this case perhaps we

should be more ready to accept his signals. If he pushes his plate away we ask him if he wants some more, and if he pushes it away again remove his plate.

In other circumstances if he throws food or tips over his plate out of temper, or, perhaps, to make us cross, we take his food away and don't give him any more. We may make him clear it up, using restitution (page 102). Any food we remove should be firmly thrown away. It seems wasteful at the time, but if we can teach the child to eat properly we will probably waste less in the end.

Of course if the child spills his food or drink by accident we clear it up, or get him to, without making a fuss.

6. Slowness over eating

Sometimes a child, far from bolting his food, is so slow over eating that the meals almost merge into each other. How we deal with this will depend partly on why he is so slow, and partly on how he feels about his food. Terry, who was 14, was fond of his food but seemed to have got into the habit of lingering over it, to put it mildly. He was told that he would be allowed the following times to eat his meals:

Breakfast:
cereal:	7 minutes
hot dish:	12 ,,
bread and butter:	7 ,,

Mid-day meal:
meat and vegetable:	15 minutes
sweet:	8 ,,

When a course was given to him a kitchen timer was set to go off at the end of the allotted period, and he was told that anything he had not finished when the timer rang would be thrown away. No particular notice was taken of Terry during this time, he was not urged to hurry or warned about how much time had gone by. When the timer rang his plate was removed and the food thrown away, and, in spite of his protests, Terry was never given any extra time. When he finished within the time he was praised. Terry soon learnt to finish within the time allowed. After this the timer, although still set, was moved away where he could not see it; he still managed to finish within the time so the programme was discontinued. Three months later he was still eating at a normal speed.

Terry seemed to enjoy the challenge of 'Beat the Clock' but other children may need some other reinforcement for their success. Maisie for example was allowed a comic to look at whenever she completed her meal on time. As with all the programmes there is no hard and fast rule: what we do depends on the individual child we are working with, how we run the programme depends on how the child responds to it.

The main points

1. Teaching feeding is often enjoyable because food is reinforcing to most children.

2. It is important that the child should be seated in a correct position.

3. Self-feeding:
    (a) Stand behind the child to teach him.
    (b) Begin by using foods he likes.
    (c) Use prompting, fading and backward chaining.
    (d) Don't fade prompts too quickly.
    (e) In spoon-feeding, teach and reinforce putting the spoon back on the plate separately.
    (f) Use games to teach cutting with a knife, encouraging a sawing movement.
    (g) In teaching drinking teach and reinforce separately putting the cup down.

4. Managing and taking foods:
    (a) Introduce new textures of food very gradually.
    (b) Offer new foods, or those the child dislikes, in very small quantities alternating them with something the child does like.

5. Table-manners:

(a) If a child enjoys his food, his plate may be taken away for a short time (30 seconds) if he:

    uses his fingers

    troughs (make him sit upright)

    snatches (don't let him eat what he has snatched).

(b) Bolting food: take plate away between mouthfuls, or take away his plate or hold his arm down when he tries to gobble.

(c) Throwing and tipping plates:

    take away the child's food and don't give any more

    use restitution if appropriate.

(d) Slowness:

    give the child a certain time to finish his food

    don't nag him to hurry or give him extra time.

Some practice problems

*1. Supposing you were a Chinese parent. How would you set about teaching a child to use chopsticks? (Aren't you glad you don't have to!)

*2. Make a list of foods that we sometimes eat with our fingers, sometimes with cutlery. How would you teach a child when he should use one and when the other?

*3. How would you teach a child to set a table?

*4. Lucy can feed herself very well but as soon as she has finished eating as much as she wants she tips the plate over – not, apparently, to be tiresome but to show that she has had enough. How would you deal with this?

13. Language

Language is the skill with which mentally handicapped children have perhaps the most difficulty. It is often the child's lateness in talking and in understanding speech that makes his parents realize that he is handicapped. Parents are very concerned when their child seems to be really slow in talking, and rightly so, for the ability to communicate with other people is of tremendous importance to all of us. A child who cannot communicate is handicapped to a degree that no other difficulty can match.

So teaching language is extremely worthwhile, but it is difficult, and is often very slow. It is quite impossible to give any idea of how long any part of the teaching will take as children vary so much in this ability and parents in the amount of time they can spend on it. Don't give up easily, though. A child who seems to be making little progress may be storing up the teaching for use later. 'We didn't seem to be getting *anywhere*, but now six months later he's beginning to use lots of words and seems to enjoy it.' The first words are the slowest to come: once a child has got started, new words are likely to come rather more quickly and easily.

Language can be divided into two, equally important, parts: comprehension (the understanding of language) and expression (usually thought of as speech, but including also written, picture and sign language). We can teach comprehension alone, or comprehension and expression together. The thing to remember is how important comprehension is: if a child is unable to communicate (that is, unable to speak or to convey meaning to us by signs or gestures) it may still make a big difference to him if we can teach him to understand even a few of the things that we say to him.

Organizing the teaching

One way of teaching language to a child is in semi-formal, sitting-at-a-table sessions (and this is how I have described the teaching). In this case we should choose a time when the child is lively and interested, and we should keep the sessions short – five to ten minutes is quite enough.

On the other hand, it may be better not to have special language-teaching sessions but to make use of any opportunity that presents itself during the day. So, if we know that he wants to listen to a record or have a drink we say to him, 'Say record', or 'Say drink' (or milk or orange or whatever it is he wants). Then he only gets his record or his drink if he says either the word or as much of it as he is capable of, and the record, or the drink, is then a natural reinforcer.

The big advantage of this informal way of teaching is that we will always be teaching names of things or of activities that the child wants or is interested in; so the words he learns are those that are really important and useful to him, and he will be the more willing to learn them. This principle should also apply if we teach in more formal sessions.

Which method you use is up to you. Of course there is nothing to stop you using a little of each if you want to.

As before, all the teaching depends on reinforcement. This deserves some special consideration in teaching language. The most important aspect of whatever we use as a reinforcer is that, when it follows a piece of the child's behaviour, that piece of behaviour occurs more often: in other words the child learns and does what we want him to more often, because he is very keen to get the reinforcer, which means that the reinforcer has to be something that the child wants very much. If that happens to be food, then that is what we have to use. However, there is a slight disadvantage in using foods, especially when the child is learning to make sounds or say words, in that he has to stop making the sounds in order to eat it, and this can slow the teaching up a bit. So if the child is equally fond of several things – sweets, crisps, drinks, a coloured light flashing – then it may be better to use one of the ones he does not have to chew –

drinks slip down quickly and the coloured lights may take only a few seconds. But, as always, the crucial point about a reinforcer is: does it have the effect of increasing the behaviour? Then no matter how preferable the drinks and lights, if they do not work but the crisps and sweets do, we are better off using the latter.

Teaching comprehension

1. *Responding to instructions*

This is a simple kind of comprehension training. We teach the child to carry out certain simple actions when we ask him to do them. Even very severely handicapped children, who appear to take little notice of what is said to them, can learn to respond to some simple instructions. Again we make use of principles and methods that have already been discussed: mainly prompting, fading, and reinforcement. The sequence of events is:

we give the instruction (tell the child to do something)

we prompt him to carry it out

we reinforce him.

Later on we fade the prompt just enough to let the child do as much of the action as he can while still making sure that the action is completed, and eventually we fade out the prompt completely. Now when we give the instruction he carries it out without any help.

It is tempting at this point to think that the child now 'understands' the instruction but there may still be some way to go before we can be sure of this. If we have used a gesture along with the words – a finger pointing at the chair while we say, 'Richard, sit down' – we shall have to fade out the gesture before we can say that he is really responding to the words. Gestures can help a child in the early stages to understand what we are saying, but it is best not to let him rely on them; other people may use different gestures which may muddle him, so this is another reason for fading the gestures. Again, when we have taught a child to respond to one instruction we will have to teach him to respond to another, and to respond to either when they are given at random, before we can feel confident that he really understands and is responding to the words.

Instructions often taught to begin with include 'Sit down', 'Stand up', 'Come here', 'Give it to me', 'Close/open the door'. How to teach 'Sit down' has already been discussed in chapter 5, page 70. 'Stand up' is taught in much the same way, prompting the child to stand instead of sit. For 'Come here' we would start with the child at no more than arms-length away, so that when we have given the instruction we can reach out to him and prompt him to move closer to us – or, alternatively, a second person can do the prompting. For 'Give it to me' we sit across a table from the child, with an object on the table – say, a toy car. After the words 'Give it to me', we take the child's hand, put it round the car and guide his hand with the car in it to put the car into our hand. In later sessions we gradually fade the prompt until he will hand over the car when he is told to.

Another very useful instruction for the child to learn is 'Look at me'. Getting his attention in this way can help all sorts of learning. To teach 'Look at me' we sit closely in front of the child, give the instruction and hold up the reinforcer at eye-level, if necessary right between our eyes so that when the child looks at the reinforcer he is very likely to meet our gaze, even if only fleetingly; at once we give the reinforcer. Gradually we lengthen the time for which he has to look us in the eye, only giving him the reinforcer if he looks, say, for a second, then up to two or three seconds; and we fade the reinforcer from eye-level until when we say 'Look at me' the child will do so without looking first at the reinforcer. Similarly we can teach 'Look at your work' to get the child to pay attention to what is in front of him on the table.

Other instructions can be taught that seem useful to the particular child. ('Put on your coat', 'Fetch your hair brush'.) A spin-off from all this is that a child who can understand even a few instructions seems to those around him a much more responsive and rewarding person than one who has to be physically manhandled through every action. He seems in fact more of a person; it would be worth teaching him to respond to instructions for that reason alone.

2. *Understanding of words*

As well as teaching the child some simple instructions we can begin to teach him what certain words mean; words that tell us the names of things (ball, cup, car), what things are like (green, big, hot) or where things are (on, under, behind). To do this we sit across the table from the child, as we did when teaching him 'Give it to me' – and if we have already taught him that it will make the present task that much easier. It is very important to choose things the child is already interested in. So for Allen, who loves playing with a ball and is also very fond of drinks, we might start with 'ball' and later go on to 'cup'.

Allen sits on one side of the table, opposite his teacher (who could be his mother or his father, a sister or brother, aunt, uncle, grandmother, teacher at school – anyone who had decided to do the teaching). For the moment we will assume his teacher is female. The ball is on the table between them. The teacher says, 'Allen, give me the *ball*'. Allen has already learned the command 'Give it to me', so it takes only a little prompting to get him to pick up the ball and put it in his teacher's hand: his teacher quickly gives him a small piece of his reinforcer (in Allen's case, a small piece of onion-flavoured crisp). Soon Allen will hand over the ball without prompting when his teacher asks for it. In order to build in generalization (pages 81–3) the teacher brings in different balls – a small blue rubber one, a big red plastic one, a woolly ball, a wooden ball – so that Allen learns that the word ball can be applied to several similar-shaped things and not just to one particular ball.

Next the teacher puts on the table another object, a wooden brick perhaps, about ten inches away from the ball. Now when he is told, 'Give me the *ball*' Allen hesitates a little, but he is able to pick up the ball with a little guidance from the teacher, hands it over, and is reinforced. The teacher repeats the performance, varying the ball's position from time to time: sometimes the ball is on the left-hand side, sometimes on the right; sometimes it is on the side of the table nearest to Allen, sometimes nearest the teacher. This is so that in teaching Allen the meaning of the word ball he is not by accident learning that, for him, it means 'The thing nearest me on the table' or 'The thing on my right-hand side'. When Allen can hand over the ball without prompting and whatever its position, then the teacher goes on to pair the ball with other objects – a pencil, a doll, a shoe, and so on.

Once Allen seems thoroughly to have learnt the word 'ball' his teacher goes through the same process with 'cup'. When that has been learnt, both objects are put on the table and Allen is asked sometimes for the cup, sometimes for the ball. Again the positions of the cup and the ball on the table are varied, and as always Allen receives reinforcement; as he gets more skilful he might go on to an intermittent rather than a continuous schedule, receiving reinforcement only every now and again rather than after each correct response.

Notice that when Allen's teacher chose the words she was going to start with to teach she chose not only things which he was interested in but also things whose names sound clearly different from each other. 'Ball' and 'cup' are very different, so that Allen would have little difficulty in distinguishing which she had said. If on the other hand she had used 'cup' and 'cap' the similarity of the sound of the words might have made the task extra difficult and discouraging for him. (See page 85.) Later on as Allen becomes more skilful and more accustomed to listening to language (and providing his hearing is good) he will be able to learn to discriminate between words which are increasingly alike – first perhaps 'cup' and 'car', then 'cup' and 'cake', later on 'cup' and 'cap' or 'cup' and 'cut'.

Other words can be taught in the same way. Allen could also be taught to understand adjectives; to give the *red* ball or the *yellow* ball, the *round* counter or the *square* counter. Similarly, when he has learnt a number of words and has learnt to obey the instruction 'put it' as well as 'give me', he can learn prepositions: 'Put the brick *on* the chair', 'Put the brick *in* the box'.

I have emphasized that we should teach the child one thing thoroughly before moving on to another. What do I mean by 'thoroughly'? Essentially this means that having learnt something the child will never again fail on this particular task, but in practice we have to decide how long to go on with one task before moving on to another. It is difficult to lay down hard and fast rules, as children vary in how much practice they need. In general 'over-learning' (plenty of practice on something they have learned) has been shown to help mentally handicapped people to remember what they have learnt, so a little more practice is probably better than a little less. As a guide-line I would suggest going on with a task until the child gets it right five–ten times in succession. It is important though not to let the child get really bored with the task – mentally handicapped children do seem to get bored, just like the rest of us.

Learning to talk

As well as being able to understand what is said to him it is also important for the child to be able to speak to us: to be able to tell us what he wants, what he feels, what he thinks, what he hopes and what he fears. One of the great worries of those caring for a severely mentally handicapped child is the difficulty of knowing when the child is ill or in pain if he is unable to express this in words.

For a child who cannot speak at all there are two ways we can begin to teach him: one uses *shaping* (pages 68–9) and the other uses *imitation* (pages 79–80). Using the first method, shaping, we would start by reinforcing the sounds the child made, especially those that were something like speech sounds. Later, we would only reinforce those sounds that came closer to speech sounds, and later still the ones that were most like the words we wanted him to learn – 'Da-da', 'Ba-ba' or 'M-m'.

Using the second method, imitation, we would try to teach the child to imitate the sounds that we made to him. Since imitating sounds is fairly complicated and almost impossible to prompt, many people think it easiest if the child has already developed an *imitative set*; this is done by teaching him to imitate a series of movements and actions using modelling, prompting and fading the prompts, and continuing the teaching until the child is ready to try to imitate an action the first time he sees it, with little or no prompting (see pages 79–80). When he has learnt this and when he has learnt to imitate small movements as well as large ones, he can be asked to imitate movements of the head – turning, shaking, nodding and so on – and then to imitate movements of the face and mouth. He can be asked to imitate the mouth movements that go with certain speech sounds – 'oo', 'ah', 'ee', 'o', 'p' and 'm'. These are good ones to start with as they are made with clear, definite mouth shapes; and if the child had difficulty in imitating these mouth movements it is possible for the teacher to prompt them to some extent – pushing the child's cheeks together for 'oo', pressing his lips together for 'm' and so on.

At this point, the teacher, while making the mouth movement, will also make the sound: 'Do this Allen: oo'. If Allen then tries to copy the mouth movement *and* produces a sound – any sound – he receives lots of reinforcement; a big hurdle, that of imitating what he heard as well as imitating what he saw, has been cleared. Later it will be possible for his teacher to reinforce him only if the sound Allen makes comes rather closer to the one that was modelled.

If Allen only imitates the mouth movement, and not the sound, his teacher will have to look for a way to get him to make sounds that can be reinforced. The teacher may make use of the shaping method described above: another trick to try involves blowing. The teacher blows on her own hand, and then on Allen's hand, so that Allen feels the effect the blowing has on his hand; then the teacher can encourage Allen himself to blow on his own hand. The teacher can blow away a piece of fluff, or blow out a candle, or make a little piece of paper or a feather flutter by blowing on it; then she can try to get Allen to produce the same interesting effects. When Allen blows readily the teacher blows harder, and more throatily, until she makes a sound: when Allen does this, too, then he can be reinforced for making the sound.

Once Allen is making sounds his teacher can begin varying

the sounds that he is to imitate. It is a good idea to begin by modelling sounds that Allen already makes, so that it is easy for him to imitate them and receive reinforcement. The teacher can go on to modelling the vowel sounds and the consonants set out on page 191 – 'oo', 'ah', 'ee', 'p', 'm' and 'b'.

These are the first sounds normal babies produce, so it seems sensible to start the teaching with them. The next, which most babies produce around 18 months to 3 years, are 'n', 'w' and 'h' and after that 'k', 'g', 'd', 'ng', 'f', 'y', 'l' and 's' appear.

When Allen can make some of these sounds the teacher chains them together to make sounds like a baby's babble – 'Ba ba', 'm-m-m' and so on. Later these become words to be imitated – 'Mum'. Although his teacher will want to teach Allen words made up of sounds that he can already say, another thing to take into account in deciding which words to teach him is, of course, what are the things he is interested in. A child who loves cars will be more interested in the word 'car' than another whose main interest is his teddy-bear: a child who really wants his biscuit or his milk may learn early on to say 'bi' or 'mi'. (At this stage of course such incomplete words are enthusiastically reinforced; later on it will be possible to hold back the reinforcement until something nearer the real word is produced.)

Let us say that Allen has learnt the sounds 'K' and 'ah', amongst others, and that he is very fond of toy cars. So his teacher decides to work at teaching him to say 'car'. At first the teacher models each sound separately, reinforcing Allen for imitating them one at a time:

Teacher :   Allen, say K
Allen :   K
Teacher :   Good boy, that's fine! Now say Ah
Allen :   Ah
Teacher :   Well done Allen!

As Allen copies each sound more readily the teacher reduces the time interval between them, and only gives the reinforcer after Allen has imitated both sounds:

Teacher :   Allen, say K
Allen :   K
Teacher :   Now say Ah
Allen :   Ah
Teacher :   That's lovely Allen! You are clever!

Later the teacher models the two sounds together with a little gap between them:

Teacher :   Allen, say K – Ah
Allen :   K – Ah

Later again, when Allen is able to imitate this easily, the sounds are joined up to make 'Car'. Of course it is possible that Allen will join up the sounds more quickly, and, when the teacher models 'K-Ah' Allen will say 'Car'; in this case the teacher moves on to modelling 'Car' and does not insist on Allen's imitating 'K-Ah'.

Later Allen can learn words that have three or four sounds chained together – 'c-u-p', 'd-i-nn-er', taught in just the same way. From this he may go on to learn to imitate the names of many things around him.

Using words spontaneously

Learning to speak, to say words, is an important step for a child who is developing communication; of at least equal importance is that he should learn to use words spontaneously. A child who finds that words are useful to him and uses them spontaneously to indicate what he wants has the beginnings of real communication; the child who only produces words when prompted to do so has only the beginnings of speech.

Supposing Allen has learnt to say the word 'car', and will imitate this when his teacher models it. Now his teacher holds up a toy car (Allen has already learnt to associate the word with the toy), asks him 'What is this?' and prompts the answer 'Say, car':

Teacher :   What is this? Say, car
Allen :   Car

Later the teacher fades the prompt.

Teacher :   What is this? Say, c . . .
Allen :   Car

Later still the teacher just mouths the first sound, leaving Allen to supply the word.

Teacher :   What is this? Say (mouths)
Allen :   Car

Later still the teacher will fade out the 'Say' until at last, when she holds up the car and says 'What is it?' Allen answers 'Car'.

Occasionally a child will repeat the whole prompt, and instead of saying 'Car' will say 'Say car'. If this happens the teacher can either drop the 'Say', or can whisper 'Say' and speak 'Car' in a loud and firm voice, to make it easier for the child to imitate only 'Car'.

Next Allen is encouraged to ask for what he wants. The teacher holds up two things that Allen has learnt to name – say, a car and a ball – and says to Allen, 'What do you want?' If Allen does not reply, the teacher looks to see which one seems to be attracting most of Allen's attention and prompts him to ask for it.

Teacher :   What do you want?
Allen :   (Doesn't reply but looks hopefully at the ball)
Teacher :   What do you want? Say, ball
Allen :   Ball

Later this prompt too is faded, and when Allen has learnt to ask for what he wants, whichever object he names he is given to play with. In the same way Allen can be offered a choice of two foods, and be given whichever one he names to eat, and so on. Later, when he is well able to do this, the teacher begins to fade out 'What do you want' until eventually Allen is able to ask for things without being questioned first.

Teaching verbs

Verbs, or action words, can be taught in much the same way, using play. Allen is prompted (or told, if he understands well enough) to do something – run, jump, climb on a chair. Then the teacher says, 'What are you doing? Say jumping'. Allen imitates this (having a moment to get his breath back first) and in time the teacher fades the prompts as before.

Again it is a good idea to teach the child verbs describing activities which he is very fond of: as well as being a good way to catch the child's interest, this also provides the teacher with the chance to use the activity itself as a reinforcer, preventing the child from going on with the activity until he has made the response required of him.

Adjectives and prepositions

The same methods can be used to teach other kinds of words. Colour names and shape names can be taught when the child has acquired several names of objects and people. 'What colour is this? Say green', 'What shape is this? Say round.'

Opposites – big, little etc. – are usually not learnt by normal children until they are 3–4 years old, and mentally handicapped children would also learn them later.

Eventually the object name and the adjective can be chained together – 'What is it? Green car'. Later still the child may be able to learn a longer phrase, like 'It's a green car', using the same techniques of backward chaining and fading the prompts.

What is it? Say, it's a green . . .
What is it? Say, it's a . . .
What is it? Say, it's . . .
and so on.

Prepositions are useful additions to the child's vocabulary.

The easiest to teach are 'in' and 'on' and 'under'. We can use the question 'Where is it?' and the prompt, 'Say, it's *on* the table' or, 'It's *in* the box' and so on. We will need to be quite clear about the differences between the prepositions, so later we would teach him to answer the question 'Where is it?' with 'It's *in* the box' or 'It's *under* the box', 'It's *on* the shoe' or 'It's *in* the shoe'.

Many of these parts of speech may of course have cropped up already in teaching comprehension – 'Give me the blue ball': 'put it on the table'. It may be helpful for the child to learn to understand these words, and to respond to them when he hears them before he begins to try to use them in speech. Words that a child already understands and responds to may be easier for him to learn to say, and perhaps more useful to him, than those he does not first learn to comprehend.

Other ways of communicating

If a child is unlikely ever to be able to speak (for instance because he is deaf as well as mentally handicapped, or for any other reason) it may be worth looking to see whether he can learn to communicate in some other way. There are three other ways of communicating to consider: picture language, one of the systems of signs, and written language (or any combination of these).

1. *Picture language*

This is the simplest, but also the most limited, of the alternatives. The aim is to teach the child to use pictures to convey what he wants: for instance, to show a picture of a cup when he wants a drink, of a lavatory when he wants to use one, of a toy when he wants to play with it, and so on. Fourteen-year-old Derek could understand some speech but could not speak at all and was unable to learn to use sign language (Paget-Gorman). His teacher decided to try using pictures. At first she made sure that he understood that pictures of objects 'stood for' the objects themselves: when he was asked to match pictures with objects Derek was able to put the pictures with the right objects. Next, she went on to teaching comprehension using pictures instead of words: when she showed Derek a picture, say of a toothbrush, he had to pick out the actual toothbrush and give it to her to get his reinforcement. He learnt this quickly. Next, in 'expression teaching' his teacher indicated the object and Derek had to pick out the right picture: later still he would use the pictures, picking out and pointing to the right one, from a necklace of pictures he wore round his neck, to get things he wanted – a sweet, a drink, a pencil or scissors. Later again it is hoped that he may be able to learn some verbs, using pictures of people doing things – walking, sitting, eating, washing and so on.

Learning to use this kind of communication made a great difference to Derek; instead of having to pull people to the thing he wanted he could select the picture of it, and could be given it more reliably and quickly. However, it *is* a limited system. It is hard to imagine how pictures could be provided to represent some parts of speech – adverbs like 'quickly', adjectives like 'nice', or prepositions like 'before' and 'after'. So whenever possible it would be preferable to teach one of the other systems, signing or written language.

2. *Sign language*

Many children without speech, especially deaf children who are not mentally handicapped, use gestures to try to indicate what they want to convey. The families of these children, and other people around them, may get very good at knowing what their gestures mean, so that it hardly seems necessary for the child to learn a recognized sign system. However, there are two reasons why this may be better: first, when he moves out of the circle of people who know him very well his gestures may not be so well understood – perhaps not understood at all by some people – while a system of signs that is widely understood and taught will enable him to communicate with many people beyond his immediate circle. Secondly, most sign systems contain signs for many objects, ideas and feelings which the individual child or family might be hard put to it to invent, so a sign system probably allows for a greater range of communication than would the child's own gestures, even if these were readily understood.

There are several sign systems in existence. The best known in this country is finger-spelling, used by many deaf adults, in which each finger of a hand stands for a vowel, and finger and hand movements are used to represent consonants. For example, B is made by making a circle with forefinger and thumb of each hand and touching the two circles together at fingertips, U by pointing to a little finger, and S by linking the two crooked little fingers – B US. Deaf people become extremely skilled at spelling out and understanding words made by this method, but it is slow and laborious compared with systems which use a sign to indicate a whole word.

There are several such systems. British Sign Language uses, besides finger-spelling, quite simple hand signs, and abbreviated speech: for example instead of saying 'Do you want a drink of water?' they would sign 'Want water?' The Paget-Gorman Sign System on the other hand aims at an accurate representation of English, signing all the parts of speech – all the 'ing's' and 'to's' and 'the's', using past and future and other tenses of verbs, leaving nothing out. The Bliss System does not use hand signs but instead a system of symbols which are laid out on a board and the person wanting to communicate points in turn to the symbols that make up his sentence.

These are a few of the sign systems available. If you want to know more about them, and how to use and teach them with a mentally handicapped child, they are described in detail in a book called *Starting Off* by Chris Kiernan, Rita Jordan and Chris Saunders, published by Souvenir Press, London. Which of the systems you will want to teach will depend partly on your child and his abilities, but partly also on which one is most widely used in your area. Obviously he will benefit most from learning a system which other people around him, in schools, and clubs and workshops, will be most likely to understand and use, so it would be worth asking your local Social Services department which system is used most in your area; or if you have any difficulty write to: Royal Association in Aid of the Deaf and Dumb, 7 Armstrong Road, London W3.

3. *Written language*

Some children find it very difficult to understand, or to make use of, gestures or signs. In this case, the best alternative if the child is severely mentally handicapped, as Derek was, may be to teach him picture language. If however he is more mildly handicapped it may be possible to teach him some written language. This was done with Andy (see page 101). His teacher already knew that Andy, although quite deaf and with many behavioural problems, was only mildly retarded. She knew, too, that he loved doing school work, and that he was able to match letters and make them up into words to match words put in front of him. So she began teaching him comprehension and expression, just like that used by Derek's teacher, only instead of using pictures Andy had to give the objects when he was shown the word printed on a card, and had to select the printed word when she indicated an object. Soon she was able to teach him to obey instructions by showing these to Andy in printed form: 'Wash your hands', 'Go to the toilet', 'Give me the red brick'. Andy also had to produce the right cards for 'knife' 'fork' 'spoon' and 'dinner' before he could have his meal; and he was taught his own name, and those of the people around him, by matching the printed names first to photographs and later to the people themselves. The next step is to build up Andy's ability to write: obviously if he can write down the things he wants, instead of as at present carrying round a chatelaine of word cards, his communication system will become much easier for him to use.

Final note

It is important to realize that it is quite all right to teach one of these alternative communication systems to a child even if he may later develop speech. It is not at all likely that this will discourage him from using speech if he can. On the contrary it has been found that children who were taught comprehension of spoken words and of signs at the same time learnt to understand the spoken words more quickly than children who were taught using spoken words alone. So signs are likely to help rather than to hinder a child to learn speech.

The main points

Language consists of two major parts, comprehension (understanding communication *from* others) and expression (conveying communication *to* others).

I *Teaching comprehension*

1. Responding to instructions:
   (a) We teach this by giving the instruction, prompting the child to respond, and reinforcing his response
   (b) later we fade the prompts
   (c) we teach one instruction thoroughly, then another, then mix them.

2. Names:
   (a) start with names of things the child likes
   (b) start with names of things that sound very different – e.g. 'box' and 'shoe', not 'box' and 'book'
   (c) teach one name thoroughly, then another, then mix them
   (d) keep teaching sessions short, and reinforcers powerful, to avoid boredom.

II *Teaching expressive language*

1. Shaping: at first reinforce sounds the child makes, then only those nearer to the sounds you want him to make.

2. Imitation:
   (a) teach imitation of many large, then smaller movements
   (b) go on to head and mouth movements
   (c) if the child does not imitate the sounds the teacher makes with the mouth movements, either: shape these (see II.1. above) or: teach by blowing.

3. Teach several separate sounds, then chain two (or more) together to make words.

4. Use words that refer to things the child is interested in.

5. Spontaneous speech:
   (a) hold up object, say, 'What is it? Say . . .': fade prompts gradually
   (b) hold up two objects, say, 'What do you want?' Prompt reply if necessary: fade prompts
   (c) verbs – prompt an action:
   Say, 'What are you doing?'
   Prompt reply if necessary.
   Fade prompts.

6. Adjectives:
   (a) teach in same way – colour names, shape names, later on size
   (b) chain together adjective and name of object

7. Prepositions – in, on, under.

III *Other communication systems*

1. Picture language.
2. Sign language.
3. Written language.

Teaching one of these will not be harmful even if the child may eventually develop speech: it will be more likely to help.

Some practice problems

Note: for those of you whose children have already learnt to speak, you may need to look back to the time before they had learnt to do so.

1. What is your child interested in, the names of which you could use as early words for him to learn?
   Foods? Toys? People? Activities? Animals?

2. Are there any particular words or phrases that you would like

your child to learn, other than the ones mentioned here, which would be specially helpful in your particular family set-up? (Come indoors, Give Grannie's specs to me, Put the parrot down, Shut the rabbit's cage.)

3. Can you think of any other ways in which you could try to encourage a child to use speech spontaneously?

*4. Which of the alternative communication systems (picture, sign, and written language) would you try out for a child who was at present unable to speak and was:

    (a) mildly retarded, timid but affectionate
    (b) severely retarded and very sociable
    (c) deaf, mildly retarded and very withdrawn
    (d) severely retarded and with partial paralysis affecting his hands.

14. Play

Play is one of the most important parts of a child's life. Besides helping him to learn useful things like positioning, turning and balancing things and how the action of one thing affects another, and besides stretching his imagination and learning give and take with other children, play occupies the child. When he plays he is busy and happy and does not need constant attention from other people; his parents can have a few blessed moments to themselves. Some mentally handicapped children do not know how to play: so we try to teach them.

There are three main kinds of play:

1. Play with toys.
2. Social play (playing with other children).
3. Imaginative play.

1. Play with toys

Normal children spend much of their time playing with toys, and indeed with anything else they can get hold of – sugar-bowls, saucepans, the contents of Mum's handbag, and so on. Some handicapped children, however, do not play with toys, and instead may spend their free time doing things they shouldn't. Other handicapped children may have a special affection for one particular toy which they refuse to be parted from, and it is often hard to persuade these children to play with anything else, especially if they become upset when the 'special' toy is removed. Other children again are interested in toys but treat them so badly, throwing or breaking them, that toys have to be taken away from them. These problems will be discussed in a moment.

Why is toy-play important?

For many children play is the thing they do most of the time. When they play with toys they take in all kinds of information about their surroundings, and about themselves. For example, when building a tower out of bricks the child learns how to pick up a brick, how to let go of it, how to make his hand move the brick a little to the right or left according to what his eyes tell him so that the tower will not fall over; he learns how balancing the bricks gets harder the higher the tower, what happens when the top brick is not on quite straight, what happens when you pull out a brick at the bottom of the tower, and so on. This kind of learning is important for the child's development and play with toys (or objects) teaches skills to the child which are useful to him later on. So it is especially important for the handicapped child to learn to play, since he of all people needs to learn as many useful skills as possible.

Another powerful reason for teaching play is that the handicapped child should be taught, whenever possible, to do anything and everything a normal child does. And an even more pressing reason for most parents is the need to be able to leave their handicapped child to occupy himself for short periods of time: a child who cannot occupy himself even for a minute is unbelievably wearing to be with.

Selecting toys

Before embarking on ways of teaching a child to play with toys we should think about what toys to give him. Two things should be taken into account – his likes and dislikes, and the level of development that he has reached.

Likes and dislikes

The more fascinating a toy is to a child the more he is going to play with it (with or without help), so we want to choose toys that he will specially like. If he does not at present play with

toys at all we can see what sort of everyday things he likes, and how these could be included in a toy for him. If he loves noise then (provided of course that we can stand the row) we should choose noisy toys – squeezy animals with a very loud squeak, pegs to be hammered into holes, posting boxes where the shape makes a noise when it falls through the hole, and so on. If there seems to be nothing that he is particularly fond of then it may be best to borrow different toys from the local toy library if you have one in your area. The number of toy libraries in existence is growing, and toys can be borrowed from them, just as books can be borrowed from the public library. Toy library staff are extremely helpful about choosing the right toy for the child, and can often suggest ways to encourage the child to play with and enjoy it. They understand, too, that if toys are played with they may get broken and, as a rule, breakages are not charged for. So, by borrowing toys from the library we can see which ones appeal to the child before buying possibly expensive toys. (See Appendix 2 for the address of the Toy Libraries Association.)

Age level

It can be difficult to choose toys that are neither too easy nor too difficult for a child, especially if he is good at some things but poor at others. Children who like toys usually push aside those that are too easy or too difficult. However, when a child is not very interested in toys at all it is difficult to get much guidance from his behaviour with toys as to which are roughly at his level. In this case it is worth asking the child's teacher, or the local psychologist if there is one, or the toy library staff, for advice. If all else fails we just have to try out some toys at random. We start with easy toys, as we can always move on to harder ones, whereas starting with toys that are too hard can be discouraging. Many parents of normal children find they tend to buy toys that are too difficult (I did, for one) so that the children only begin to play with the toys months later, by which time they are no longer excitingly new. Since it is obviously easy to over-estimate a child's level, it seems best to start with toys which might be below the child's level rather than above.

The following is a very rough guide to toys for each age level. (For more comprehensive guides to toys for different age groups see Appendix 3.) With a handicapped child we cannot always go by how old he is, but rather by the age his kind of behaviour suggests. For example an 8-year-old child might be doing things more like a 3-year-old. In this case some of the toys for him are listed under the 3-year age group.

Age	Toys
0–6 months	Rattles, bells, mobiles, mirrors, own hands, odd items to look at, hold, mouth and so on.
6–12 months	Toys that wobble (e.g. those on suction pads), noisy toys (that squeak), bells and rattles, pull-along toys, big building bricks, odd items (cups, spoons, etc.).
12–18 months	Posting boxes (simple ones, single or 2-hole), form-boards (few pieces only), stacking toys (can't do it by size though), building bricks, peg-boards, crayons (scribble and strokes, not pictures), balls,

	hammer and peg toys, sand and water play, picture books (looking at pictures).
18 months–2 years	3–4 hole posting boxes, form-boards and stacking toys, hammer and peg toys, crayons (beginning to imitate strokes), picture books (beginning to understand names of objects in pictures, and names a few), building bricks, cars and dolls, soft toys.
2–3 years	Multi-hole posting boxes, form-boards and stacking toys, paper cutting and sticking, threading, colour matching, simple constructional toys, crayons and paints, picture books.
3–4 years	Simple jig-saws (up to 6 pieces), complex form-boards, crayons and pencils (beginning to copy simple things), simple picture matching, constructional toys, doll's houses, cutting and sticking.

Teaching children to play with toys

Learning how to use toys

Denis was 5 years old and very, very active. He spent his time at home rushing up and down the stairs, jumping on the beds, galloping round the garden, turning chairs over, and so on. He showed no interest in toys, except occasionally to put them in his mouth and blow them out on to a hard surface (making a good bang), and he could not be left alone to play because he would throw the toys and upset the furniture.

Careful observation of Denis suggested that most of his troublesome behaviour was due to over-activity and to his liking for noise – part of the fun of overturning furniture seemed to be the noise it made. So it was decided that Denis should be taught to play properly with some very simple toys, with the aim that eventually he would play with them for a short time by himself. The toys chosen were simple stacking toys, a simple posting box and a hammer toy in which balls were banged through holes with a hammer.

His teacher had five-minute sessions with Denis, as often as she could manage it. She made him sit down at a table during these sessions, and taught one toy at a time. With the stacking toy she prompted him to stack one ring on another, with her hands moving Denis' hands to pick up the ring and put it on another. Then she reinforced him, giving him a kiss and a jelly-tot (which he loved). The prompts were gradually faded until Denis could do the stacking toy with only slight prompts and eventually without any at all. At this stage he would stack one ring on another, get reinforcement, then stack another ring and get reinforcement, and so on. He could not get the sizes of the graduated rings right, but if the rings were laid out in the right order he could put them on correctly. In the same way Denis learnt to hammer the balls through the holes, and to post the shapes through the posting box. He could not match lots of different shapes to holes, so very simple one-shape and then two-shape posting boxes were used.

It took several months to teach Denis this much. Now his teacher, and his mother who is doing the same thing at home, give him reinforcement every second time he puts on a ring, hammers a ball through or posts a shape; soon they will move on to reinforcing him every third time, and so on. Eventually when he can do the tasks completely – stack all the rings or bang all the balls through – for one reinforcement it should be possible to begin to get him to play alone (like Olga, see page 210). Since he is so fond of noise it seems likely that out of the three toys he has learnt to use the one he will most successfully play alone with is the hammer toy, just because this is likely to be the one he will enjoy most.

Denis is fairly typical of the child who shows no interest in ordinary toys, although his energy and activity probably made Denis more of a menace than most. The methods his teacher used are suitable for most children: we choose a small number of toys of the right level, and then use *prompting* and *fading* (pages 69–73), *backward chaining* (see pages 74–5) and reinforcement (see pages 36–47) to teach the child to play with each toy. Once he can play with these toys it should be a little easier to teach him to go on to play with other toys, though, as he may not spontaneously generalize his play (see pages 81–3), he may need more teaching whenever he meets new toys.

Playing with new toys

Timmy (see page 41) was like Denis in that he showed no interest in ordinary toys. However he did have a special toy from which he would not be parted, a small plastic cup which he hung over his thumb and twiddled. It became known as 'Timmy's twiddler' and it would keep him 'occupied' for hours. The trouble was that while he twiddled he could not learn anything new; he just was not interested in other things while he had his twiddler. If, on the other hand, the cup was taken away from him he would scream and pull at his hair and face until the cup was returned to him. (Timmy punished people for removing his cup by screaming and pulling his hair, which they hated: while anybody who returned his cup was negatively reinforced by his stopping the screaming and hair-pulling.) One way and another Timmy had taught people not to take away his cup.

If Timmy were to learn anything it would be necessary to remove his twiddler, despite his protests. So his teacher decided to start removing the twiddler for very short periods and to begin teaching him to play with toys. The teaching methods were identical with those used with Denis, except that during the teaching part while Timmy had no twiddler he tended to enliven the session with screams of protest (his hands were being prompted through the required actions and so he had no chance to pull at his hair or face). The reinforcer for Timmy was the twiddler; each time he had done what was wanted of him his teacher gave him back his twiddler for about ten or twenty seconds. Timmy gradually learnt the routine, and, after he had done what was wanted, would reach out his hand for his twiddler. Since he was never now given back his twiddler when he screamed or pulled his hair, but was only given it when he was not doing these things he also learnt to scream and pull his hair less. He has never learnt not to scream or pull his hair at all, but perhaps this was because he was about 12 years old when the teaching started so that these were long-standing habits. Similarly, although it was possible to teach him to play to some extent with a few toys, he never learnt to play with them alone.

Timmy is a good example of a child who is so attached to one toy that he will not willingly play with any other. Many of these children make much more progress than Timmy did; it depends a great deal on how bright the child is and how devoted to the special toy. Other ways of dealing with things the child is very strongly attached to are discussed in chapter 15, 'Phobias and Obsessions'.

Playing alone

Olga was 11 and could play with simple toys but would never play by herself. As soon as her mother left the room Olga would get up and follow her and pester her with questions, leaving the toys behind. Her mother's observations showed that, left to herself, Olga would play for up to five minutes with water (pouring, tipping, emptying and filling containers), for less than a minute with a simple form-board, and for less than two minutes with stacking rings. If her mother or father sat next to her Olga would play for a good deal longer.

It was decided that Olga should have two kinds of teaching sessions; one to teach her to play with new toys, using the same methods as those used for Denis, and the other to teach her to play on her own with toys she was used to. In this second programme Olga was given one of her own toys to play with and her mother then moved quietly away to the other side of the room. After a short time (about half a minute) she went over to Olga and, if she was still playing, reinforced her with praise and a drink. If Olga had stopped playing she was not reinforced but was told to go on with her playing. These sessions only lasted about ten minutes, and the time between reinforcements was gradually lengthened (over the weeks) from every half a minute to every few minutes. A few months later Olga's mother found she could withdraw for quite a few minutes to another room and Olga would continue playing on her own. She did of course still need to help Olga to learn to play with new toys, but it was nice for Olga (and for her mother) that she could now play on her own with toys that she knew well.

This kind of programme, with perhaps small changes to suit different children, should be useful for most of those who are already able to play with some simple toys and who need to learn to play without supervision. Children are usually more willing to play alone with simple toys which they know well than with more advanced toys, so it is a good idea to teach a child to occupy himself using toys that are well within his range. We can then teach him to play with more advanced toys in separate sessions, as Olga's mother did. When these have been mastered then of course they can be used in the 'playing alone' times too.

Playing properly

Duncan was $2\frac{1}{2}$ years old and, on the whole, very well behaved. However, when he had toys within reach he would pick them up in turn and throw them round the room. His parents would scold him and pick the toys up for him. In the baseline observations ten toys were given to him ten times each, and the average length of time he held the toys before throwing them was found to be six and a half seconds. Each time Duncan threw a toy he looked round to see what his parents' reactions were; it seemed that he threw his toys partly to get their attention. So it was decided that his parents would treat his throwing by extinction (see page 96) – that is, they would no longer scold him, or pick up the toys, or pay any attention at all to his throwing. In addition, since Duncan seemed not to know what he *should* be doing with the toys, his parents taught him, in quite short sessions of about five minutes at a time, how to play properly with the toys. The reinforcers that they used were praise and clapping; these, as we might have expected (because Duncan had already shown that he was eager for his parents' attention), were very good reinforcers for him. The result was that within about eight weeks Duncan was holding his toys and playing with them for an average of about one minute instead of six and a half seconds, and beaming all over his face whenever he was praised or clapped. His playing continued to improve over the next months and Duncan was transformed from a little terror in the playroom to a boy whom it was a pleasure to have around.

Duncan did not play with toys properly because he had unintentionally been reinforced, by all the attention his parents gave him, when he threw them. Children like Duncan often improve rapidly once the wrong kind of play is no longer reinforced. It is a good idea also to do as Duncan's parents did, and teach and reinforce the proper ways of playing with toys, since it may be quite difficult for the children to learn this of their own accord. Then the reinforcement given for the proper play takes the place of the reinforcement that used to be given for the wrong kind of play; which means that the child gets at least as much of the good things in life as he was getting before.

2. Social play: playing with other children

Most very young children take relatively little notice of each other when playing, but by about the age of 2 they begin to play alongside other children. Gradually between about 2 and 3 years old, they begin to respond more and more to each other and to play together. Children probably learn a lot about getting along with other people through play – how to take turns, how to be a leader at one time and a follower at another, how to be friendly and how to cope with unfriendliness.

Some handicapped children do not play cooperatively with other children and we may want to teach them to do so. It may be easier to teach this in school, where there are plenty of other children around, than at home, where there may be only one or two brothers or sisters. Nevertheless, if we want to we can make a start on teaching cooperative play at home, using a brother or sister (as in the example of Robin on page 213) or perhaps a neighbour's friendly child. Here again suitable toys can help. Some toys such as see-saws, and most ball games, need more than one player to play them, as do many of the table-top games such as snap or snakes and ladders. So these are good ones to choose for teaching a child to play with others especially if we think the child would enjoy them. Which ones we choose will of course depend partly on the child's ability – see-saws and simple ball games come at the lower end of the scale. Many other toys can with a little ingenuity be turned into social games; for instance doing a jigsaw can be a social affair if each child has half the pieces and they have to take turns to put pieces in. This can be an especially useful thing to do if, for instance, the child does not like the kinds of things which need two people to do them, like see-saws, but does enjoy jigsaws.

Very simple social play

Sometimes a child will not play with other children because he is not interested in contacts with people at all, neither with adults nor with other children. If we want to teach him to play, perhaps as a step towards his making and enjoying contacts with others, then the play will have to be very simple – rolling a ball or playing (with help) a simple table game like snap with another child, or sitting on a see-saw with another child at the other end, each helping to make the see-saw work. Teaching this kind of play will probably need, first, a cooperative second child as helper; and second, prompting and reinforcement of 'playfulness' in the child being taught. Deliberate reinforcement of the child's play may need to be continued for quite some time, as if it is stopped he might stop being willing to play. But if reinforcement is given over and over again alongside the social happenings going on at the same time – contacts with the other children, praise and encouragement from them perhaps – then eventually these social happenings themselves may become reinforcing. If they do, the child has taken a big step forward.

Responding to children as well as adults

Some children only find pleasure in contacts with adults, and not in contacts with other children such as brothers and sisters. Where a child responds to adult praise, hugs, cuddles and so on it is as a rule not so hard to teach him to play with other children, usually by reinforcing the play with adult attention.

Four-year-old Robin managed to get his parents' attention in various devious ways, such as turning up the volume on the radio or television, swinging on the curtains, turning on taps in

the kitchen and, when all else failed, kicking or pinching his
6-year-old sister. Robin's sister was a kind and patient girl who
never retaliated, but just endured her brother's assaults. Whenever Robin attacked her their parents would give Robin 'a
good talking to' but Robin seemed oblivious to the niceties of the
concept of 'fair play' and, as time went on, he bothered his sister
more rather than less. Fortunately Robin adored doing simple
jigsaws which his mother normally helped him with. A programme was set up in which both his sister and his mother helped
Robin with his jigsaws, each of them praising and petting him
for a good performance. Gradually Robin's mother began to
withdraw for a short time (just a few seconds at first) returning
every now and again to reinforce Robin before withdrawing
again. Robin's sister also gave reinforcement, praising and petting
him as she had seen her mother do and eventually, after weeks
of sessions, Robin's mother did not need to return at all during
the ten-minute sessions. Then other games were introduced, in
which Robin's sister could take more part, such as constructional
toys. Although Robin's sister never really enjoyed the games
(they were rather young for her) she did begin to like the
sessions because Robin's obvious enjoyment of them was
reinforcing to her, and moreover she no longer got bitten and
kicked. Robin, for his part, had learnt to play cooperatively with
at least one person.

Learning to be friendly

Sometimes we find a child who is reinforced by the company and
reactions of other children, and might be expected to be a good
candidate for learning to play happily with other children.
However, it may be that the reactions the child finds reinforcing
are the screams of agony or rage given by the other children
when he attacks them. If this is the case we will want to alter
the way he behaves to other children so that he will do fewer
aggressive and more friendly things. Of course, if he did anything friendly this would be strongly reinforced by the adults
around (it would probably be too much to expect the other

children to give this reinforcement, at least at first). The aggression we could in theory try to deal with in either of two ways – *extinction* (see page 96), or *punishment* (see page 100).

The first idea, extinction, would involve persuading the child's victims not to provide the reinforcement (the screams) but this is too much to ask of them. Also, even if some heroic victims were able to suppress their usual reactions to pain the child would be likely to discover new victims who would bellow nice and loudly (very young children perhaps, who could not understand instructions to ignore pinches or bites or whatever, let alone carry them out); or he could develop more intensive tortures which even the heroic victims could not ignore. So extinction is to all intents and purposes impracticable.

Probably a better solution is to find a way of punishing the child's aggressive acts (using whichever of the methods discussed in chapter 7 seems most suitable) while still reinforcing the friendly ones. This after all is a natural pattern: normally children *are* punished for being aggressive in that if they kick someone they tend to get kicked back. Some handicapped children, however, when they are attacked do not respond by hitting back, so the aggressive child misses out on the punishment that would normally teach him not to be aggressive. In other cases a handicapped child's brothers and sisters may not retaliate because they have been told not to by their parents, who may feel that the handicapped child 'can't help it'. In preventing their other children from retaliating in a normal way the parents may, however indirectly, allow the handicapped child to continue being aggressive.

So when we want to teach a child, who finds the distress of other children reinforcing, to behave more reasonably we may have to punish the aggressive things he does. It is probably better if the adults do the punishing rather than teach the victims to retaliate, as this is less likely to result in catastrophe. And, of course, we should be alert to spot and reinforce any sign of friendliness. If this does not happen very often then some special teaching, like that given to Robin, might help to speed up the learning of friendly responses.

3. Imaginative play

Much of an older child's play involves representation: things stand for other things, as when doll's house furniture stands for real furniture, or children stand for other people when they dress up as nurses or cowboys. Imaginative play is an important part of a child's development, although its place in his development is not altogether clear. Some experts feel that imaginative play comes before and helps the development of language: others, that language comes before imaginative play, which just reflects a high level of language development. Either way, most children do not show a lot of imaginative play until they have a good deal of understanding of language, and it is not easy to teach imaginative play to children who are showing no signs of understanding or using language.

In the few cases where people have tried to teach children imaginative play they have usually found that although they could teach the child one particular play, such as pouring imaginary tea from a teapot and pretending to drink it, the child did not go on to play new imaginary games on his own. In other words the child did not generalize (see page 81). So it is perhaps not worth trying to teach imaginative play to a child who shows no signs that he is ready for it. If, on the other hand, a child is teetering on the brink of imaginative play – cuddling dollies, or putting a teddy to bed occasionally – we should certainly reinforce such play and provide suitable things for the child to play with. Certain kinds of equipment – cars and garages, dolls, doll's prams and houses, tea-sets, play houses, and all kinds of clothes for dressing up – can act as cues for imaginative play. If we provide these kinds of materials the child will be more likely to play imaginatively, especially if we help him by playing the games with him.

The main points

1. Playing with toys is an important way for the child to learn new things.

2. We should choose toys which suit the level of development the child has reached.

3. A child who likes a toy is more likely to learn to play with it.

4. To teach a child to play with toys we use reinforcement (chapter 3) and prompting, fading and backward chaining (chapter 5).

5. If reinforcement is given by the teacher then it must continue to be given (unless the child comes to find the toy itself reinforcing). Otherwise his play will fade away.

6. A 'special' toy which the child is very attached to can be used as a reinforcer.

7. Once a child can play with some simple toys, he can be taught to play on his own, usually by 'fading out' the adult helper.

8. If we get rid of a bad behaviour with toys we may still have to teach the child to play properly with the toys.

9. Children can be encouraged to play with other children if the right sort of toys are available.

10. Children who do not play with other children may be either:
   (a) quite uninterested in the company and reactions of people: these children can be taught only simple social play, using deliberately-provided reinforcement
   (b) reinforced only by adult company and reactions: if these are first paired with responses from other children, and then faded out, these children may come to enjoy being with other children
   (c) reinforced by distress of other children: they will need to be taught either to be friendly (using reinforcement) or not to be aggressive (using extinction or punishment).

11. Imaginative play cannot easily be taught to children with little or no language.

12. We can encourage imaginative play by providing the right kind of materials and reinforcing the right kind of play.

Some practice problems

1. What toys do your children find reinforcing?

*2. What kinds of toys do you think blind children might find reinforcing, or deaf-blind children?

*3. How could you teach a child not to keep asking 'Mum, I'm fed up – what can I do?'?

*4. What would you do if you wanted to teach a child to play with other children when the child in question actually *avoids* other children and becomes upset if other children approach? (But he does find adult attention reinforcing.)

15. Getting Over Phobias and Obsessions

Phobias

Sometimes children develop fears that are quite out of proportion to the dangerousness of the thing they are afraid of. Simon (see page 153) was so frightened of having a bath that for six years he refused to have one at all. Andy (see page 101) was terrified of dogs and could not stay in the room with even the smallest chihuahua. Dino (see page 54) went into a panic if anyone attempted to touch his legs. Other children have been afraid of going in cars, sitting on lavatories, getting dirt on their clothes, having their hair washed, going into large shops and many other things which in themselves are not dangerous.

These fears are quite common too in children of normal intelligence and in adults. Just why they develop is not always clear. Sometimes there may be an obvious reason: sometimes we can guess at a possible reason. Claire's parents (see page 224) wondered whether she had ever been hurt by uncomfortable shoes, but they could not pin it down to anything definite. Sometimes there seems to be no imaginable reason for the fears (as in the case of Matthew, page 227). But not knowing why the problem arose does not mean that it cannot be dealt with.

The methods used to help handicapped children to get over their fears are much the same as those used for normal people; the two main ones are called *graded practice* and *flooding*.

Graded practice

The object of this method is gradually to accustom the child to what he fears, starting at the point where he is hardly afraid at all and gradually working up to the point that he needs to reach – where his ordinary life can go on without being disrupted by his fears. We begin by making a list of the things the child finds frightening, starting at the lowest level, with aspects of the thing that the child finds not frightening at all. For example, although Andy was frightened of any real dog he was not at all frightened of stuffed toy dogs. Next on the list come aspects of the thing that the child finds very, very slightly worrying: in Andy's case large life-like models of dogs. So we move very gradually up the scale until we come to the aspect of the thing that the child is likely to have to cope with in ordinary life. In Andy's case this was friendly dogs of any size quite close to him: this was what he was likely to meet in the streets and shops and people's homes. This list of aspects of the feared thing, graded very carefully in very small steps from the least-frightening to the most-frightening-necessary, is called a *hierarchy*.

So for Andy his hierarchy of dog-frighteningness went as follows:

1. Stuffed toy dog
2. Model of a small dog
3. Model of a large dog
4. Film of a small dog in the background
5. Film of a small dog in the foreground
6. Film of a small dog in closeup
7. Film of a large dog in the background
8. Film of a large dog in the foreground
9. Film of a large dog in close-up
10. Small dog behind a wire fence, 3 metres away
11. Large dog behind a wire fence, 3 metres away
12. Small dog behind a wire fence, 1·5 metres away
13. Large dog behind a wire fence, 1·5 metres away
14. Small dog behind a wire fence, 60 cm away
15. Large dog behind a wire fence, 60 cm away
16. Small dog on a lead 18 metres away
17. Large dog on a lead 18 metres away
18. Small dog on a lead 9 metres away
19. Large dog on a lead 9 metres away
20. Small dog on a lead 4·5 metres away
21. Large dog on a lead 4·5 metres away
22. Small dog on a lead 3 metres away

23. Large dog on a lead 3 metres away
24. Small dog on a lead 2 metres away
25. Large dog on a lead 2 metres away
26. Small dog on a lead 30 cm away
27. Large dog on a lead 30 cm away
28. = No. 16 without lead, 29 = No. 17 without lead, and so on, through to No. 39
40. Andy pats small dog
41. Andy pats large dog

The list is a long one, and goes in small steps (they could, if necessary, have been made even smaller, by, for instance, using a medium-sized dog as well, or by using first very short and then gradually longer times for Andy to see or be in company with the dog). It is also pretty complicated (the programme was carried out in a special children's clinic) and some of the steps might be impossible to arrange in a normal situation. This need not matter. The important thing to remember is to make the steps as small as we reasonably can so that moving from one to the next will not be frightening for the child.

When we have made out our hierarchy, we take the first item on it and we present it to the child. If the child seems worried by it we stop right there – it shows we haven't gone down far enough in the hierarchy. If he seems completely unconcerned we go to the next step up in the hierarchy and present him with that; and so on until we see the faintest tinge of uneasiness in the child. At that point we start the treatment.

Treatment consists of presenting the child with the first item in his hierarchy – the thing that makes him only just anxious – and making the situation, complete with the just-feared thing in it, a pleasant, rewarding, enjoyable one for him; until he loses even that tiny twinge of anxiety. After a while we should be able to present this item to the child without his showing the slightest distress. Then we move up to the next step in the hierarchy and repeat the process; presenting the next item to the child and making the situation a relaxed, happy one for him. So we gradually work up the hierarchy, until eventually the child is no more afraid of that thing than anybody else would be in the same circumstances.

For Andy this meant getting him to the point where he was quite happy in the company of even large friendly dogs. He was not expected to be unafraid of nearby barking dogs – many adults would be afraid in that situation, and quite right too. But Andy was no longer sent running and terrified from harmless dogs, and his life became that much more peaceful and manageable.

The way this treatment works is thought to be something like this. A child with a phobia is afraid of something that is not actually dangerous. He is so afraid of it that he always runs away from it or in some other way avoids it. So he never actually experiences the thing that he fears, so he never learns that it will not hurt him. In graded practice we do two things: present the child with something that is only slightly frightening to him, so that he does not very much want to run away; and we make the situation such a pleasant one that he does not want to run away at all. So he stays in the situation, with the (just-) frightening thing, and he finds he comes to no harm. He stops being afraid of the slightly-frightening thing, and we may then go on to repeat the process with the next item up in the hierarchy.

Let us look at an example in detail. Dino had lost most of the use of his legs following an attack of polio and moved about only in a wheelchair. It was thought that he could probably learn to walk with crutches if he wore calipers to support his legs. However, Dino, with a history of a broken leg and some painful experiences in hospital, was terrified of having his legs touched and flew into a screaming tantrum if anyone attempted to do so. It was impossible to measure him for calipers, let alone get him to wear them. So Dino stayed in a wheelchair, until the psychologist working with him decided to try graded practice to get him to allow people to handle and move his legs.

She constructed a hierarchy: the first item was a brief touch of his hand and hand games, working up to the highest items – holding and moving his feet or legs.

The sessions were run as games, as Dino enjoyed these and found them relaxing. First the psychologist modelled the response: she got someone to touch her hand, and showed that this did not frighten her.

'That didn't hurt at all! That was just a touch. Touches don't hurt, Dino. Look, you try it.'

She touched Dino's hand. 'That didn't hurt did it?'

Dino was quite untroubled by this low-on-the-hierarchy item: 'No that didn't hurt.'

'Well *done* Dino, that was magnificent. You are a very sensible boy.'

Gradually the psychologist progressed from touching Dino's hands and arms to touching his body, then his legs. After eight sessions he would allow his legs to be touched and moved. Things looked good so another attempt was made to put calipers on. Dino reacted with panic, screaming and lashing out uncontrollably. The psychologist realized she had tried to go too fast and that fitting and wearing calipers had to be included in the hierarchy. She went straight back to graded practice and the next few sessions were spent going over the steps in the hierarchy that Dino had already mastered. Then another hierarchy was drawn up, starting with touching Dino's legs with things quite different from calipers (a pencil, an ashtray) then with string, bandages and straps: then all of these were laid one at a time across his legs, then the strings and straps were tied loosely, then done up firmly round his legs. Small parts of the calipers were brought in, and built onto gradually until he was able to put up with complete 'practice calipers'. During this time he had been measured up for his real calipers and in his eighteenth session he put on his own boots for the first time and in the twenty-second allowed the calipers to be strapped on properly. Dino felt enormously proud and excited, and delighted with the praise and pleasure of everyone around him. The whole process had taken four months.

The programme had not gone at all smoothly. Dino was a difficult, touchy, anxious and aggressive boy, and often the psychologist had to wait quietly for him to stop shouting and flailing about, and then go back again to previous steps to allow him to work up slowly to and beyond the point where he had thrown his tantrum. But her patience and persistence resulted in success, and what success. Dino came of a proud Sikh family who had felt humiliated by having a crippled son who could not walk. When after weeks of practice with parallel bars and walking frames, he showed them that he could walk his status in the family rose almost visibly. On his thirteenth birthday, twenty months after the treatment was begun, he was given the much-coveted turban that marked his acceptance as an adult Sikh, and which it had once seemed impossible for him ever to attain.

Another little girl, Claire, at the age of $2\frac{1}{2}$ developed an intense fear of her own shoes.* It is said of normal adults that when they develop a phobia it is of something potentially dangerous, 'snakes or spiders, but not pyjamas'. But the mentally handicapped child may well become phobic about something entirely harmless, as did Claire. She refused to wear shoes, and screamed if she even saw child-sized shoes, though she was not worried by adult-sized shoes. Eventually her parents decided to try graded practice.

Clarie was very fond of boiled eggs, and always had one for her tea, so her parents felt that teatime was likely to be a very relaxed, enjoyable time for Claire. They bought a pair of soft slippers in Claire's favourite shade of blue. When Claire was next having a boiled egg they brought the slippers into the room until Claire could just see them; then they took them away again. Claire had shown no sign of distress and continued to eat her egg. The next time her parents kept the slippers in the room for a little longer while Claire ate her egg; later they were able to bring the slippers gradually nearer and nearer, until they were right beside her chair. On another day while she was eating her egg they put one slipper on Claire's foot, and took it quickly off again. Later they were able to leave the slipper on for longer, later still to put on the other one. In time she was quite happy to

---

* The way that Claire's fear was dealt with is described briefly in *Autistic Children: A Guide for Parents*, Lorna Wing, Constable, 1971. With the author's permission all the steps that were actually followed in helping Claire to overcome her fears are described here·

wear the slippers for the whole of teatime. Then, greatly daring, they stood her down on the floor in her slippers – and quickly popped in a mouthful of egg that they had reserved for this moment. After this Claire ran about everywhere in her slippers. Then one day, while she was eating her egg, her father took off one slipper and put on a shoe. No problem. Later in the week the same was done with the other shoe. After this Claire wore shoes like everyone else and as though she had always worn them.

This programme, as it happened, ran smoothly, without hitches or drawbacks. But it might not have done. If a difficulty had arisen her parents would have gone back, as Dino's psychologist did, and repeated the last few successful steps of the hierarchy: then, at the point where trouble had come, they would have put extra steps in the hierarchy so as to take things more slowly. For instance, after getting to the point where she was running round in the slippers Claire might have found the change to shoes on her feet too sudden and too frightening: then her parents would have gone right back to introducing the shoes very gradually into the room, as they had done with the slippers.

Flooding

Sometimes it is just not possible to use graded practice to deal with a child's fears. It may be that there simply isn't time for the lengthy process of graded practice to take place, in which case another possible method to use is flooding. This method works not by gradually working up to the feared situation but by presenting the feared situation straight away, in all its most nerve-wracking aspects – and not allowing the child to get out of, or avoid the situation.

The reasoning behind this treatment goes like this: as before the child is afraid of something that is not dangerous; he therefore never learns that what he fears is harmless, because he never gives himself time to experience it. His getting out of the feared situation may actually reinforce – strengthen – his fear: he may think that only his escaping ensures his safety and he never gives himself the chance to find out that if he did not escape, if he stayed in the situation, he would come to no harm.

So in using flooding the child is in some way forced to remain in the feared situation: and if it is humanly possible, he is forced to stay in it until he calms down and is no longer afraid (but see pages 228–9).

How this is done depends on the child and what he is afraid of. Simon (see page 82) who refused to use any toilet but that in his own home, was forced to sit on different toilets: he was physically held down until he stopped squirming and complaining, accepted them as tolerable and finally used them. A big moment for Simon's family came when they took him for the day to the seaside and he used a seaside toilet!

When Claire (see page 224) was older she would, apparently without any reason, go into screaming panics. Eventually her parents discovered that this happened when she got damp, even if it were only a tiny spot of damp on her cuff. At first they took every possible precaution against her getting this damp spot; they kept her away from ponds, wash-basins, water jugs and garden sprinklers, and put an umbrella over her even before the rain began to fall. If her cuff got wet they changed her dress immediately. At last they saw that life could not go on like this. They altered their tactics. They allowed Claire's cuff to become damp and they held her firmly, not allowing her to throw herself on the ground to rub off the damp or to rip off her cuff, and made her stay put with her damp cuff. After many sessions like this Claire seemed to realize that a damp cuff was not a sign of impending disaster. In time she made no more fuss over it than anyone else would.

Flooding does work in many cases, and it can be quicker than using graded practice. But it is also often hair-raising, as the child may become frantic with terror before he finally calms down, and this can be a very distressing time, especially for his parents. So graded practice is as a rule the treatment of choice for phobias. It is calmer, gentler, less fraught for everybody. Probably most of us would prefer to use it whenever possible. But if graded practice is not possible for any reason then it is worth considering using flooding.

Modelling

I mentioned on page 222 that Dino's psychologist modelled being unafraid of having her hand touched. Modelling is a useful extra technique to use along with either graded practice or with flooding. In either case some other person models for the child the unafraid behaviour we want him to show, and this may help him to show it himself. As with modelling in other situations (see page 81) it may be most effective if the person doing the modelling is someone the child is fond of, or someone like himself, like another child.

Obsessions

Obsessions are closely related to phobias. Instead of avoiding something a child with an obsession seems to feel compelled to do something, to carry out some action. Adults of normal intelligence who have obsessions sometimes say they have an indefinable feeling that disaster will strike unless they carry out their rituals – continual hand-washing, going back repeatedly to turn off gas taps or to shut doors, or other kinds of ritual.

Since handicapped children with obsessions behave in a very similar way to adult obsessionals, it can be assumed that their reasons for their rituals are much the same. Adults or children, the treatment is to prevent them carrying out their obsessive rituals, and in time they learn that this does not lead to disaster. This technique is rather similar to flooding, in which the phobic person learns that experiencing something, and not avoiding it, does not lead to disaster.

Matthew was 13 years old, a tall handsome boy whose mother had had german measles early in her pregnancy. Matthew was severely mentally handicapped, partially deaf, could not speak and had many of the handicaps of an autistic child, amongst them obsessional behaviours. He insisted on certain things being exactly as he wanted them, and always exactly the same. The windows in his house could not be fully opened or closed but had to be opened about three inches, exactly the same amount always all round the house. If the family went for a walk they

had always to go along the same route. When they sat together
in the evening every member of the family had to sit upright,
knees together and heads turned slightly to the right – they were
not allowed to cross their legs, or speak or read a paper. If
anyone attempted to do something contrary to his obsessions
Matthew would throw terrible temper tantrums. He had smashed
up most of the home – light fittings, armchairs, TV, the fridge –
and the family were very afraid, if they frustrated him, of his
attacking his four-year-old sister, the family dog, and little
children living nearby. At this point, when the family were
spending every evening unable to read, speak or move, they
asked for help.

To begin with Matthew went into the local small unit for
mentally handicapped children. The staff there got to know him
and how to handle him. Because he was in new surroundings
he did not show all his old obsessions, but he would still throw
tantrums when he did not want to do something. The staff of
the unit found that if he was dealt with quietly and firmly and
was not allowed to get out of whatever he was supposed to do he
would calm down and behave reasonably. His mother, and later
his two sisters and his father, visited and were able to work with
him in the neutral surroundings of the unit.

Then came the day for Matthew to pay a visit home. He went
accompanied by his teacher and psychologist. As soon as he
went into the sitting-room of his home, Matthew made a dive
at the window, which was shut, and struggled to open it to
his required degree. The psychologist retrieved him before he
could do so and brought him to sit on the sofa. Matthew threw
himself sideways, screamed and tried to bite the psychologist.
She made him sit up. Again and again he tried to get to the
window, screaming and sobbing, flailing and biting. The
psychologist and teacher decided that if he would sit quietly for
five minutes they would call it a day. He never did. At the end of
an hour he was still fighting and kicking. His parents and sisters
were in tears. For practical reasons it was impossible to stay any
longer so the psychologist and teacher took him out to the car
and back to the unit, convinced that the visit had been a total
failure.

Matthew was taken home again the following week. He did not attempt to touch the windows. This time the visit passed in peace, smiles, and congratulations on all sides, especially for Matthew.

Soon after this Matthew returned home to live. By now his family knew how to manage him. When he tried to impose one of his obsessional rituals they simply did not let him do so – and this included not letting him hurt people around him or damage the house. They had learnt that if they refused to allow him to do these things Matthew, after a period of storms (which became shorter and shorter as time went on) seemed to lose the urge to do them and this gave his family the courage to be firm. They went on a variety of walks around the neighbourhood, and in the evening could read their papers, cross their legs, and talk to each other if they wanted to. Matthew the Tyrant reverted to being Matthew the much-loved son and brother.

Since Matthew could not talk it was impossible to learn what had been going on in his head on and after that traumatic morning, so we can only guess that he had some vague feeling that something terrible would happen if the window was not opened the required three inches: that he desperately tried to get it open to avert the catastrophe: that he did not get it open and realized that the catastrophe did not occur: so he no longer felt it necessary to have the window at that precise angle. This may be a far too simple, or a far too complicated, explanation for Matthew's behaviour, but it is the nearest we can get.

Obsessional objects

Sometimes a child's obsessions take the form of his refusing to be parted from a particular object. Many small children go through a phase of this sort (like Linus in *Peanuts* with his blanket); it may be somewhat inconvenient to the child's parents but not impossibly so, and sooner or later the child himself loses interest in the object and discards it. But the handicapped child may become so obsessed with his object that he will not put it down even for a moment, and because his hands are fully occupied with it, cannot learn to do other things like feeding himself or playing with toys.

One way to deal with an obsessional object is similar to graded practice – we gradually reduce its size until it disappears. Peter's object was a blanket, and Claire's an old X-ray film that she had managed to get hold of. In each case their parents snipped a tiny piece off each day until Peter had just a few threads of blanket and Claire a tiny square of X-ray film which she kept tucked in the palm of her hand. Eventually even these fragments disappeared and the children were free to do other things with their hands.

If the obsessional object is something that cannot be so easily cut down, like a toy fire-engine or a watering-can, it may be possible to persuade the child to part from it for increasing lengths of time: first for just a second or two, then ten seconds, half a minute and so on. Ideally the period for which it is taken away will at first be so short that the child will not have time to get upset. If, however, in spite of our efforts he does get upset we have to be very calm and firm and ignore the screams and the tantrums; after a second or two we return the object, and after a rest repeat the process until the child realizes that if he loses his beloved object he soon gets it back again. Then when he is quite calm about losing it for a second or two we can very gradually increase the time, perhaps introducing some other interesting toy or activity while the object is out of the way. The child may in the end learn to do without the object altogether, but if he only learns to do without it for short periods, like half an hour, at least in those times he can do something else with his hands. Timmy (see page 41) who at first would not be separated from his twiddler, learnt to put it down while he was having his meals. In time he learnt to put it down when he left the house; after that he spent all day at school without it, which made him a great deal easier to teach.

The main points

1. A phobia is a fear which is much greater than the dangerousness of the thing feared warrants.

2. The most usual way to treat phobias is by graded practice.

3. The first step is to draw up a hierarchy – a graded scale – of the feared thing.

4. The hierarchy goes from the hardly-frightening aspect of the thing to the most frightening that the child needs to cope with.

5. Treatment starts by presenting the first item in the hierarchy when the child is in a pleasant situation.

6. When he shows no concern at the first item we move up to the next item; and so on.

7. In flooding the child is prevented from escaping from the feared situation.

8. Modelling – someone else demonstrates not being frightened in the feared situation.

9. An obsession is an overwhelming and repeated urge to do some unnecessary action. Response prevention may be used to treat obsessions.

10. Obsessional objects may be either gradually cut down or removed for increasingly long periods.

Some practice problems

*1. Linda has many fears. She is afraid of cats, of very high places (6 metres or more), and of getting dirt on her hands. Her family live in a bungalow and have a poodle as the family pet. She goes to a small village school and her classroom is on the upper floor. Supposing you could treat her fears only one at a time what order should you take them in?

*2. Bill is terrified of spiders. He does not mind photographs but films of moving spiders make his flesh creep a bit. Can you draw up the possible first (least frightening) six items in his hierarchy?

16. Keeping Going

At the beginning of this book I suggested that, while some people might read it from general interest, others might want to make use of it to help and teach their children. So you may have set up projects to teach putting on a jumper, imitating sounds, eating with a knife and fork, responding to words. In the first flush of enthusiasm perhaps you worked very hard, kept good records, got perhaps some surprising and gratifying results. But first enthusiasms simmer down; it may be hard to see how to keep up this level of effort for long. This chapter is written for you: a few ideas to help you carry on.

I'll start with the bugbear of:

Record-keeping

Keeping records is one of the more arduous parts of the work in behaviour modification that we do, and yet it is one of the most valuable. By our records we can see progress when otherwise it might be overlooked: spot particular things happening in particular situations (Joe throws most of his temper tantrums after tea and before he goes to bed, Jane can do up buttons below but not above her waist); we can see when our efforts are clearly not having the effect we want and can try something else. Records do help.

So don't abandon records altogether. However, you probably can lighten the load a bit, particularly for the times when everything is going pretty well. What I am suggesting is that once you have got a programme under way, don't record everything that happens every time; instead, keep your records spaced out at regular intervals, recording what happens every fourth or seventh or tenth session, or at whatever interval you choose to take. For instance, if you were teaching Melanie spoon-feeding you would carry out the teaching at every meal (or at every breakfast, or whatever you had decided) but you would record how many spoonfuls she fed herself, how much prompting she needed, and so on, only on, say, Thursdays. If you were trying to increase the number of times Valerie obeyed verbal requests you might want to have separate records for week-days and week-ends (since she is likely to be given many more requests at weekends, and because the weekend situation is so different from the week, with Dad around more of the time and other people coming and going a good deal): so you might keep records for Sundays and Wednesdays: or Sunday afternoon, or two hours on Sunday, and Wednesday morning before school, whatever seemed suitable to you. The important thing is to keep careful records of everything that happens in the times you have chosen: much better this than recording half of what happens for most of the day. Of course, if what you are recording is something that happens only occasionally – say, heaving flowerpots through a window, or offering to wash up – there is nothing to stop you continuing to record these every time they happen: if you tried to record them in selected short periods you might never catch them.

Keeping regular, but not continuous, records like this makes record-keeping less of a drag and perhaps more practicable in the long run. There are just a few things to watch out for.

First, try to ensure as far as you can that the time you pick for your recordings is a fairly typical one. For instance, we would not choose to record Valerie's obedience the day that an aunt, who doesn't think it fair to be hard on the child and does everything for her, regularly comes to tea. (Neither would we, if the aunt happened to come to tea on the day set aside for recording obedience, decide to scrub the recording for that day but go ahead with it and note down that the day was an unusual one.) Similarly if Melanie's favourite food was ice-cream we would not have ice-cream *always* on Thursdays: ice-cream would be on the menu sometimes on Thursdays, sometimes on other days. Make sure, too, that the length of time for which you make your recordings stays the same: you don't want to try to compare the number of words spoken per two hours before treatment with the number of words said per half hour afterwards (although you can do this if your recordings are made in percentages – see page 124).

Second, we should try to make sure that the teaching continues, and that we put as much effort into it, on the days when we were not making recordings as on the days when we were. One of the spin-offs of record-keeping is that it does seem to make the work more worthwhile: just because we are easing the burden of recording for ourselves we don't want the work itself to fall off.

Third, as I hinted earlier, these discontinuous but regular records are adequate and practical when everything is going along well. If you hit a difficult patch, and things are not going well, it may be helpful to go back to keeping fuller, continuous records. This is because you may get better information about what it is that is going wrong from the continuous records. Do you have more difficulty on certain days? When certain people are around? or not around? when your child is more likely to be tired? or when he has been involved in certain activities? when he is in certain places? and so on. You are more likely to get this sort of information from continuous records, and so be able to see what changes you could make in your programme.

To sum up: record-keeping can be wearisome (I am smitten to the heart by the memory of someone saying to me '*Please* can we have a break over Christmas?' and feel sure that at least part of the break that was needed was from record-keeping) but it is worthwhile and rewarding. Find a reasonably typical time, at whatever regular interval seems to you appropriate, and keep records only then. If you run into difficulties with your programme it may be worth going back to more continuous records.

Of course, if what is driving you mad is the pressure of carrying out the teaching sessions themselves, then you should consider spacing them out a bit – mad parents are unlikely to be a great help to the child. However, spacing out the teaching may slow up the child's learning, whereas spacing out recordings should not. So, if you decide to space out the teaching sessions your child gets, you should be prepared for him to learn rather more slowly.

What to do when you are stuck

It is easy enough to carry out programmes when everything is going swimmingly. It is not so easy when things go wrong, the programme doesn't seem to work, the child stops progressing. What then? I certainly do not have all the answers but here are a few tips that may help.

1. *Examine the problem*

Look as closely as you can at what has been happening. Look at the methods you have used to try to solve the problem: if they have failed, try to see the possible reasons for their failure – every reason you can think of, not just the most obvious or probable. Work out as clearly as you can what the difficulty is. Write it down.

At this point you are not trying to find solutions, just to get a clear picture of the problem.

2. *Discuss it*

Two heads are better than one. It is a lonely business trying to grapple with difficulties in a programme on your own. Try, however, to discuss it with somebody who has some knowledge of and interest in behaviour modification or you may find yourselves at cross purposes – common sense is not quite the same. Other parents who have also been trying to use these methods may be willing to help, and may in their turn enlist your help with their problems. You might get in touch with your Regional Officer for the NSMHC, or with a local psychologist (see pages 259–60); they might be able to help.

3. *Solutions*

Once you have got quite clear what the problem is, possible solutions often (though not always) become much more obvious. For example when Jack was learning to put on his socks (page 138) he got stuck at the stage where he had to pull the sock over his heel. It wasn't until his teacher saw, in discussion with several other experienced people, that the difficulty lay in the position Jack sat in, with his heel resting across the other knee, that she saw that he needed to have his foot free of contact. Even so her first solution – to get Jack to put his foot on the floor – failed; after that she gave him a chair to rest his foot on, and Jack quickly learnt to pull on his socks.

Sometimes the best way to deal with a problem may not be to tackle it directly but to try to deal with it by working on something else. This often applies with, for instance, children who are aggressive, or who injure themselves; instead of using punishment we may try to lessen the frequency of the bad behaviour by encouraging – reinforcing – other, better things. Or again, you may look to see whether a simple change in the child's surroundings – a higher chair at the table, a gate to keep him out of the kitchen, an electric night-light, a zip instead of buttons, a lock on the china cupboard, can help to change his behaviour in the direction we want it to go. These two methods are, of course, DRO (Differential Reinforcement of Other behaviour) and changing the surroundings which appeared in chapter 7, pages 104–6. Because they are indirect ways of tackling a problem they are easy to overlook. It is worth keeping them in mind, especially when more direct methods don't seem to be working.

On page 74, I suggested that if a programme stopped working there were two questions you should ask yourself: first, are the reinforcers really effective? and second, has the task been broken down into small enough steps? Whether the second applies will depend on what you are working on (it probably would not apply if, for instance, you were trying to deal with tantrums) but the first may always apply. It is extremely common for a child to lose interest in a reinforcer, and you should not be discouraged if he goes right off something on which until recently his whole happiness apparently depended. It is then important to look for what *is* now reinforcing to him, and not to think 'reinforcers don't work'. It is a question of finding the right one. With some children this can be very, very difficult; but it is crucial to what we do.

Finally, two small points. When you are considering possible solutions to your problem, try to be flexible and to keep an open mind as to what will be worth trying. Obviously you have to choose the most likely solution to try out but it may help if you try to define clearly *why* one is more likely to succeed than another: in particular when everything seems unlikely it may be necessary to stop saying '*That* won't work', and give it a try. In this case you will need to keep careful records of what you do, and, probably, set a time limit for how long you will try it.

This brings me to the last point: a programme must be given time to work, and should not be said to have failed until it has been going long enough for success to be possible. One of the repeated findings of many researches is that the mentally handicapped can learn, and often do learn to do tasks as well as people of normal intelligence, but it takes them much longer to reach the same standard. The crunch comes when you ask, how long is long enough? There is no specific answer to that question – the answer will depend on the task, the child, how often you have your teaching sessions, and so on. The important thing is not to give up almost as soon as you have started. Over and over again I have heard people say, 'The programme's no good, it isn't working' – and it was only agreed on yesterday. It may help if, when you set out on a programme, you decide on a period of time for which you will keep it up – say, a week, or ten days, or twelve teaching sessions. At the end of that time, but not before, unless disaster strikes (and not counting small adjustments to the programme) you will look at it again, and decide whether to carry on or whether to change the programme. You don't want to struggle on indefinitely with something that is clearly not useful, but neither do you want to abandon a promising programme before it has had a chance to succeed.

The following check-list may help you to pin-point problems.

1. *Reinforcement*

If social (praise, hugs, etc.): are these really enthusiastic and clear?

If edible (sweets, fruit, cheese, drinks, etc.): has he got tired of it? (try something else).

Is the schedule of reinforcement right? (is the reinforcement given often enough? or too often?)

Does he get the reinforcement too freely at other times? (e.g. biscuits for elevenses and tea *and* for his teaching sessions).

Are you giving the reinforcement quickly enough? (*immediately* after the good behaviour).

Would a different reinforcer help? (e.g. a favourite toy instead of a sweet, a lick on a lolly to back up the 'good boy').

2. *Teaching new skills*

Have you broken the task down into small enough steps?

Are you giving enough physical prompting?

Have you faded out the prompts too quickly? not enough?

Are you making sure that the child gradually does a little more, and then a little more still, for each reinforcer?

Is the task one that the child is really likely to be able to succeed in? or is it a bit too ambitious? It is not always easy to tell in advance what it will or will not be possible to teach to a particular child, and sometimes we just have to go ahead and try teaching it to him (see pages 67-8). But if after a time of careful teaching, and if none of the suggestions in this section make a difference, it may be better to go back to an easier task and work up, or to leave this task for a while and return to it later.

Is the child bored? (this is usually because he is no longer interested in the reinforcer: it can be that he is bored with the task).

Are the sessions the right length? (i.e. not too long).

Would it be better to have more frequent sessions?

3. Bad behaviour

Are you sure the 'bad' behaviour is not still being reinforced (e.g. by a brother/sister/uncle/teacher)?

Are you quite clear what is the reinforcer for the 'bad' behaviour?

If you are using punishment, has it 'worn off' – has the child got used to it? (if so look for a new one or use DRO).

Very important: If you have stopped reinforcing his 'bad' behaviour does the child get plenty of reinforcement for his good behaviour instead?

If absolutely desperate: try re-reading chapters 3 to 8: see if this suggests anything that you haven't already used: try it boldly, keeping careful records of what happens.

To encourage the others

You may find that you are able to achieve quite considerable changes with your child. A persistent wetter may become toilet-trained, a silent child begin to use words, an uncooperative child become more amenable. If you feel that what you have done could be of interest or benefit to other parents, think about writing a short account of it for publication, either in your local newsletter, or in *Parents Voice*, or in one of the journals. Your local psychologist or NSMHC representative should be able to give help if you want it. Nothing succeeds like success, and I can imagine few things more encouraging to parents than to hear what other parents, through their own initiative and effort, have been able to do for their own children.

Good luck!

Appendixes

Appendix 1: Answers to the Practice Problems

These are some answers I can suggest to the 'Practice problems' marked with an asterisk in the text.

Chapter 3: Reinforcement

4. Housework, for example; it must be one of the most under-reinforced of all activities. I bet you can count on the fingers of one hand the number of times it's even noticed – 'How nicely the bedroom has been dusted!' or, 'This shirt is beautifully ironed'. It is lucky housewives get some satisfaction from the sight of dust-free surfaces and wrinkle-free shirts or they might be unlikely to dust or iron very often.

5. When the child gets the sweet she stops complaining of the pain: her parents experience relief from her complaining and are negatively reinforced – they are more likely to give her a sweet on another occasion. But the child receives a sweet when she complains, so her complaining is positively reinforced: she is likely to complain more often.

The outcome is likely to be that the child will complain of more and more pains. If her parents realize that what they are doing – giving the sweets – is increasing her complaints they might decide to act differently. They would of course keep a sharp look-out for any genuine illness but if they thought there was nothing the matter with the child (as they clearly did when they 'cured' her with a sweet) they might say pleasantly that little girls with pains shouldn't eat sweets; they might distract her with something to look at or do; and when some time had gone by without her complaining she might then be offered a sweet. If the child found that she never got sweets when she said she had a pain she might complain less.

Chapter 4: Tokens

3. The first move is to check on the exchange reinforcers – are they powerful enough? Is she really keen to get them? If she is carelessly mislaying her tokens it may be that she doesn't much care about them because she doesn't much care about the exchange reinforcers. If we suspect this is the case we should look around for something that she would like very much.

If, however, we think that she *does* care about the exchange reinforcers then we might try to devise some better way for her to store her tokens once they have been given to her: a necklace with a fool-proof clasp, or a string attached to her belt ending in a tag (these two would only work with tokens that have a hole in the middle); or a purse with a flap with a Velcro fastening on a belt. Or the tokens could be put into a rack or jar where she could see them but would not have to carry them about.

4. We should have to use something that was available on the desert island; but it must not be something so easily available that the child (or whoever the programme was for) could pick it up easily and so come into possession of quantities of unearned 'tokens'. So it would have to be something that only we had access to; the tail feathers of our pet parrot who would allow no one else to touch him, or a particular kind of shell, the source of which only we knew. Or we could use something quite commonplace like pebbles or peeled twigs but mark it with something that only we had – the cochineal we happened to have saved from the shipwreck, or the only ball-point pen on the island.

This question obviously has some relevance for real life. The child should not be able to cheat by pretending he has earned more tokens than he really has. So the tokens, or stars or whatever, must be kept carefully out of reach.

5. All sorts of things may contribute to the failure of a slimmer's programme, and I can only suggest a few of them.

Has the slimmer chosen adequate exchange reinforcers? In my own programme I once caught myself thinking, 'Well I don't care about the reinforcer anyway'. I had to change the reinforcer, fast.

Is the reinforcer immediate enough? Especially in the case of slimming. The pleasure to be got from eating is so strong and so immediate that only a very powerful reinforcer, the prospect of which is clearly in front of the slimmer, has a hope of competing with food. For this reason (immediacy of reinforcement) it is probably better too for the tokens to be earned for what is or is not eaten, rather than for weight loss, which is rather far removed from the crucial factor of eating. The effect might be even greater if tokens were also earned for *not buying* the food.

Does the slimmer have a reasonable hope of getting the reinforcement? or is the programme too stringent? If hopelessness has set in it may be better to relax the rules slightly and then build up gradually.

If penalties are incurred for failure, are these too severe? Again, this happened in my programme, when the penalty (not having a bath) was so unpleasant that I kept letting myself off. The programme worked better when I fixed on something (no orange juice for breakfast) that, though I disliked it, I was prepared to impose on myself.

If the programme is entirely self-controlled it could be beneficial to enlist the help of someone else to monitor successes and failures. Having to confess to my family that I had not earned my orange juice made me more likely to ensure that I did earn it.

Family support may be especially important for the slimmer. She (or he) needs her family to back her up, to urge her on, to encourage rather than deride or to undermine the programme as one kind-hearted but misguided husband did, who gave his wife a large box of chocolates because he felt so sorry for her.

6. There are several things we could do.

   (*a*) If he was very slow we might gradually speed up Charlie's dressing by requiring him to do it in a shorter time. At first he might have no time limit at all, then to earn the tokens he might have to get dressed within forty-five minutes, then forty minutes, and so on until he was dressing within a reasonable time.

   (*b*) We could extend the things he needed to do to earn the sweets – washing himself, or helping to lay the table.

Neither of these would reduce the number of sweets he got. If we thought it *very* important to do that we could:

(*c*) Reduce the number of tokens he earned, and tell him, first, that he would now get one token for the pair of socks; then, when he was used to that, that he would get one token for vest and pants; and so on; *or*,

(*d*) Increase the 'token price' of the sweets; we could tell him that three tokens were needed now for two sweets; *or*,

(*e*) Include other kinds of reinforcers that he could exchange for his tokens; some special treat for breakfast, five minutes cuddling, five minutes with a tape-recorder – anything we could think of that he might like as an alternative to the sweets.

Chapter 6: Imitation: Learning by Copying

1. Most sports – tennis, golf, football – are taught very largely through imitation, though occasionally a teacher will use a certain amount of prompting especially on hand and arm movements.
Here are a few more:
Singing
Dancing
Plaiting
Stirring and beating in cookery.
Can you think of others?

2. Prompting could be used, but would be clumsy and tedious. Most could be done to a certain extent by following instructions, either verbal or written; but imitation is a much easier and surer way to teach.

3. Sleeping in a bed.
Sometimes children who are used to sleeping in their own bed will not sleep if they go in a strange bed. Usually they accept the new bed after a night or two, or they may be helped by bringing some familiar things from the old bed – their teddy-bear, a special pillow or blanket.

5. (*a*) Rain falling. A wet weather forcast. Seeing other people in mackintoshes or with umbrellas. A threatening sky.

(*b*) Traffic already on the road. Road signs (*Tenez la droite*).

(c) Somebody wearing a deaf aid. Noisy surroundings. Somebody not replying, or saying 'Eh' when we speak in a normal voice. Somebody at a distance.

(d) Seeing a charity flag seller. A request – 'That will be 50p'. Being given a bill. A ring on the front door bell following a muffled rendition of the first verse of 'Oh come all ye faithful'.

(e) An alarm clock going off. A baby crying. Hearing other people about. A full bladder. Somebody shaking you or saying 'Get up'. A smell of fire.

Chapter 7: Learning Not To

1. Either you would have to arrange to meet your *bête-noire* personally or, if he/she were going to appear in public, you would have to organize the entire audience to carry out the treatment. You would also have to find out what was the reinforcer maintaining the bête-noire's 'bad' behaviour, but I think we can expect that in most of these cases it is applause. Then, whether in private or public meetings, if you are using extinction (a), when the 'bad' behaviour appeared it would be met by blank silence. Similarly if you were using time-out (b), the bête-noire would receive a good deal of applause which would stop abruptly when he produced the 'bad' behaviour.

2. (a) Extinction and DRO. We would expect that attention is the reinforcer. Look rather uninterested in the stories of her illnesses but become immediately interested if she talked about anything else. We might also prompt her to show the kind of behaviour that would be reinforced by leading the conversation on to other topics – such as how she grew the fruit and flowers, and how good she was at this.

(b) Restitution or fining or time-out. We could insist on their getting up out of their chairs to pick up the sweet papers and put them in the waste-paper basket – perhaps empty the waste-paper basket as well. Or we could fine them, fines to be taken out of pocket-money. Or we could time them out from whatever pleasurable event was going on at the time – switch off the TV for five minutes, for instance.

(c) Extinction. But make sure she has been to the lavatory before you set off for your shopping. And it might be a good idea to make the conversations few and brief, and to hand out reinforcement if she did not interrupt (DRO).

(d) I am really stumped by this one. I think I would put up with it, or try to forestall it by expressing appreciation first. But it does get boring to have to do that for every meal. Has anybody any better ideas?

(e) Change the surroundings – put the butter somewhere where he can't get it. And make sure he gets a drop of cream every now and again in his saucer.

Chapter 8: Records and Graphs

1. (a) Either by grading the prompts; or by probes, in which case we would probably still need to assess how much prompting the child needed to thread, say, five beads each time we did a probe (see page 115). Later when the child had got pretty good at threading we might count the Number of Things Achieved – how long, for instance, it took him to thread five beads.

(b) Probes, in which we would perhaps record each time the proportion of the time that the child spent interacting with another child. (We would probably use duration recording – see page 25).

(c) We could count the number of things that went over the fence each day: or just on one day a week (probe).

(d) Either count the number of letters known: or as usual do probes to see how many are named in single sessions.

2. If we turned both sets of figures into percentages we could plot them on the same graph.

The number of dry nights per week could be worked out as a percentage of the highest number of dry nights it is possible for him to have: in one week the highest number he could have is 7. So we work out the number he actually got each week as a percentage of 7. In Week 1 that would look like this: $\frac{2}{7} \times 100 = 29$ per cent.

For 'Cooperation' we could work out the number of times Henry obeyed requests as a percentage of the number of requests made to him. In Week 1 there were 27 requests and Henry obeyed 4 of them: $\dfrac{4}{27} \times 100 = 15$ per cent.

The figures for the nine weeks go like this:

Week	% Dry nights	% Cooperation
1	29	15
2	14	40
3	43	58
4	57	43
5	71	57
6	57	86
7	43	79
8	86	91
9	100	93

Now we can plot these figures on a graph.

Henry: *Dry Nights : Cooperation*

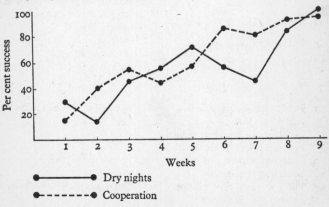

●————● Dry nights

●– – – –● Cooperation

Chapter 9: Dressing and Undressing

1. (a) *Mitts*

Adult

1. Puts mitt over child's hand, guides thumb almost in
2. Puts mitt over child's hand, guides thumb half-way in
3. Puts mitt over child's hand, guides thumb to thumb hole
4. Puts mitt over hand
5. Puts mitt half over hand

Child

1. Holds cuff of mitt, pulls mitt fully on
2. Holds cuff, pushes thumb in and pulls mitt fully on
3. Holds cuff, pushes thumb right in and pulls mitt fully on
4. Holds cuff, finds thumb hole, pulls mitt on
5. Pulls mitt on to hand, finding thumb hole
6. Puts mitt on

(b) *Woolly hat*

1. Puts hat on to child's forehead, pulls back and down over ears
2. Puts hat on to child's forehead, pulls back and down nearly over ears
3. Pulls hat half-way over ears
4. Pulls hat to ears

5. Puts hat to forehead

1. Pushes front of hat back on forehead
2. Pulls right down, adjusts front
3. Pulls down and adjusts front
4. Pulls hat out (if he does not do this he is liable to end up with his ears folded down in half) over ears and down, adjusts front
5. Pulls hat down, out, and down and adjusts
6. Puts hat on

(c) *Wellington boots*

1. Finds support for child to lean on (wall, back of chair etc.) lifts one foot, puts it into boot until heel almost down
2. Puts foot half-way into foot of boot, heel raised
3. Puts foot into boot until toe touches the bottom

1. Pushes foot flat and fully into boot
2. Pushes foot fully into boot
3. Slides foot into foot of boot

Adult	*Child*
4. Puts foot half-way into leg of boot	4. Pushes foot down leg and into foot of boot
5. Puts foot into mouth of leg-opening of boot	5. Pushes foot right down leg and into foot of boot
6. Provides support for child	6. Lifts foot, puts it into boot and pushes it fully down
	7. Leans for support, and puts foot into boot

2. (*a*) Probably (I think) putting in the first arm (steps 8 to 9): otherwise pulling it over his head (step 10) especially if it is a jumper with a close neck, like a polo neck.

(*b*) Finding the second armhole (step 6). Always the bogey in my experience.

(*c*) Pushing the (black) lace under the (white) loop, and through to make the second loop (step 3). Everything else is plain sailing compared with this.

3. (*a*) A woman's one-piece swimsuit: and, perhaps, other garments which are dry when you put them on and wet when you take them off.

(*b*) Rubber gloves, if you take them off right side out. They are quite easy if you peel them off, like surgeons do, but then you have the bother of putting them right side out again (unless you are a surgeon I suppose, in which case you leave it to a minion).

(*c*) Wellington boots. Especially if they are a bit big they are very easy to slip on, but taking them off entails quite a tricky bit of pressing the toe of one foot against the heel of the other.

Chapter 10: Washing

1. We would concentrate the teaching on the bath, though it would not hurt to repeat things at the wash basin when he was washing his hands. We would teach him the difference between the hot and cold taps: these would be clearly marked, with a large red (for hot) and blue (for cold) sticker. We would test the water in each, and get Bobby to test it and show him the stickers and emphasize 'Cold', 'Hot'.

Then we would run some water into the bath, rather cool perhaps, test it, and get Bobby to do so: we would say (something like), 'Wants more *hot*' and prompt him to turn on the hot tap. We would keep testing, and getting him to, until the right temperature had been reached: then we would say, 'Enough!' and prompt Bobby to turn off the tap. Then, if he wanted to, he would be allowed to get into the bath and play in it.

We would repeat the process with too hot water and adding cold, being especially careful and only letting Bobby put in a fingertip. Then we would go on to letting Bobby do the testing first, and reinforcing him if he made the right decision, either that the water was a reasonable temperature, or that it needed more of either hot or cold.

Finally, at the end of the teaching process, Bobby would test his bathwater temperature every night, and we would check it until we were quite sure he could be safely left to do it on his own. We wouldn't worry too much if the water was a bit too cool but be very, very careful about its being too hot.

2. For me, there seem to be four ways.
   (*a*) As a routine – on getting up and on going to bed, before meals and after going to the toilet.
   (*b*) If my hands feel sticky.
   (*c*) If I have been handling something dirty or unhygienic.
   (*d*) If I can see dirt on them. How much dirt there needs to be depends on what I am about to do; if I am going to do cooking, or sewing, or handle clothes straight from the washing machine the smallest speck will suffice to send me to the wash basin; if I am going to garden, or bath the dog, or go for a walk I would not be so fussy.

Chapter 11: Dry Pants, Dry Bed

1. *Similarities:* both use prompting – we lead the child to the potty and hurry the pet into the garden; both the child and the pet may be given rewards – praise, petting, Chocolate Flake, whatever is appropriate – when they use the potty or the garden;

each may be given mild punishment – disapproval, scolding, a smack for the pet – if they instead use pants or the sitting-room carpet. In each case punishment may be more effective if it follows immediately on the misplaced wetting rather than later; both may be expected, in time, to learn to give some signal when they want either to go to the toilet or to be let out into the garden.

Differences: I suppose the major one is that language is likely to play a much greater part in teaching the child than the pet; while many other subtleties exist in the situation of the child but not of the pet – the child may in some cases soil or wet deliberately in order to annoy the adult; so ignoring this behaviour may be effective although ignoring the pet's accidents would not be a useful way to train him. Physical punishment will be more likely to be used for the pet and reward for the child. The signal that the child learns to give is likely to be a specific one, whereas if our pet raises a paw to the back door for all we know he only wants to go out in the sunshine or chase the birds off the lawn. Finally the child has to learn many associated skills – pulling down pants, climbing on to the toilet, wiping himself, climbing off, pulling up pants, flushing the toilet – which have no place in the pet's training.

All in all, although many of the principles of teaching are similar, the details of it vary: toilet training is a more complicated and subtle process for the child than it is for the pet.

2. The child might be frightened of or unhappy on the potty. In this case we would try to make sitting on the potty a happy time for him: we would give him his favourite toys, play or sing with him, perhaps give him little bits of his favourite food, in the hope that he would begin to relax enough to use the potty.

Or he might associate wetting so strongly with the feeling of wearing nappies or pants that they have become to him the cue for wetting, and he cannot allow himself to wet when he is not wearing them. We would wait until it was warm enough to let him run about all day without any pants on, and then try again.

Or he may just do it to annoy, in which case we would remain very calm and unperturbed; and we would try sitting him on the pot, getting him off it, then just before the two minutes was up, we would sit him down again. And if by chance he then performed, ply him lavishly with every reinforcer at our command.

Chapter 12: Eating and Table-manners

1. I think this would have to be taught by imitation, with a minimal amount of physical prompting, because the very fine finger adjustments needed would, I think, be very difficult to prompt. If the child was not able to learn by imitation I should gratefully recall that the Chinese use a spoon a good deal and would teach this skill to the child instead.

2. Chips, toast (in fingers if buttered, with knife and fork if under scrambled egg), lettuce, tomato, cucumber, apples, cream cakes, chicken drumsticks.

The cues that tell us whether or not we should use our fingers are quite complicated. They depend partly on the state of the food – hot or cold, dry or a bit messy, as for instance a dressed salad; partly on the situation – a dinner party or a picnic; partly on what other people are doing. This last might be the most useful guide for the child; if we could teach him to see what other people do before he starts to eat he might make fewer mistakes. Otherwise a few simple rules might help: 'It's *hot*, use your knife and fork,' 'We're *in the garden*, you can use your fingers'.

It *is* complicated, so perhaps it is just as well that it does not matter very much.

3. Imitation, and/or prompting, and breaking down the activity into small steps. We could show the child how to put a knife on the right-hand side of one person's place: then at each person's place. Then we could go on to a knife and fork: then knife, fork and plate: and so on.

We could also change the surroundings by putting a large sheet of paper, with knife, fork, spoon, plate and cup drawn on it, at each person's place, and the child would put the objects in their place over the picture of each one. Later we fade this prompt by making the drawings gradually fainter and fainter, while making sure that the child can still succeed at every stage.

4. We would give Lucy a plate on a suction mat (see Appendix 4). We would watch her like a hawk as she reaches the end of the meal. As she went to tip the plate we would prevent her from doing so; and we would prompt her to say, or make a sign, or produce a picture card, for the word 'Finished'. Then we would reinforce her and take her plate away. We would do this at every meal until she found it was no longer necessary to tip her plate.

If, despite our efforts, Lucy managed occasionally to tip her plate over, we would retrieve the plate and make her say or sign that she had finished.

Chapter 13: Language

4. (a) Sign language (signing) as first choice, because of its flexibility and economy of time, and because it allows a more normal, conversation-like exchange that this child might enjoy and benefit from.

(b) Signing if he can manage it – and if he is very sociable and attentive to people he might well manage at least some signs. If not then picture language.

(c) A toss-up between signing and written language. I would try signing first, as more economical of his time if he can use it, but would be prepared to move on to written if he made little progress with signing.

(d) Too retarded (probably) for written language, and too physically handicapped for signing, for this child I would go for pictures.

Chapter 14: Play

2. Deaf/blind children can enjoy: Play-doh; plasticine, sand, water, including baths and swimming; movement – swings, push-carts, rockers, bouncy cushions; 'feely box' and 'feely toy' – these are not so far as I know available commercially but are quite easy to make. A 'Feely box' consists of a box con-

taining all sorts of things which feel interesting and different from each other – soft, hard, knobbly, smooth, scratchy, silky, furry, round, square, tubular and so on. The box might have, amongst other things, shells, pieces of macaroni, big round beads, square beads, soft woolly balls, small bricks covered with sandpaper and others covered with mock fur. The child can feel about in the box, encountering different and unexpected textures. A 'feely toy' is based on the same idea but the different materials are built onto a board, or stitched onto a doll or a teddy-bear – an example of this kind of toy is described in an article by Geraldine McCormack and Mona Tsoi, 'Toys for the multiply handicapped child', *Apex*, Vol. 4, 1976, pp. 24–6.

Blind children may enjoy all these but can also enjoy noise – music-makers – humming tops, rattles, drums, xylophones, hammer toys; squeaky toys.

The National Association for Deaf/Blind and Rubella Handicapped have an excellent list of toys and activities for deaf/blind children – see Appendix 2.

3. First, we would make sure that there were plenty of things that the child *could* do: outdoor things if possible like a swing, tricycle or bike, slide or climbing-frame; indoor things like jigsaws, building bricks, constructional toys, materials for drawing, painting, colouring, cutting and sticking; picture books and comics; the makings of imaginative play – dressing-up things, dolls, cars and garages, tea-sets and toy guns. We would make a list of these, using pictures if the child could not read.

Then we would tell him that he would get a little reward, or a star to stick on his chart, every time he came and told us what he was going to do instead of asking what he could do (we might have to set some limit on how often this could be – three times in half an hour perhaps). If he did come and ask we would prompt him to look at his list and decide for himself.

4. We would use graded practice (see chapter 15, page 219) prompting and reinforcement. Supposing it is Rex, whom we want to help to play with other children. We would set up a very pleasant situation in which Rex got lots of adult attention. Then we would bring another child, Mark, into the far end of

the room. (It helps if Mark is himself a friendly sociable person.) Gradually over many sessions we would get Mark to draw nearer and nearer to Rex, always making sure that Rex was quite calm and relaxed. When Mark was able to be quite near to Rex we would have him first look, then smile at Rex, then pass him an object, then touch him. We would teach Mark to give social reinforcement to Rex in just the same way as we did: to begin with Mark could give the reinforcement simultaneously with us – for instance we would smile and stroke Rex's cheek and say 'Well done, that's *lovely*!' at the same time. Gradually we would fade out our part in the reinforcement so that eventually it was given only by Mark. We would go on to prompt Rex to give an object to Mark, to touch him, to begin to play some simple game that Rex enjoys with him; and keep our warmest reinforcement for the occasions when he does so.

All this is likely to take quite some time and several sessions: we would not expect to get Mark sitting right next to Rex at the first attempt, but would expect to take it very slowly.

Chapter 15: Getting Over Phobias and Obsessions

1. Since Linda does not have to cope with either high places or cats in her daily life the first fear we would tackle is that of getting dirt on her hands. This problem may crop up at any time, and especially if she does painting or cookery, while it could also make it difficult for her to learn to wipe herself at the toilet.

Probably the second fear to tackle would be that of cats, as she could encounter a cat if she visited relatives or her friends. Lastly, we would expect to try to help her to get over her fear of high places.

However, this order could be re-arranged if, as we got to know Linda better, we found there were particular reasons to do so – if, for instance, we found that the next-door neighbours had just got a cat that often strayed into Linda's garden. The order in which we would tackle the problems would be that which would give the greatest benefit to Linda.

2. 1. Film of stationary spider (long shot).

2. Film of stationary spider (close-up)
3. Spider in film moves one leg.
4. Spider in film moves one inch.
5. Spider in film moves three inches.
6. Spider in film moves across the screen.

We should have to discuss these with Bill or try them out to see whether they were suitable steps, or whether he needed smaller ones. We could go on to toy spiders, toy spiders that move, dead little spiders, dead big ones, small live ones in a confined space and far away from Bill, then coming gradually closer. And so on.

Appendix 2: Useful Addresses

Association of Parents of Vaccine Damaged Children, Mrs Rosemary Fox, 2 Church Street, Shipston-on-Stour, Warwicks. Tel: Shipston-on-Stour (0608) 61595. Please write, and include a stamped addressed envelope.

British Epilepsy Association, Crowthorne House, Bigshotte, New Wokingham Road, Wokingham, Berks RG11 3AY. Tel: 0344 63122

British Psychological Society, St Andrews House, 48 Princess Road East, Leicester LE1 7DR.

Down's Children's Association, Quinborne Centre, Ridgacre Road, Birmingham 32. Tel: 021 427 1374

Invalid Children's Aid Association, 126 Buckingham Palace Road, London SW1. Tel: 01-730 9891

Kith & Kids, Mr Maurice Collins, 6 Grosvenor Road, Muswell Hill, London N10. Tel: 01-883 8762

MIND (NAMH), 22 Harley Street, London W1N 2ED. Tel: 01-637 0741

National Association for Deaf/Blind and Rubella Handicapped, J. Pryce-Owen (Secretary), Suffolk House, 10 The Butts, Coventry. Tel: 0203 23308

National Children's Bureau, 8 Wakley Street, Islington, London EC1. Tel: 01-278 9441 (Information and advice centre)

National Society for Autistic Children, Mrs M. Everard, 1a Golders Green Road, London NW11 8EA. Tel: 01-458 4375

National Society for Brain Damaged Children, Hon. Sec., 35 Larchmere Drive, Hall Green, Birmingham 28. Tel: 021-777 4284

National Society for Mentally Handicapped Children, 117 Golden Lane, London EC1Y 0RT

National Society for Phenylketonuria and Allied Disorders, 26 Towngate Grove, Mirfield, West Yorkshire.

Royal Association in Aid of the Deaf and Dumb, 7 Armstrong Road, London W3. Tel: 01-743 6187

Spastics Society, 12 Park Crescent, London W1N 4EQ. Tel: 01-636 5020

Toy Libraries Association, Seabrook House, Wyllyotts Manor, Darkes Lane, Potters Bar, Herts EN6 2HL. Tel: Potters Bar (77) 44571

See also 'Useful Books' – *Handbook for Parents with a Handicapped Child*, which contains the names and addresses of many other societies and organizations.

For other useful addresses, see 'Toys and play', page 262, for where to obtain toy catalogues; and 'Aids and Equipment', Appendix 4, for useful mail-order addresses and addresses to write to for general advice.

Appendix 3: Useful Books

Teaching handicapped children

Helping the Retarded, E. A. Perkins, P. D. Taylor and A. C. M. Capie, Institute of Mental Subnormality, 1976. £2·95. (Covers much of the material found in this book but in a different way.)

Isn't It Time He Outgrew This? or, a Training Program for Parents of Retarded Children, V. L. Baldwin, H. D. B. Fredericks and G. Brodsky, Thomas, Springfield, Illinois, 1973. (American – useful, and enjoyable to read.)

Let me Speak, Dorothy Jeffree and Roy McConkey, Souvenir Press, 43 Great Russell Street, London WC1B 3AP. £2·50. (How to teach language. Written particularly for parents.)

One in Seven is Special, Ronald Brown, National Society for Mentally Handicapped Children, 1974. 30p. (How a family taught their own handicapped child, using behaviour modification.)

Starting Off, Chris Kiernan, Rita Saunders and Chris Jordan, Souvenir Press, London, 1978. £3·95. (Teaching for the most severely handicapped.)

Teaching normal children

Children & Parents, H. A. Peine and R. Howarth, Penguin, 1975. 50p. (Behaviour modification used with normal children. Easy to read.)

Elementary Principles of Behaviour, D. L. Whaley and R. W. Malott, Prentice Hall, 1971. £9·05. (More technical, and American, but entertainingly written, and has many examples of work with handicapped children and adults.)

Toys and play

Play Helps: Toys and Activities for Handicapped Children, Roma Lear, Heinemann Health Books, 1977. £2·50. (Full of ideas on toys to buy and to make, and games to play with handicapped children, grouped according to the senses – 'Making the most of' – sight, hearing, touch, taste and smell. Cheerful text and illustrations.)

Toys and Playthings: in development and remediation, John and Elizabeth Newson, Penguin, 1979. £1·50. (General book on toys with 2 chapters concerning handicapped children in particular.)

Toy catalogues obtainable from:
James Galt & Co. Ltd, 30 Great Marlborough Street, London W1. Tel: 01-734 0829

Kiddicraft Ltd, Godstone Road, Kenley, Surrey, CR2 5YS. Tel: 01-668 4181

Educational Supply Association, P.O. Box 22, Pinnacles, Harlow, Essex. Two catalogues that are specially useful for handicapped children: Play Specials and Extra Specials, for older and larger children.

Children with particular handicaps

Autism

Autistic Children: A Guide for Parents, Lorna Wing, Constable, 1971.

Cerebral palsy

Handling the Young Cerebral Palsied Child at Home, Nancie Finnie, Tindall, Bailliere & Cassell, 1968. (A mine of information and practical advice.)

Down's syndrome

Improving Babies with Down's Syndrome, Rex Brinkworth and Dr Joseph Collins, National Society for Mentally Handicapped Children. 1973. 70p. (Full of ideas for stimulating and teaching the babies right from the start.)

Judith: Teaching our Mongol Baby, W. W. Smith. National Society for Mentally Handicapped Children. 30p. (How a family worked to teach their own child with Down's syndrome.)

Young Children with Down's Syndrome, Janet Carr, Butterworth, 1975.

General

Handbook for Parents with a Handicapped Child, Judith Stone and Felicity Taylor, Home & Schools Council Publication, 1972. 15p. Obtainable from: Case Publications, 17 Jackson's Lane, Billericay, Essex. (Contains a fuller list of societies than is given here, and of other sources of help.)

Practical Help for Parents of Retarded Children: Some Questions and Answers, A. D. B. Clarke and Ann M. Clarke, Hull Society for Mentally Handicapped Children, 1969. (Transcript of a Brains Trust in which parents asked the questions and two psychologists with wide experience in mental handicap supplied the answers.)

Magazines

Many of the special organizations produce magazines, for example, *Parents Voice*, published by the National Society for Mentally Handicapped Children; *Communication*, published by the National Society for Autistic Children; *Link*, published by the Association for Spina Bifida and Hydrocephalitis; and *Spastic News*, published by the Spastics Society.

It is worth trying other organizations for useful publications and newsletters.

Appendix 4: Aids and Equipment

Washing

Bathing: Non-slip bath mats may make the child feel more secure and independent. Obtainable from any chemist.

Hair washing: Shampoo shield helps to prevent shampoo and water going over the child's face. Obtainable from: Mothercare Ltd, Cherry Tree Road, Watford, Herts, WD2 55H.

Toilet training

Musical potties: When the child wets in one of these the urine closes an electrical circuit and starts the music playing. Some children seem to love the music, but the big advantage of these potties is that they tell you at once when the child has wet so that you can reinforce him immediately. Obtainable from: Nursery Educational Aid Centre, 54 Shepherd's Bush Market, London, W12 4DF.

'Watford' potty chair: This has high sides and a wooden safety bar across the front, so that the child feels secure and cannot easily leave the seat. Potty slides in under the seat and is removable for emptying. From: Newton Aids, Unit 4, Dolphin Industrial Estate, Southampton Rd, Salisbury. Tel: 0722 20441.

Toddler trainer seat: To fit onto ordinary lavatory seat. Obtainable from Mothercare Ltd (see above).

Grow-tall step: To help the child reach the lavatory seat, and to rest his feet on when he has got there. Obtainable from: Mothercare Ltd (see above).

Crossland toilet aid: Provides head and trunk support for older children who have difficulty in sitting upright. Fits over ordinary lavatory. Obtainable from: Crossland Plastics, Unit 4, Freightway, Sandbeds Trading Estate, Wakefield Road, Ossett, W. Yorks.

Eating and Table-manners

Rubazote: If cutlery handles are too narrow for the child to hold comfortably they can be made thicker with Rubazote. This is thick soft rubber tubing which can be cut to any length required and slipped over the handle. Invaluable too for pencils and paint brushes. Obtainable from: Nottingham Handcraft Co., Melton Road, West Bridgford, Nottingham NG2 6HD.

The minimum length supplied is 2 metres. For shorter lengths contact: British Red Cross Aid Dept., 76 Clarendon Park Road, Leicester, LE2 3AD. Minimum length 20 centimetres (about 8 inches) for 20p.

Non-slip plastic mats: These help to hold plates and cups steady – alas they do not prevent crockery from being hurled. Obtainable from: Phoenix Supply Co., 28 Sanderstead Road, Croydon, Surrey. Tel: 01-688 7442

The material can be supplied as individual mats or in rolls. Larger pieces are useful to provide a secure, non-slip surface for chairs or small tables.

Suction devices: Plate-holders, and small feeding bowls, are obtainable which are held down more firmly by suction.

Plate holders (about 8 centimetres high, 12 centimetres in diameter) obtainable from J. & A. Carters Ltd, Westbury, Wilts. Tel: 0373 822203

Feeding bowl obtainable from Mothercare (see 'Hair Washing').

Plate guards: Scooping up the food is the most difficult step in self-feeding. A plate guard makes this a little easier: clipped on to the edge of the plate it makes the edge higher, so making it easier for the food to fall into the spoon rather than off the edge of the plate. Obtainable from: British Red Cross Society, 9 Grosvenor Crescent, London SW1

The 'Manoy' plate, made with one high side, may be used

instead of a plate and a guard. Obtainable from: Homecraft Supplies, 27 Trinity Road, London SW17. Tel: 01-672 7070

Two-handled mugs: Easier for some children to manage than a cup or beaker. Obtainable from: Spastics Society (see Appendix 2); *or:* Sherrards Centre, Digswell Hill, Old Welwyn, Herts.

Straws: Useful to help a child gain control of his lips and tongue, and just for the fun of using a straw. The following do not disintegrate as quickly as ordinary straws: (*a*) Flexistraws, obtainable from Boots. (*b*) Plastic tubing, obtainable from Boots wine-making counters.

Pelican bibs: The rigid pocket at the bottom of the bib saves some food descending to the floor. Small sizes available from Boots or Mothercare. Adult size from Cindico Ltd, Skerne Road, Driffield, N. Humberside. Tel: Driffield 42521

Language

See 'Useful books', Appendix 3.

Play

See 'Useful books', Appendix 3.

General Advice on Aids and Equipment

1. The Disabled Living Foundation, 346 Kensington High Street, London W14. Tel: 01-602 2491
2. The Spastics Society, Family Services and Assessment Centre, 16 Fitzroy Square, London WIP 5HO. Tel: 01-387 9571
   Both are mines of information which they keep constantly up to date; and they are very helpful to individual inquirers.

Index